Post-Watergate Morality

Post-Watergate Morality

Edited by Lester A. Sobel

Contributing writers: Mary Elizabeth Clifford, Joseph Fickes, Hal Kosut, Stephen Orlosfsky, Lauren Sass
Indexer: Grace M. Ferrara

Facts On File
119 West 57th Street, New York, N.Y. 10019

Post-Watergate Morality

© Copyright, 1978, by Facts on File, Inc.

Published by Facts On File, Inc.,
119 West 57th Street, New York, N.Y. 10019.

Library of Congress Cataloging in Publication Data
Main entry under title:
Post-Watergate morality.
   "Consists largely of the record that Facts on
File compiled in its weekly reports."
   Includes index.
   1. United States—Moral conditions. 2. Cor-
ruption (in politics)—United States. I. Sobel,
Lester A. II. Facts on File, Inc., New York.
HN90.M6P67   170'.973   78-11919
ISBN 0-87196-261-6

9 8 7 6 5 4 3 2 1
PRINTED IN
THE UNITED STATES OF AMERICA

Contents

Introduction

WHETHER JUSTLY OR OTHERWISE, POLITICS and government service often seem to be linked in the public mind with corruption, inefficiency and sloth. And not only in the mind of the public. Political and government workers are well aware of the suspicions with which their calling is regarded. To some extent, it seems, many of them even share these misgivings about their fellow office holders—with or without good cause.

One of the most popular jokes in Washington, a tale told frequently by elected officials and civil servants, is the story of a poor citizen in financial straits. In desperation, he mailed a letter to "God," pleading for fifty dollars to help him out of his difficulties. A postal worker, displaying the judgment considered typical of public employees, directed the message to Washington, where it wound up as close to the addressee as was in the power of the Postal Service to deliver it—on the desk of the President. The President sympathized with the poor citizen and sent him a five-dollar bill from his own pocket. A few weeks later, the President received another letter from the same author. "Thanks for the money," it said. "It helped. Now I need fifty dollars more. Only don't send it through the politicians in Washington. Last time they kept out forty-five dollars for themselves."

Any newspaper reader knows that good reasons are made public repeatedly for suspecting the rectitude of at least some la-

1

borers in the political and governmental vineyards. Headlines
and television news broadcasts of recent years have been heavily laden with reports of such disquieting developments as Watergate, Koreagate, Congressional sex scandals, corporate payments to American or foreign political figures, abuses of police
powers, unconscionable wastage of government money, and ultimately—to many horrified American citizens, incredibly—the
resignation in disgrace of first a Vice President and then a President of the United States.

Political corruption seems to have existed ever since civiliza-
tion reached a level of organization making government and politics possible. Bribery of public officials was common, and was
denounced, in ancient Egypt. Vote-buying was the norm in ancient Rome. In colonial Virginia in 1757, a candidate for election
to the House of Burgesses was denounced on charges that he
had plied voters during his campaign with 28 gallons of rum, 50
gallons of rum punch, 34 gallons of wine, 46 gallons of beer and
two gallons of cider royal. Since there were only 391 voters in
the district, the liquor expenditure averaged nearly half a gallon
per voter. The criticized candidate, George Washington, won
election and went on to perform many valued acts of public
service.

There are many reasons ascribed for the decline in morality
that observably takes place with time in many areas of government and politics—as it also does in private business. Most frequently cited in this context is Lord Acton's letter of April 5,
1887, in which he noted that "power tends to corrupt and absolute power corrupts absolutely." Bismark had been quoted earlier (1881) as saying that "politics ruins the character." Rep.
Otis Pike (D, N.Y.) amplified one aspect of this view. In a statement in the *Congressional Record* March 2, 1977, Pike observed:
"There is such a thing as wanting to be reelected too badly.
There is such a thing as needing a job too much. In my judgment, . . . this is the largest single cause of political corruption
of which I am aware."

Most Americans are probably distressed at the widespread
distrust in which public figures are held—even in cases in which
they find this distrust logical. There are people, however, who
do not agree that immorality in public office is prevalent enough
to make the suspicion completely justified.

"If the polls are to be believed," said Sen. William D. Hathaway
(D, Me.) in testimony before the Senate Special Committee on

Official Conduct Feb. 1, 1977, "the level of trust our constituents place in Congress, and in government in general, is unfortunately low. The reason for this are no doubt complex. . . . But one reason is that some voters and, more tragically, non-voters seem to feel that those in political life are solely interested in lining their own pockets or taking junkets to the exclusion of helping those who elected them. These sentiments are difficult to understand since the vast majority of men and women in public life whom I have come to know are extraordinarily dedicated and hardworking and scrupulously honest. There have unfortunately been an infamous few who have abused and debased public office. And these individuals, with the assistance of vigilant and persistent press, have managed to shape and dominate public perceptions and thereby obscure the positive examples and clean records of so many others. This sort of feeling on the part of a significant portion of the electorate represents a cancer on our democracy which we must take every step to eliminate. . . . We have various Senate rules, the Federal Election Campaign Act and provisions of the criminal code already in place, but it is appropriate that we reexamine all of these standards on a comprehensive basis and draft a code of conduct. But at the outset we should realize that no matter what system we devise there will continue to be a few who will attempt to abuse public office—we cannot alter human nature. . . ."

Senator Hathaway's view found its supporters—in Congress, at least. The House (of Representatives) Republican Task Force on Reform said a week later: "It is no secret that the public's perception of the Congress is at an all-time low. The American people, disillusioned by the continuing accounts of scandal, question the very integrity of the legislative branch. The conflicts of interest, the misuse of public moneys, and the allegations of personal enrichment while in government service undermine the public faith. The abuses of a few members tar the reputations of all members. Congress for too long has tolerated activities which skirt the boundaries of acceptable ethical behavior. . . ."

Many of the abuses of trust that so distress Americans, particularly the crimes of the Watergate period, have been detailed and discussed in the FACTS ON FILE books *Watergate & the White House* (three volumes), *Money & Politics* and *Corruption in Business*. This book continues the account of such developments during the years immediately following the Watergate period. The material in this volume consists largely of the record that FACTS ON FILE compiled in its weekly reports on world events. As in all FACTS ON FILE works, there was a conscientious effort to keep this book free of bias and to make it a balanced and accurate reference tool.

LESTER A. SOBEL

New York, N.Y.
August, 1978

The End of Watergate

Watergate Forces Nixon's Resignation

The Watergate scandal, with its continuing revelations of official misconduct, in which President Richard M. Nixon was increasingly shown to be implicated, ultimately made it impossible for Nixon to remain in office. Admitting at least some guilt in the affair, Nixon resigned as President of the United States in August 1974.

Nixon resigns, Ford becomes President. Richard M. Nixon, 61, resigned as President Aug. 9, 1974. Vice President Gerald Rudolph Ford, 61, was immediately sworn in as his successor. It was the first time in the history of the nation that its president had resigned.

The resignation, a dramatic conclusion to the effects of the Watergate scandal on the Nixon presidency, was announced Aug. 8, three days after Nixon released a statement and transcript of tape recordings admitting "a serious act of omission" in his previous accounts of the Watergate cover-up.

According to Nixon's statement, six days after the break-in at the Democratic Party's national headquarters in the Watergate building in Washington, D.C. June 17, 1972, he had ordered the Federal Bureau of Investigation's probe of the break-in halted. Furthermore, Nixon stated, he had kept this part of the record secret from investigating bodies, his own counsel and the public.

The admission destroyed what remained of Nixon's support in Congress against a tide of impeachment that was already swelling. The President's support had been eroding dangerously since the House Judiciary Committee had debated and drawn, with substantial bipartisan backing, three articles of impeachment to be considered on the House floor.

The development was accompanied by serious defections in the Republican Congressional leadership and acknowledgment from all sides that the vote for impeachment in the House was a foregone conclusion and conviction by the Senate certain.

This assessment was delivered to the President by the senior Republican leaders of the Congress. Shortly afterwards, Nixon made his final decision to resign. He announced his decision the evening of Aug. 8, to a television audience estimated at 110–130 million persons. In his 16-minute address, Nixon conceded he had made "some" wrong judgments. He said he was resigning because he no longer had "a strong enough political base in Congress" to carry out his duties of office.

5

Jaworski: no agreement made. There was widespread speculation both before and after Nixon's resignation as to what legal action, if any, might be taken against him as a private citizen. A key element in the issue was the fact that Nixon had been named as an undicted co-conspirator in the cover-up case, even without the latest damaging transcripts. The grand jury had reportedly wanted to indict Nixon but had been dissuaded by Watergate special prosecutor Leon Jaworski.

In a statement released after the resignation announcement Aug. 8, Jaworski said that bargaining regarding possible immunity from prosecution had not played a part in Nixon's decision to leave office. "There has been no agreement or understanding of any sort between the President and his representatives and the special prosecutor relating in any way to the President's resignation," the statement said.

Jaworski said his office "was not asked for any such agreement or understanding and offered none."

Congressional opinion on possible prosecution was divided: the New York Times reported Aug. 9 that many members felt Nixon should be subject to the same liability to prosecution as any ordinary citizen, but some members followed the general line of argument that the disgrace of resignation was sufficient punishment. Senate Republican Leader Hugh Scott (Pa.) said Aug. 9 that the nation already had its "pound of flesh" and that it did not need the "blood that goes with it." Senate Democratic Leader Mike Mansfield (Mont.) said he would have "appreciated" some reference in Nixon's address "to the reasons which brought about this tragedy."

A telephone survey conducted by the Gallup organization Aug. 8–9 and reported Aug. 11 found that 55% of those polled opposed further criminal investigation of Nixon, while 37% believed such investigation should be pursued.

Another legal possibility concerning Nixon's future—pardon by President Ford either before or after an indictment—was indirectly dismissed by Ford's press secretary Aug. 9. Asked about such prospects at a news briefing,

J. F. terHorst said he had not spoken to Ford about the issue directly, but cited Ford's statements during his 1973 vice presidential confirmation hearings. (Ford had been asked: if a President resigned would his successor have the power to prevent further investigation or prosecution? Ford replied: "I do not think the public would stand for it.... The attorney general, in my opinion, with the help and support of the American people, would be the controlling factor.")

Nixon Pardoned, Controversy Follows

Ford pardons Nixon. Ford Sept. 8, 1974 granted Nixon a full pardon for all federal crimes he "committed or may have committed or taken part in" during his term in office.

Nixon issued a statement accepting the pardon and expressing regret that he had been "wrong in not acting more decisively and more forthrightly in dealing with Watergate."

The White House also announced Sept. 8 that the Ford Administration had concluded an agreement with Nixon giving him title to his presidential papers and tape recordings but guaranteeing they would be kept intact and available for court use for at least three years.

The pardon for Nixon was unexpected. Ford made his announcement from the Oval Office on Sunday morning after attending church. After reading a brief statement on his decision before a small pool of reporters and photographers—the event was filmed for broadcast later—Ford signed a proclamation granting Nixon the pardon.

Nixon had not been formally charged with any federal crime and the granting of a pardon in advance was a reversal of Ford's position on the issue, expressed as recently as his Aug. 28 news conference.

The announcement drew wide protest and some support. Generally, it was split along partisan lines and the Democratic protest was more heated than the Republican support for the Nixon pardon. One protester was White House Press Secretary J. F. terHorst, the first appointee of the Ford Administration, who resigned Sept. 8 as a matter of "conscience." The controversy broadened Sept. 10 when a White House spokesman, in response to a question, said Ford was considering pardons for all Watergate defendants. Following further adverse criticism, the White House shifted its stance Sept. 11 and announced that individual requests for pardons would be considered.

In his statement, Ford said Nixon and "his loved ones have suffered enough, and will continue to suffer no matter what I do." "Theirs is an American tragedy in which we all have played a part," he said. "It can go on and on, or someone must write 'The End' to it. I have concluded that only I can do that. And if I can, I must."

He cited the "years of bitter controversy and divisive national debate" and the prospect of "many months and perhaps more years" before Nixon "could hope to obtain a fair trial by jury in any jurisdiction" of the country. He "deeply believe[d] in equal justice for all Americans, whatever their station or former station," Ford said, but "the facts as I see them are" that a former president, "instead of enjoying equal treatment with any other citizen accused of violating the law, would be cruelly and excessively penalized either in preserving the presumption of his innocence or in obtaining a speedy determination of his guilt in order to repay a legal debt to society."

Ford continued: "During this long period of delay and potential litigation, ugly passions would again be aroused, our people would again be polarized in their opinions, and the credibility of our free institutions of government would again be challenged at home and abroad. In the end, the courts might well hold that Richard Nixon had been denied due process and the verdict of history would be even more inconclusive with respect to those charges arising out of the period of his presidency of which I am presently aware."

His conscience told him, Ford said,

"that I cannot prolong the bad dreams that continue to reopen a chapter that is closed" and that "only I, as President, have the constitutional power to firmly shut and seal this book." "My conscience says," he continued, "it is my duty, not merely to proclaim domestic tranquility, but to use every means I have to ensure it. . . . I cannot rely upon public opinion polls to tell me what is right. I do believe that right makes might. . . ."

The proclamation granting Nixon "a full, free, and absolute pardon" referred to the articles of impeachment recommended by the House Judiciary Committee. "As a result of certain acts or omissions" occurring during his presidency, it stated, Nixon had become liable to possible indictment and trial for offenses against the U.S. "It is believed," the proclamation continued, that a trial, if it became necessary, could not "fairly" begin for a year or more and "in the meantime, the tranquility to which this nation has been restored by the events of recent weeks could be irreparably lost by the prospects of bringing to trial a former president of the United States. The prospects of such trial will cause prolonged and divisive debate over the propriety of exposing to further punishment and degradation a man who has already paid the unprecedented penalty of relinquishing the highest elective office in the United States."

The timing of the pardon was criticized by the American Bar Association Sept. 20. The group's board of governors recommended that Ford withhold future pardons "until appropriate judicial processes have been followed." It made the recommendation "in order to avoid the possible erosion of public respect for law," it said.

A request by New York Law professor Joseph H. Koffler to void the pardon was dismissed by U.S. District Court Judge Gerhard A. Gesell of Washington Sept. 25 on the ground a private citizen lacked standing to challenge a presidential pardon.

Nixon's statement—In accepting the pardon Sept. 8, Nixon said he hoped that this "compassionate act will contribute to lifting the burden of Watergate from our country." His "perspective on Watergate" had changed, he said, and "one thing I can see clearly now is that I was wrong in not acting more decisively and more forthrightly in dealing with Watergate, particularly when it reached the stage of judicial proceedings and grew from a political scandal into a national tragedy."

He spoke of "the depths of my regret and pain at the anguish my mistakes over Watergate have caused the nation and the presidency." He knew, he said, "that many fair-minded people believe that my motivation and actions in the Watergate affair were intentionally self-serving and illegal. I now understand how my own mistakes and misjudgments have contributed to that belief and seemed to support it. This burden is the heaviest one of all to bear. That the way I tried to deal with Watergate was the wrong way is a burden I shall bear for every day of the life that is left to me."

Pretrial pardons renounced—The Senate Sept. 12 adopted a resolution urging Ford to refrain from using his pardoning power until the judicial process in each case was completed. The resolution, passed by a 55–24 vote with bipartisan support, had no force of law but merely expressed the sense of the Senate.

The resolution opposed any pardon "to any individual accused of any criminal offense arising out of the Presidential campaign and election of 1972 prior to the indictment and completion of trial and any appeals of such individual." Such a pardon "would effectively conceal the whole truth of what happened" in the Watergate case, the resolution stated.

Ford on Nixon pardon: 'no deal.' President Ford, in an historic appearance before a House subcommittee Oct. 17, 1974, defended his pardon of Nixon.

Ford was not put under oath for his testimony, in which he reiterated he had made "no deal" with Nixon on the pardon but had acted "out of my concern to serve the best interests of my country."

The hearing, which was televised, was before the House Criminal Justice Subcommittee of the Judiciary Committee.

Its members were allotted five minutes each to question the President after his 5,-000-word opening statement. The toughest questioning was by Rep. Elizabeth Holtzman (D, N.Y.), but, protesting the time limit, she did not wait for answers except to one query, whether Ford would be willing to turn over to the panel all tape recordings of his conversations with Nixon. Ford responded that the Nixon tapes were safe, "in our control," and being held for the Watergate special prosecutor. They "will not be delivered to anybody until a satisfactory agreement is reached with the special prosecutor's office," Ford said.

Holtzman said there were "dark suspicions" in the public mind about the pardon. Why was no crime cited, no guilt confessed? she asked. Other Holtzman questions: Why was the action done in haste and secrecy, and without consultation with the attorney general or the special prosecutor? Why did the pardon accompany a tapes agreement that was contrary to the public's right to know and prosecutor's access to the materials?

Ford stressed "there was no deal, period" between himself and Nixon. He said his main purpose in granting the pardon was to turn national attention "from the pursuit of a fallen president to the pursuit of the urgent needs" of the country. No conditions were placed on the pardon, and no confession sought, Ford said, although acceptance of the pardon in his mind implied admission of guilt. The tapes arrangement, while "related in time to the pardon discussions," was "not a basis" for the decision to grant the pardon. Ford said he acted at the time he did out of concern that continuation of the legal processes against Nixon and thus the preoccupation of the nation with the controversy would have consumed at least a year and probably longer.

Rep Don Edwards (D, Calif.) asked Ford to put himself in the position of a high school teacher. " . . . how would you explain to the young people the American concept of equal justice under the law?"

Ford's response: "Mr. Nixon was the 37th president of the United States. He had been preceded by 36 others. He is the only president in the history of this country who has resigned under shame and disgrace. I think that in and of itself can be understood, can be explained to students or to others. That was a major, major step and a matter of, I'm sure, grave, grave deliberations by the former president and it certainly, as I've said several times, constituted shame and disgrace."

Ford broke little new ground, except to reveal that Nixon Administration officials just prior to Nixon's resignation were considering such options as Nixon pardoning himself, or pardoning various Watergate defendants, then himself, before resigning. A third option, Ford said, was "a pardon to the President should he resign," granted by Ford, who would be his successor. Ford said the options were broached to him by Nixon aide Alexander M. Haig Jr. at an Aug. 1 meeting when Haig advised him of the critical evidence on tape against Nixon which would probably lead to Ford's accession to the office.

Ford said he told Haig he wanted "time to think" about the pardon option, then informed him the next day that "I had no intention of recommending what President Nixon should do about resigning or not resigning and that nothing we had talked about the previous afternoon should be given any consideration in whatever decision the President might make."

Ford also admitted that he made misleading public statements after that time—that he did not believe Nixon was guilty of an impeachable offense—because "any change from my stated views, or even refusal to comment further, I feared, would lead in the press to conclusions that I now wanted to see the President resign to avoid an impeachment vote in the House and probably conviction vote in the Senate."

Pardon inquiry dropped—The House subcommittee Nov. 22 voted, 6–3, against further pursuit of resolutions of inquiry into the Nixon pardon.

Nixon's Recollections

In a series of interviews televised during 1977, ex-President Nixon answered ques-

tions about the Watergate affair and other events of his years as President. The interviewer was British TV celebrity David Frost, who put together five telecasts from nearly 29 hours of taped sessions with Nixon. Nixon's fee for the interviews was reported to be $600,000 plus a share (said to be 10%) of the profits. The segments that carried material on Watergate were telecast May 4, May 19, May 25 and Sept. 3, 1977. A May 12 telecast was devoted to international affairs.

May 4 program: bad judgment conceded. Nixon told Frost in the interview segments telecast May 4, 1977 that he really had "let the American people down" by making misleading statements on the Watergate affair and not meeting his constitutional duty to see that the laws of the country were enforced.

But he insisted that he not committed any criminal or impeachable offense. He had impeached himself by resigning, he said. "I brought myself down. I gave 'em a sword. And they stuck it in, and they twisted it with relish. And I guess if I'd been in their position, I'd have done the same thing."

The Watergate interview focused largely on Nixon's knowledge of or possible participation in obstruction of justice; payment of hush money to E. Howard Hunt Jr., one of the original Watergate defendants; Nixon's anguish over the resignation of key aides H. R. Haldeman and John D. Ehrlichman, and Nixon's final assessment, under probing by Frost, that he had made mistakes.

Obstruction of justice debated—Frost pressed hard to get Nixon to acknowledge some complicity in the cover-up stemming from the break-in at Democratic national headquarters in the Watergate office building in Washington, D.C. on June 17, 1972. Using one of the "new" tapes—a conversation Nixon had had on June 20, 1972 with Charles W. Colson, a special counsel to the President—Frost sought to establish that Nixon was "pretty well informed" and already counseling a cover-up within three days after the break-in.

Frost also cited Nixon's attempt to have the CIA block the FBI investigation of Watergate, an attempt documented on the so-called "smoking gun" tape of June 23,

1972, featured in the Nixon impeachment proceedings. At that time of his intervention, Frost contended, Nixon knew of the involvement of Hunt and G. Gordon Liddy, a staff member of the Nixon campaign committee. Both men were apprehended later as members of the original seven Watergate defendants. Their involvement connected the break-in strongly to the Nixon campaign committee and directly to the White House.

Frost argued that Nixon had been aware that a consequence of his action to block the FBI investigation would be to protect Hunt and Liddy, "who were criminally liable." That, Frost said, "was a conspiracy to obstruct justice."

Nixon told Frost the important thing was his motive. His motive then was not to try to cover up a criminal action but to avoid any "slop-over" that would damage innocent people "or blow it into political proportions."

Nixon gave a personal interpretation of the statute on obstruction of justice. "One must have a corrupt motive," he said. His motive was "pure political containment," he said, and that was not a corrupt motive.

Frost countered, however, with precise information on the statute, which he said stated that motive was not a factor where intent and foreseeable consequences were apparent. He said Nixon's intent, which was to stop the investigation, was "absolutely clear" and "the foreseeable, inevitable consequence, if you'd been successful, would have been that Hunt and Liddy would not have been brought to justice." "How can that not be a conspiracy to obstruct justice?" he asked.

Hush money to Hunt—Frost also pressed Nixon persistently on the question of whether he had endorsed payment of money to the burglars, especially Hunt, to buy their silence.

Frost used two more heretofore undisclosed tapes of Nixon conversations with Colson on Feb. 13 and 14, 1973. On the first, Nixon was quoted as saying, "this tremendous investigation rests unless one of the seven begins to talk. That's the problem." On the Feb. 14 tape, Nixon said, "The cover-up is the main ingredient; that's where we gotta cut our losses; my losses are to be cut. The President's losses got to be cut on the cover-up deal."

Frost also cited 16 quotes, from a March 21, 1973 tape, when Nixon talked of the urgency of handling "the Hunt problem." Nixon said such things then as "Get the million bucks, it would seem to me that would be worthwhile" . . . "That's worth it, and that's buying time" . . . "Would you agree that this is a buy-time thing? You'd better damn well get that done, but fast" . . . "We have no choice."

Nixon told Frost he had not authorized any blackmail payments. He said he would have condoned payments to the defendants "for humanitarian purposes, to help these people with their defense." But he said he would have disapproved payment "for the purpose of keeping them quiet."

Nixon said he did have a concern that men engaged in such dangerous covert work were "likely to say anything" and that under "the pressures of the moment" they "could have started blowing and putting out all sorts of stories to embarrass the Administration."

Because of such concern, he had considered Hunt's request for money, Nixon said, but it came down in the end to a question of clemency and he considered that wrong and opposed it.

The question was whether the payment to Hunt was made at the direction of the President, Nixon said, and "it was not."

Coaching of aides on testimony—Again referring to the March 21, 1973 tape, Frost asked about "the coaching" that Nixon gave his White House counsel John W. Dean 3rd and his chief of staff, Haldeman, on "how to deal with the grand jury without getting caught." He quoted Nixon's advice: "perjury's a tough rap to prove," and "just be damned sure you say, 'I don't remember. I can't recall.'"

Nixon said he thought the advice was "proper" because he was beginning to put himself in the position of "an attorney for the defense—something that I wish I hadn't felt I had the responsibility to, to do." He said every lawyer gave similar advice to a witness going before a grand jury.

'A modified, limited hang-out'—Frost referred to Nixon's public statement of August 15, 1973 that said he had instructed Dean to write "a complete

report of all that he knew on the entire Watergate matter."

How did he reconcile this, Frost asked, with his taped requests at that time (late March 1973) for a "self-serving goddamned statement denying culpability of principal figures," a "complete statement but make it very incomplete" and, "Understand, I don't want to get all that goddamned specific."

Frost inquired as well about the apparent policy decision eventually for "a modified, limited hang-out," hang-out being disclosure of truth.

As for the "report being complete but incomplete," Nixon told Frost, what he meant was that Dean "should state what he was sure of." One day Dean would say "one thing" and another day "something else," Nixon claimed.

Nixon insisted that he had given an instruction on the report that, "If it opens doors, let it open doors."

"I meant by that I was prepared to hear the worst as well as the good," he said.

'Almost prayed I wouldn't wake up'—The remainder of the interview was largely a monologue by Nixon. Frost had wondered why, when Nixon discovered the complicity of his aides, "you didn't pick up the phone and tell the cops."

Nixon recounted the firing of Haldeman and Ehrlichman, his chief domestic affairs adviser, as one of the most "heartrending" experiences of his life.

As a prelude, he told a story of an assignment, when he was Vice President, from former President Eisenhower. Eisenhower gave him the task, he said, of firing Eisenhower's White House chief of staff, Sherman Adams. Adams had become enmeshed in allegations of impropriety attached to acceptance of gifts from a business friend.

(Meade Alcorn told the Hartford Courant May 5 that Nixon's version of this event was "not accurate." Alcorn, who was Republican national chairman at the time, said he, not Nixon, informed Adams that Eisenhower desired his resignation. Alcorn's account was corroborated by a Sept. 29, 1958 Time magazine story that said Eisenhower told Alcorn: "You've got to handle it. It's your job. . . ." Also, Adams wrote in his memoir, *Firsthand Report*, that no one

told him he had to resign but that Alcorn and another person—not Nixon—both relayed to him Eisenhower's concern about "the feeling against me among the influential supporters of the Republican Party.")

When it came to his own problem, Nixon continued to Frost, he handled it himself, although it took him two weeks.

"I frankly agreed . . . in my own mind that they had to go on the basis of the evidence that had been presented," Nixon said. But "I still wanted to give them a chance to survive." He remembered pleading with an aide that "I can't fire men simply on the basis of charges; they've got to have their day in court."

Nixon said Haldeman, a "splendid man," disagreed with the decision, as did Ehrlichman. "I knew that Ehrlichman was bitter because he felt very strongly he shouldn't resign," Nixon related, "although, he'd even indicated that Haldeman should go and maybe he should stay."

Nixon said he told Ehrlichman on the morning he accepted his resignation, "I hoped, I almost prayed I wouldn't wake up this morning."

"I cut off one arm and then cut off the other arm," Nixon said of the firings. "Now, I can be faulted, I recognize it. Maybe I defended them too long; maybe I tried to help them too much, but I was concerned about them. I was concerned about their families. . . .

"And, I suppose you could sum it all up the way one of your British prime ministers summed it up, Gladstone, when he said that 'the first requirement for a prime minister is to be a good butcher.' Well, I think the great story as far as summary of Watergate is concerned, I, ah, I did some of the big things rather well."

"I screwed up terribly in what was a little thing and became a big thing. But I still have to admit, I wasn't a good butcher."

Nixon revealed that he had seriously considered resigning when Haldeman and Ehrlichman left.

He expresses regret—Frost asked Nixon if he would admit to something stronger than "mistakes"—commission of a crime, or abuse of power or failure to fulfill totally the oath of office, or even making the public suffer "two years of needless agony." "I think that people need to hear it," Frost said, "and I think unless you say it you're going to be haunted for the rest of your life."

He had made mistakes, Nixon said, and some he regretted the most came from his public statements. Some of those statements were misleading, he said, "misleading in exaggerating."

"I said things that were not true. Most of them were fundamentally true on the big issues, but without going as far as I should have gone, and saying perhaps that I had considered other things, but had not done them.

"And for all those things I have a very deep regret. . . . It was my fault."

Nixon rejected the idea "that what brought me down was a coup, a conspiracy," although he said "there may have been" a conspiracy.

"I don't know what the CIA had to do. Some of their shenanigans have yet to be told, according to a book I read recently. I don't know what was going on in some Republican, some Democratic circles, as far as the so-called impeachment lobby was concerned."

He also mentioned the "enormous political attack I was under," a "five-front war with a fifth column." He cited "a partisan media" and "partisan" staffs of the Special Prosecutor and congressional Watergate committees.

But, Nixon continued,

"People didn't think it was enough to admit mistakes, fine. If they want me to get down and grovel on the floor, no. Never. . . ."

What he had done was fail to meet his responsibility to see that the laws of the nation had been enforced, he said. To the extent that he did not meet that responsibility, he said,

"To the extent that within the law, and in some cases going right to the edge of the law in trying to advise Ehrlichman and Haldeman and all the rest as to how best to present their cases—because I thought they were legally innocent—that I came to the edge and, under the circumstances, I would have to say that a reasonable person could call that a cover-up."

"I didn't think of it as a cover-up. I didn't intend it to cover up. Let me say, if I intended to cover up, believe me, I'd have done it. You know how I could have done it? So easily? I could have done it immediately after the election, simply by giving clemency to everybody, and the whole thing would have gone away."

He had not committed obstruction of justice nor an impeachable offense nor participated in an illegal cover-up, Nixon

declared. These were "legalisms, as far as the handling of this matter is concerned," he said. "It was so botched up. I made so many bad judgments. The worst ones, mistakes of the heart, rather than the head. . . ."

In sum, as far as the American people were concerned, Nixon said:

"I let down my friends. I let down the country. I let down our system of government and the dreams of all those young people that ought to get into government, but think it's all too corrupt and the rest. . . . I let the American people down, and I have to carry that burden with me for the rest of my life.

"My political life is over. . . . Maybe I can give a little advice from time to time."

Poll results vs. Nixon. A special poll of viewers of the Nixon interview found that 69% thought Nixon was still covering up, 72% thought he was guilty of obstruction of justice or other impeachable crimes and 75% opposed his taking a future role in public life. The survey was conducted by the Gallup Organization for the May 16 Newsweek magazine (available May 9).

May 19 program: a president's right to act illegally. Nixon told Frost in an interview segment telecast May 19, 1977 that a president had the right to commit illegal acts whenever he deemed them in the best interests of the country.

"When the president does it, that means that it is not illegal," Nixon asserted to Frost in the third of the series of their pre-recorded programs.

Speaking of the so-called Huston plan of wiretapping, burglary, mail openings and infiltration of antiwar groups, Nixon said, "If the president . . . approves something because of the national security, or in this case because of a threat to internal peace and order of significant magnitude, then the president's decision in that instance is one that enables those who carry it out, to carry it out without violating a law. Otherwise they're in an impossible position."

Nixon said there were restraints on a president, that he had to face the electorate and had to get appropriations from Congress. He had not read "every jot and every tittle" of the Constitution, he said, but he did know that it had been "argued that as far as a president is concerned that in wartime, a president does have certain extraordinary powers which would make acts that would otherwise be unlawful, lawful if undertaken for the purpose of preserving the nation. . . ."

Nixon portrayed himself as a wartime President who took actions, as President Lincoln had during the Civil War, to save a nation "torn apart" by dissent. The clamor of dissent over the Vietnam war had encouraged the enemy to think the war could be won in Washington, Nixon argued. "Without having enough support at home, the enemy, in my opinion, would never have negotiated in Paris, as they did," he said.

May 25 program: resignation was 'shattering.' Nixon told Frost in the interview section of May 25 that his resignation from the presidency meant "life without purpose" and was "a very, very shattering experience."

Besides his own resignation, and some of the incidents in the final hours of his Administration, Nixon talked of the resignation of Spiro Agnew as his Vice President, the overthrow of the Salvador Allende government in Chile in 1973, his wife's health and some items of his personal finances.

Among the highlights of his remarks:

Chile—Nixon said an Italian businessman had come to him before Allende came to power in 1970 and told him, "If Allende should win the election in Chile and then you have Castro in Cuba, what you will in effect have in Latin America is a red sandwich, and eventually it will all be red."

"And that's what we confronted," Nixon told Frost.

"But that's madness of him to say that," Frost objected.

"It isn't madness at all," Nixon replied. "It shows somebody cutting through the hypocritical double standard of those who can see all the dangers on the right and don't look at the dangers on the left."

Nixon continued that "Allende was overthrown eventually, not because of anything that was done from the outside, but because his system didn't work in Chile."

Nixon made a distinction between right-wing and left-wing dictatorships. If a right-wing variety "is not exporting its revolution, if it is not interfering with its neighbors, if it is not taking action against the United States, it is therefore of no security concern to us." As for a left-wing dictatorship, he said, "we find that they do engage in trying to export their subversion to other countries, and that does involve our security interests."

Agnew—Nixon reported that Justice Department officials had informed him, prior to Agnew's resignation, that the charges against Agnew were serious and could be corroborated and were of such magnitude that the officials would have to recommend a prison sentence.

After considering whether the impeachment process was open to Agnew, and receiving legal advice that it was not, Nixon said "Agnew had come to the point, and he realized that he had no alternative but to do everything that he possibly could to avoid going into court.

"And therefore the resignation option became absolutely indispensable. The point here was not that resignation would lead to no charges, but the point is that resignation was a step that if it were not taken, would probably mean that he would get a tougher rap."

In their meetings at the time, Nixon said, Agnew maintained his innocence of bribery. He said Agnew told him it was "common practice" for state or county officials in Maryland to receive contributions from contractors doing business with those governments.

Agnew assured him, Nixon said, "that he never did anything while he was Vice President for which he received any funds, and I totally believed him on that."

Frost asked Nixon which version he believed, Agnew's or the Justice Department's.

"I was very pragmatic," Nixon replied. It "didn't really make any difference," he said, since it was obvious, after hearing the department's version, that Agnew "was frankly going to get it."

"So under the circumstances, it became an irrelevant point," Nixon continued. "I'm not going to sit here and judge Spiro Agnew. I know that he feels he didn't get enough support from the White House. . . .

All that I can say is that it was a no-win proposition."

Nixon explained that Agnew felt "that I could have put the arm on [then-Attorney General] Elliot Richardson a little harder to get Richardson to let up on him."

Personal finance items—Nixon assured Frost that "I not only don't have any assets abroad, I never had a foreign bank account in my life."

He denied knowledge of the backdating of his gift of vice presidential papers to the government, which gained him an income-tax deduction, later disallowed, of $432,-787. All he did, he said, was to order the papers to be delivered to the archives and his aides to "follow the proper procedures and take whatever deductions the law allows."

Offered money to Haldeman, Ehrlichman—Nixon reported offering money to his top White House aides, H.R. Haldeman and John D. Ehrlichman, for their Watergate defense. The money, he said, would have come from $100,000 of a secret campaign contribution from the late Howard R. Hughes and from "other campaign funds that were possibly available for this, which we don't need to go into."

Haldeman and Ehrlichman rejected the offer of money but they recommended, Nixon said, that he pardon everybody involved in Watergate before he left office and couple that with a general amnesty for the Vietnam draft-dodgers and deserters. Nixon rejected their suggestion.

Ford's pardon—As for his own pardon by Gerald R. Ford, who became President upon his resignation, Nixon said there was no discussion of the pardon before he left office.

He had told his lawyer, Nixon said, "I'd just as soon go through the agony of a trial so that we can scrape away at least all the false charges, and fight it out on those in which there may be a doubt and then I'll take whatever the consequences are."

But his lawyer advised him, he said, that "in his legal opinion, there was no chance whatever I could get a fair trial."

Nixon said he was "so emotionally drawn, mentally beaten down, physically not up to par, that I said, 'Well, OK, I'll do it.'" Thus, he accepted the pardon, he said.

Sept. 3 program: destruction of tapes. Nixon told Frost in the interview section telecast Sept. 3 that he believed he had ordered destruction of all but the most historical of his presidential tape recordings before the Watergate investigators learned of their existence.

The instruction, which Nixon conceded might have been dubious, was given to his White House chief of staff, H. R. Haldeman. (Haldeman said he had not recalled an explicit order to this effect.)

"If the tapes had been destroyed," Nixon told Frost, "I believe that it is likely that I would not have had to go through the agony of the resignation." The tapes played an instrumental role in the impeachment hearings prior to Nixon's resignation.

On the other hand, Nixon said he did not believe that there was anything "detrimental" to him on the tapes. Nor did he believe "that they were going to come out." The possibility of exposure existed, he said, and if he had thought that the tapes contained "conversation that was criminal, I sure as the, the dickens—I could use stronger expletives, but not before this home audience—I sure as the dickens would have destroyed them."

Nixon also made these comments in the final segment:

The 18½-minute gap—Nixon had no explanation for the 18½-minute erasure in a potentially key tape of a conversation between him and Haldeman three days after the 1972 Watergate break-in. "I didn't do it," he said of the erasure.

He upheld the testimony of his White House secretary, Rose Mary Woods, that she might have been responsible for a portion of the erasure, accidentally, in reaching for a telephone while the tape was running.

Nixon memoirs on Watergate. Nixon considered the Watergate affair primarily "a public relations problem that only needed a public relations solution." according to excerpts from his memoirs.

The book, titled *RN: The Memoirs of Richard Nixon,* was published May 15, 1978 by Grossett & Dunlap. Excerpts from the memoirs, however, were published by many newspapers in installments, beginning April 30.

In the first two installments carried by the New York Times, Nixon dealt with the Watergate affair, which eventually led to his resignation from office, before turning in the third installment to other matters.

Nixon admitted in the memoirs that he had been a participant in the cover-up of Watergate and that he had misled the public about his role in it.

But Nixon maintained as he had in the past that he committed no high crime or misdemeanor that would warrant impeachment. His mistakes were more on the order of misjudgments and tactical errors, he felt, and he was forced from office by overwhelming political forces.

Among the highlights from the excerpts concerning Watergate:

He first learned about the break-in, and arrest of burglars, at Democratic national headquarters in the Watergate building in Washington, the day after it happened. He read of it in an item in a newspaper in Florida, where he was spending a long weekend. At the time, "I dismissed it as some sort of prank," he wrote of the break-in.

The memoirs related some advice from John Mitchell, who at the time of the break-in was chairman of the Committee to Reelect the President (CRP). The advice was relayed through Nixon's White House chief of staff, H. R. Haldeman. ". . . John Mitchell had told Bob on the phone enigmatically not to get involved in it . . ."

Haldeman "had also heard," Nixon went on, "that the money found on the arrested men—over $1,000 in bills—had apparently come from the CRP."

The excerpts next cited a meeting several days later between Nixon and his aide Charles W. Colson, who figured, he said, "that the break-in might have been something the Cubans organized on their own." The reference was to several Miami Cubans who had been arrested in the break-in.

"I told Colson we were just going to leave the Watergate matter where it was, with the Cubans," Nixon wrote.

Nixon acknowledged telling Haldeman several days after that, on June 23, 1972, to have the Central Intelligence Agency call the Federal Bureau of Investigation and "say that for the sake of the country they should go no further into this case."

"As far as I was concerned, this was the end of our worries about Watergate," Nixon recounted.

Later, Nixon said, "I could sense that a cloud of suspicion still hung over the White House." "Yet, I felt sure that it was just a public relations problem that only needed a public relations solution," he said.

It was not until nine months after the break-in, Nixon said, that "what I had assumed . . . was the major Watergate problem—the question of who had authorized the break-in—had been overtaken by the new and far more serious problem of the cover-up."

In reference to his former presidential legal counsel, John W. Dean 3rd, who eventually broke with the Nixon White House, Nixon wrote:

"I worried about the wrong problem. . . . I did not see it then, but in the end, it would make less difference that I was not as involved as Dean had alleged than that I was not as uninvolved as I had claimed."

As his presidency unraveled, it came to the point that he had to let go of his principal aides, Haldeman and John Ehrlichman, his chief domestic affairs adviser. At that point, he was aware that any involvement of theirs would brush off onto him.

"I told myself that I had not been involved in the things that gave them criminal vulnerability," Nixon wrote. "But there were things that I had known. I had talked with Colson about clemency" for the Watergate burglars, "and I had been aware that attorneys' fees and family support were going to the defendants."

"I was faced with having to fire my friends for things I myself was a part of.

"I was selfish enough about my own survival to want them to leave; but I was not so ruthless as to be able to confront easily the idea of hurting people I cared about so deeply. I worried about the impact on them if they were forced to leave, but I worried more about the impact on me if they didn't."

In the second installment of the excerpts May 1, Nixon told of his belief, now, that from the time of the disclosure of the existence of the presidential tape recordings, "and my decision not to destroy them, my Presidency had little chance of surviving to the end of its term."

Nixon said he had "raised the idea" of whether the tapes should be destroyed, but he decided, he said, "that the tapes were my best insurance against the unforeseeable future."

"I was prepared to believe that others would turn against me just as John Dean had done," he continued, "and in that case the tapes would give me at least some protection."

Nixon attributed the adverse public reaction to the tapes, once they were released, partially to the style of the conversations.

"There is noble talk in the Oval Office to be sure, high-minded and disinterested," he wrote. "But there are also frustration, worry, anxiety, profanity and, above all, raw pragmatism when it comes to politics and political survival."

"With the . . . transcripts, I was in the position of telling the American people things that they did not want to know."

Watergate Prosecutors

Jaworski announces resignation. Leon Jaworski announced Oct. 12, 1974 his resignation as Watergate special prosecutor. The resignation, effective Oct. 25, was submitted to Attorney General William B. Saxbe. It was accepted by President Ford, according to White House Press Secretary Ron Nessen.

Jaworski simultaneously submitted an interim report on his activities.

A large part of the interim report was devoted to the question of the "the validity" of the pardon granted Nixon by Ford. The legal right to grant the pardon, and the legality of one granted prior to filing of charges, were "so clear, in my opinion, as not to admit of doubt," Jaworski said. He had also concluded that there was nothing in the charter and

guidelines of his office "that impairs or curtails the President's free exercise of the constitutional right of pardon."

For him to challenge the pardon for a court test of its legality, he said, would be "intellectually dishonest," "a spurious proceeding in which I had no faith; in fact, it would be tantamount to unprofessional conduct and violative of my responsibility as prosecutor and officer of the court." Jaworski explicitly denied there was any connection between his resignation and the pardon or the suggestions that Nixon be indicted to test the pardon.

Says Nixon guilt evident—In an interview published by the Wall Street Journal Oct. 16, Jaworski conceded that the pardon of Nixon had prevented an indictment and trial but he said the pardon itself, and evidence that was or would become public, would show Nixon guilty of obstruction of justice. "The evidence will show he's guilty, just as much as a guilty plea," Jaworski said. He said a pardon "isn't just a beautiful document to frame and hang on the wall. You are offered a pardon only because it is believed you can be charged and convicted. You accept it only if you want to be cleared."

Jaworski said he had not spoken out until a jury had been chosen for the Watergate conspiracy trial of Nixon aides and until he had announced his resignation. He denied the resignation had resulted from the pardon and said it was a mistake to think more evidence against Nixon would have become public if the case had gone to trial. "If he had gone to trial," Jaworski said, "he could have invoked his Fifth Amendment guarantees against self-incrimination, pleaded nolo contendere, or even pleaded guilty, and we wouldn't have learned any new details."

Ruth new special prosecutor. Henry S. Ruth Jr. was named Watergate special prosecutor Oct. 23. The appointment was made by Attorney General William B. Saxbe, who said it had been cleared with President Ford, the Democratic and Republican leaders of Congress and the ranking majority and minority leaders of the House and Senate Judiciary Committees.

Jaworski had recommended Ruth, 43,

deputy special prosecutor for 18 months, as his successor.

Ruff replaces Ruth—Attorney General Edward H. Levi Oct. 7, 1975 announced the appointment of Charles F. Ruff as Watergate special prosecutor to replace Ruth, who was resigning to join the Urban Institute. Levi said the office no longer required a fulltime director and Ruff would divide his time there with a faculty position at Georgetown University Law Center.

Watergate prosecutor reports. The Watergate Special Prosecutor's office issued a report Oct. 15, 1975 with proposals on how to prevent recurrence of the illegalities it had been investigating. The report was issued by outgoing prosecutor Ruth.

The report said only "a few" inquiries remained active. Its work had resulted in the convictions of more than 50 individuals and 19 corporations. The latter were convicted of having made illegal financial contributions to political candidates.

Among the unresolved cases was the office's probe of the 18½-minute gap in a key presidential tape recording of a conversation on June 20, 1972. The grand jury concluded that "a very small number of persons could have been responsible for the erasures," the report said, but there was insufficient evidence to prosecute any specific individual.

On another case, the office found "strong circumstantial evidence" that there had been "deliberate" deletions in the transcripts of recorded conversations released by the White House in May 1974, but prosecutors were unable to establish the "criminal intent" necessary for indictment.

The office's recommendations were said to be aimed at preventing future "criminal abuse of power by government officials in high places," the unchecked growth of "secrecy in the federal executive branch" and "an undemocratic condition wherein money is power, and skillful, cynical public relations cements that power."

The report opposed the establishment of a permanent special prosecution office because it would lack accountability. In an extraordinary situation like Watergate,

the accountability was there, directly to the public, because of the "high visibility" of public interest, the report said.

The report's other recommendations:

■ Congress should clarify in a proposed constitutional amendment whether a sitting President was subject to criminal prosecution.

■ The post of attorney general, and other high Justice Department posts, should not be held by persons who served in high-level campaign posts for the President.

■ The same restriction should be applied to nominees for heads of such agencies as the Federal Bureau of Investigation, Internal Revenue Service and Secret Service.

■ Such investigative agencies should be responsive to broad policy direction from the President but prohibited from becoming part of the President's political apparatus.

■ Information given on a confidential basis to federal law enforcement agencies should be protected by law from disclosure.

■ An Administration should establish and disclose the power claimed in national security investigations involving foreign intelligence searches and seizures.

■ Congressional oversight should be exercised concerning law enforcement and intelligence agencies.

■ The Central Intelligence Agency, the FBI and the IRS should have written policies stating the purposes for the intelligence to be gathered and the methods used to gather it; the policies should be submitted to a presidentially appointed domestic intelligence board with authority to make public recommendations and hear justifications for the policies.

■ The Justice Department should have an aggressive policy to prosecute government contractors, unions and corporations for illegal political contributions.

■ Officers and shareholders of corporations with government contracts should be liable to prosecution for illegal political donations and the statute of limitations for such crimes should be extended to five years.

■ The Federal Election Commission should have authority to establish standards for campaign conduct and to investigate campaign tactics.

Harder Look at Appointments

In what may have been at least a partial reaction to the suspicions raised by the Watergate affair, Congress members in 1974 gave what appeared to be unusually strict examination of persons nominated by President Ford for appointment to federal posts.

Rockefeller becomes Vice President after close scrutiny. Nelson A. Rockefeller, nominated by President Gerald Ford Aug. 20, 1974 as Vice President, underwent harsh questioning by both houses of Congress before he won confirmation by 90–7 Senate vote Dec. 10 and 287–128 House vote Dec. 19.

At hearings of the Senate Rules Committee, Sen. Robert C. Byrd (D, W. Va.) led the attack on the issue of whether Rockefeller money posed a problem of undue power for a vice president. Byrd also aggressively interrogated Rockefeller on the pardon President Ford extended to former President Nixon.

Byrd told Rockefeller Sept. 24, "With all due respect, I am a great admirer of yours, you're about the hardest man to pin down I've ever seen." Rockefeller told Byrd, "You've got an ability to put someone on the spot beyond what I've ever seen."

However, Byrd said after the Sept. 24 session that he agreed with the committee chairman, Sen. Howard W. Cannon (D, Nev.), that there was nothing in sight that would endanger confirmation.

Cannon had stated that view Sept. 11 in announcing the committee's vote to ask Rockefeller to make a full public disclosure of his worth in lieu of a requirement for divestiture of holdings or establishment of a blind trust. Public disclosure, he said, would permit the public and the press to be a "watchdog against conflict of interest." Arriving in Washington Sept.

22 for the hearings, Rockefeller pledged to do whatever Congress required to resolve the conflict-of-interest issue, including the method of a blind trust.

A preliminary figure of $33 million was disclosed Sept. 12 as the estimate of Rockefeller's immediate personal worth. The total was upped Sept. 19 to $182.5 million–$62.5 million as the net worth of himself and his wife plus the income from two trusts worth $120 million. Rockefeller in releasing the figures to counter "incomplete and therefore misleading data" leaked to the press, said the $33 million total did not include the value of art ($12.5 million) and real estate ($8 million) he had pledged to the public. Another $9 million difference largely came, he said, from updated appraisals of the art and real estate.

Rockefeller Sept. 23 read parts of a 72-page autobiographical statement submitted to the committee. It included summaries of his tax returns for the past 10 years. He stressed his family's tradition of philanthropy deriving from the "ethic" of social responsibility from wealth. His own contribution to various philanthropic and charitable institutions totaled $33 million, he said, not counting the $20.5 million pledged in art and real estate.

To correct a possible public misconception about the family influence in the oil industry, he said he owned no more than .2% of the outstanding share in any oil company and the family did not hold more than 2.06% of the stock of any oil company. He said he did not own any shares in the Chase Manhattan Bank, which was headed by his brother, David, although one of the trusts of which he was a beneficiary did own 325,000 shares worth $25.4 million.

Among the personal financial data he disclosed: his total holdings amounted to $218 million, mostly in trusts; he was the life beneficiary of trusts totaling $116.5 million; his wife was the beneficiary of securities and trusts totaling $3.8 million and his six children held assets totaling $35.6 million; he had paid $69 million in taxes during his lifetime; his income over the past decade totaled $46.8 million, of which about $1 million a year in tax-free securities held by two trusts, was not subject to taxation.

Byrd spoke of the Rockefeller family's "economic power" as a "stranglehold" on segments of the economy. Rockefeller, rejecting the idea of "empire," said the family had "interests" but not "controlling interests."

Byrd sought a commitment from Rockefeller on the Nixon pardon issue, which had been the opening line of inquiry used by the committee's chairman, Cannon. Cannon had asked, in light of Ford's statement at his vice presidential hearings that the country "wouldn't stand for" a prior pardon of a president, "What assurances do we have that your responses will be anything more than empty phrases given at the moment?" Rockefeller affirmed a "total inclination" against granting such a pardon, adding that at the same time he "would not amend the Constitution—and renounce the power that the Constitution gives to a president."

Sen. Mark O. Hatfield (R, Ore.) asked his stand on U.S. interference in foreign countries, "such as in Chile" by the Central Intelligence Agency (CIA). Rockefeller said "a gray world" did exist among nations, "sad and tragic" as that was, and in the case of Chile the CIA activities had the approval of "top administrators in our government" and he assumed "they were done in the national interest."

Rockefeller Sept. 24 was again questioned on the family wealth and Nixon pardon issues. He told Cannon that Nixon "accepted a pardon, which in my opinion was tantamount to admitting guilt."

Byrd questioned whether Rockefeller would be able to "perceive the national interest against the background of your own wealth." Can't we agree, he asked, that "the influence is tremendous—tremendous, colossal influence?" "Can't I add the word, 'potential'?" Rockefeller rebutted. "Very well," said Byrd.

Byrd Sept. 25 challenged Rockefeller for a commitment that he would not invoke executive privilege to keep any member of the executive branch from testifying to Congress on non-security matters. Rockefeller said he could think "of no cause at the present time in which I would invoke the doctrine" but said it

would be "irresponsible to make a flat commitment."

Rockefeller also disclosed that he had received and rebuffed appeals for financial aid from former Nixon aide John D. Ehrlichman and former Vice President Spiro T. Agnew after they had left office.

Cannon said Oct. 9 that he would make public the response of Rockefeller to the committee's request for full details of financial gifts Rockefeller had made over the years to various associates. Recent disclosure of substantial gifts to such persons as Secretary of State Henry A. Kissinger, former New York State Republican Chairman L. Judson Morhouse and William J. Ronan, chairman of the Port Authority of New York and New Jersey, put the nomination of Rockefeller as vice president into immediate controversy.

The gift to Kissinger—$50,000 in early 1969 after Kissinger left the Rockefeller staff and before he joined the Nixon Administration—was disclosed by the Gannett newspaper chain. A Kissinger spokesman confirmed the report Oct. 4, saying Rockefeller had told Kissinger at the time he wanted to make him a gift "at the close of their some 15 years of association."

Reports of the Morhouse gift surfaced at the same time. Morhouse, a former member of the New York State Thruway Authority, had been sentenced to two-three years imprisonment in 1966 on bribery and unlawful-fee charges stemming from a state liquor authority scandal in New York. The conviction was upheld by higher state courts, but Rockefeller commuted his sentence in 1970.

Rockefeller's press secretary Hugh Morrow confirmed Oct. 5 the Kissinger and Morhouse gifts and said Ronan also received a gift but did not specify the sum. Rockefeller had made "many gifts to institutions and individuals" over the years, Morrow said, and had paid the appropriate gift taxes. Any impropriety was denied. The Kissinger gift had been made out of gratitude for long-time service, Morrow said. The Morhouse gift—$86,000—was made to ease "overwhelming financial problems," he said, and in Ronan's case, it was "friendship and the governor's desire to help keep a good man in government."

According to Morrow, Rockefeller loaned Morhouse $100,000 in 1969, when Morhouse was GOP state chairman, then an unsalaried post. Because of Morhouse's illness and financial problems, Rockefeller canceled the outstanding balance of the loan—$86,000—in 1973 and paid federal and state gift taxes of about $48,000.

The gift to Ronan was also in the form of a debt cancellation, Morrow said, and was made after Ronan resigned in April 1973 as chairman of the (New York State) Metropolitan Transportation Authority, carrying a $75,000 a year salary, and before he became chairman of the Port Authority, an unsalaried post. The size of the gift to Ronan was disclosed Oct. 7—$550,000. Ronan, who currently was a paid adviser to the Rockefeller family and a trustee of the New York State Power Authority ($12,500 annual salary), had borrowed that amount in a series of loans over the years, Morrow explained Oct. 8, and Rockefeller canceled the entire debt in the spring of 1973 as a gift that "could be related," Morrow said, "to the year-end bonus given to executives of large corporations." The gift tax paid by Rockefeller in this instance totaled $330,000.

Morrow said Rockefeller had received a "personal and confidential" letter from Cannon requesting information "on certain facts the committee has had for several weeks," a reference to gift-tax returns filed with the panel. Morrow told reporters Oct. 7 Rockefeller had also made "nominal contributions" to a number of Senate and House campaigns.

Senate Republican Leader Hugh Scott (Pa.) said Oct. 8 he had "seen nothing which has impaired the integrity of Gov. Rockefeller in any way," but Sen. Jesse A. Helms (R, N.C.), a Rockefeller critic at the confirmation hearings, called Oct. 8 for a reopening of the hearings.

Rockefeller was also linked Oct. 10 to a derogatory biography of Arthur J. Goldberg, published during Rockefeller's campaign in 1970 against Goldberg for governor of New York.

In response to reports that the Congressional probers were looking into the book affair, Rockefeller issued a statement Oct. 10 saying that he was unaware of it at the time but his brother Laurance had invested $60,000 in the book as a business venture. The book, "Arthur J. Goldberg, the Old and the New," by Victor Lasky, was expected to "sell well," the statement said, but "was a total flop" and Laurance sustained a net loss of about $52,000 but did not take a tax deduction on the business loss. "Had he only told me about it at the time," Rockefeller said, "I would have been totally opposed to it and would have strongly advised against his participation in any form."

He said he learned about Laurance's investment through the Federal Bureau of Investigation (FBI) during a background check because of the vice presidential nomination. Rockefeller said he told the FBI he had heard of the book at the time "but knew nothing about its preparation or financing." An aide had told him early in the 1970 campaign, Rockefeller said, that Lasky was working on a Goldberg biography but he "really didn't pay any attention because I never felt that such books coming out during campaigns cut much ice one way or another. I never heard any more about it until the book was out and someone showed me a copy, which I never even opened."

The Rockefeller campaign organization in 1970, however, reportedly received 100,-000 copies of the book.

Later Oct. 10, Goldberg expressed shock that the Rockefellers "would participate in such a dirty campaign trick" and said they owed him an apology "for financing a scandalous and libelous book."

Rockefeller apologized to Goldberg Oct. 12 by telephone. Citing the "derogatory" book, he said: "It is quite clear that when the project was brought to my attention, I should have immediately taken steps to see to it that it was stopped as utterly alien to and incompatible with the standards I have always tried to observe in my political life. I take full responsibility for the whole regrettable episode."

On the money gifts, Rockefeller made public Oct. 11 a list of 20 current and former public officials and staff aides to whom he had given about $2 million over the past 17 years. The list, prepared for the Congressional inquiries, was released because of leaks to the press, which Rockefeller deplored as "very unfair in terms of the privacy of individuals and also unfair in the sense of giving an atmosphere of uncertainty and suspicion."

Among those on the list were William J. Ronan, listed as getting $625,000 ($75,000 more than previously reported); Alton G. Marshall, president of Rockefeller Center, Inc. and once secretary to Rockefeller (when the latter was governor), listed as getting $306,867; Emmet J. Hughes, who had been a Rockefeller speechwriter and political adviser, $155,000; Edward J. Logue, chairman of the New York State Urban Development Corporation, $131,389, of which $100,000 was an outstanding debt from a loan of $145,000; James W. Gaynor, former New York state commissioner of housing and community renewal, $107,000; Henry L. Diamond, former New York state commissioner of environmental conservation, $100,000; and Victor Borella, former labor aide to Rockefeller as governor, $100,000.

During the second phase of the Senate Rules Committee's confirmation hearings, Rockefeller Nov. 13 indicated unhappiness about the book, which he called a "hasty, ill-considered decision in the middle of a hectic campaign." "Let's face it, I made a mistake," he said in revising his earlier testimony about the book's publication. Rockefeller admitted that he, rather than his brother Laurance, had initiated the financing venture. The project had been broached to him, Rockefeller testified, by his political aide Jack Wells, who said he was seeking investors for the book, which he felt would be profitable. Wells described the book as "a high-level, analytical" biography of Goldberg, Rockefeller said.

Rockefeller said he "sent a message" to his brother asking if he could help find investors, but Laurance "didn't have time to find other investors and simply authorized his people to underwrite" the book. That was Laurance's "only connection" with the project, Rockefeller said, admitting that he was "embar-

rassed" and "humiliated" by his role because "I did an injustice to my brother." He stressed that his previous "incorrect" version of the financing came from faulty recollection and that he was, "delinquent in not clearing this up sooner."

When Sen. Robert Byrd (D, W.Va.) suggested the belated disclosure of the true financing was "a throwback to what we have had over the past two years," reminiscent "of the dirty tricks of the Nixon era," Rockefeller protested, "No sir. I must bitterly object to that."

Rockefeller also was questioned Nov. 13 about his substantial money gifts. Chairman Howard Cannon (D, Nev.) questioned whether they "placed the recipients into what we might call psychological servitude."

The money was not "designed to corrupt," Rockefeller said, nor did it "corrupt either the receiver or the giver." "I'd not do this for someone in government who was not working for me and was not a close personal friend," he said.

Pressed by Sen. Claiborne Pell (D, R.I.) about whether he would continue the practice if he became vice president, Rockefeller said he was "hesitant" to renounce it solely on "humanitarian" grounds. "I would have to think that under certain circumstances I would want to help," he said. "There might be a case where I would feel in humanity that I ought to do something."

There were several further financial disclosures Nov. 13: Rockefeller's net worth was estimated by the Congressional Joint Committee on Internal Revenue Taxation at $73 million, higher than Rockefeller's own latest estimate of $62 million; a total of $3,265,374 in political contributions was made by Rockefeller over the past 18 years, $1,031,637 of it to his own presidential campaigns. The Rockefeller family's political contributions exceeded $20 million.

Rockefeller had made public Oct. 28, and made available to the committee, a list of loans totaling $507,656 made over the past 17 years to friends, associates and family members. The largest—$84,000—was to Robert B. Anderson, former Navy secretary and Treasury secretary. The form of the loan was in stock purchases in the International Basic Economy Corp., a Rockefeller-controlled corporation with extensive holdings in Latin America, which Anderson paid for with a 10-year installment note at a 3% interest rate, but sold in a short time back to Rockefeller for the price paid for the shares. The loan was made in 1957, before Anderson was named to the Treasury post and repaid shortly after his appointment.

Rockefeller was questioned primarily Nov. 14 about his money gifts. He conceded that his generosity could be "misinterpreted" and offered to "cut it out." He volunteered to pledge in writing to forego gifts or loans to federal employes if confirmed except for "nominal" gifts, such as for birthdays or weddings, or "in the event of medical hardships of a compelling human character." After some partisan squabbling over whether to keep the latter restriction or require public disclosure of such gifts, the commitment as testified to was let stand.

Sen. Byrd brought out in questioning that several of Rockefeller's loans or gifts of money had been made while the recipients held public office in New York.

The Senate committee ended hearings on the nomination Nov. 18. The House Judiciary Committee opened its hearings on the nomination Nov. 21.

Rockefeller promised the House panel, if he were confirmed, to put all securities he owned outright in "blind" trusts and to instruct the trustees of his existing trusts to act as though they were handling blind trusts, or those over which he would neither have control nor knowledge of its operation. In opening the hearing, Chairman Peter W. Rodino (D, N.J.) said "we must attempt to measure the network of Rockefeller family wealth and place it into the perspective of both the American economy and the American political system." Rep. Don Edwards (D, Calif.) indicated the Rockefeller family holdings could constitute a "conflict of interest" if he became vice president. Rockefeller responded with this comparison: in a single week, he said, the three largest U.S. insurance companies invested $156 million, the nation's pension funds invested $200 million and the Arab oil states took

in $1 billion. "These figures dwarf to the point of absurdity the funds my family owns," he said. "The Arabs in a week accumulate more money than my family in three generations of work."

Rockefeller also disputed the suggestion that public officials who received gifts from him would have "never forget" their benefactor. "You lose more friends than you gain by giving money," Rockefeller said. "It's a strain on a relationship."

Gibson's name withdrawn. President Ford Nov. 12, 1974 withdrew his nomination of Andrew Gibson as head of the Federal Energy Administration after controversy developed over the disclosure that Gibson's former employer, Interstate Oil Transport Co., had agreed to pay him $1 million over 10 years under a financial agreement negotiated when he joined the firm. Gibson, who had quit Interstate in May after serving as president for 16 months, had already collected about $120,000 in pay and was due to receive $88,000 annually over a 10-year period.

The withdrawal was at Gibson's request. In a personal letter accepting the withdrawal, Ford expressed his "continuing high regard" for Gibson and promised to appoint him to "another responsible position in government" if an investigation of his background by the Federal Bureau of Investigation (FBI) proved satisfactory.

Gibson asked Ford that the FBI check be completed despite his withdrawal in order that conflict of interest charges, raised when news of the separation contract was first revealed Nov. 6, could be refuted. In his letter to Ford, Gibson said the terms of his agreement with Interstate were "specific and unconditional" and would not inhibit him "in the discharge of my official responsibilities as federal energy administrator."

However, because the national energy situation required immediate attention, and the Interstate controversy promised to provoke a lengthy confirmation fight in the Senate, Gibson asked Ford to withdraw his name, according to the letter.

White House Press Secretary Ron Nessen said Donald Rumsfeld, White

House staff coordinator, took full responsibility for mismanaging the appointment. (The actual personnel selection had been made by a Rumsfeld appointee, William N. Walker, who himself held office temporarily pending results of the official FBI report on his background. FBI files on former Administration employes like Gibson and Walker, who had quit as FEA general counsel in June, required updating when they were rehired.)

Nessen said Gibson had orally informed Walker's office of the severance contract before President Ford announced his intention to nominate Gibson, but that written details of the contract were not provided to Walker until after the announcement was made. Ford and Rumsfeld were not told about the contract until after news accounts raised the conflict of interest possibility.

Assistant Senate Majority Leader Robert Byrd (W.Va.) had urged Ford Nov. 11 to withdraw the Gibson nomination "without further ado" because of the "blatant conflict of interest" involved. "I cannot see the Senate confirming that nomination," Byrd warned.

FEA conduct code issued—Federal Energy Administrator John Sawhill Aug. 29 had issued strict new standards of conduct for FEA employes requiring that high and middle level agency officials file financial disclosure reports.

The conduct code prohibited officials from participating in FEA matters in which they or their families had financial interests, and barred FEA employes from accepting free food or drink from "interested parties," such as FEA contractors or firms regulated by the agency.

Flanigan also dropped. The White House announced the withdrawal Nov. 16, 1974 of the nomination of Peter M. Flanigan to be ambassador to Spain. Controversy over Flanigan's role in the Nixon Administration had developed in committee hearings, and the nomination (made Sept. 17) had been delayed, requiring resubmission after the Congressional recess. The White House announcement said Flanigan had requested that his nomination not be resubmitted.

At a Senate Foreign Relations Committee hearing Oct. 2, Sen. Thomas F. Eagleton (D, Mo.) had denounced Flanigan's nomination as "a disgrace to the United States." Eagleton cited Flanigan's dealing with diplomatic appointments and campaign contributors and with the International Telephone and Telegraph Corp. and its controversial antitrust settlement.

Flanigan denied any impropriety and asserted his motivation always was to act in "the national interest." He acknowledged telling former Nixon fund raiser Herbert W. Kalmbach that a potential ambassadorial nominee, Ruth Farkas, later named ambassador to Luxembourg, was "a good prospect for solicitation." Kalmbach's sworn testimony—which Eagleton quoted—that Flanigan had advised him to contact Farkas since she was interested "in giving $250,000 for Costa Rica," was attributed by Flanigan to a misunderstanding on the telephone.

Kingsley withdrawn. The White House announced Nov. 19, 1974 the withdrawal of its nomination of Daniel T. Kingsley for a seat on the Federal Power Commission (FPC). The withdrawal, at the nominee's request, was related to Kingsley's role in the Nixon Administration, where he was a special assistant to the president in the White House personnel office. He resigned Dec. 19, 1972. The Senate Watergate Committee cited Kingsley in association with a plan to place political supporters of Nixon in government agencies.

The nomination to the FPC had been made by Nixon and resubmitted by President Ford but hearings had been delayed by the Senate Commerce Committee pending investigation of the Watergate-related issue.

Other Developments

Civil suit settlement final. The Democratic National Committee and the financial trust representing former President Nixon's re-election committees formally agreed in court Aug. 9, 1974 to a settlement of lawsuits resulting from the Watergate burglary and wiretapping.

The trust was to pay $775,000 to the Democratic Party, former Democratic National Chairman Lawrence F. O'Brien and the Association of State Chairmen. O'Brien said as part of the agreement he would turn over his share—$400,000—to the Democratic Party with the request "that it be applied to a program designed to re-enlist the confidence of the American people in the two-party system."

The accord also provided that the DNC would not file Watergate-related suits in the future. The Republicans agreed to drop libel countersuits.

Final acceptance of the tentative agreement had been held up partly by Rep. Shirley Chisholm (D, N.Y.), who had said June 19 that she would not sign a waiver against future lawsuits against the Republicans. As part of the tentative settlement, the 11 Democratic presidential and vice presidential candidates had been requested to sign such waivers.

A DNC spokesman said Aug. 15 that the GOP trust accepted assurances in the final settlement that "good faith" efforts had been made to prevent future suits, but suits by individual Democrats would not be legally precluded.

Reelection funds seized. The Internal Revenue Service Feb. 22, 1977 seized $550,508 of the $1.3 million in surplus campaign funds that remained from former President Richard M. Nixon's re-election campaign in 1972.

The IRS action was disclosed in records filed with the FEC and reported by the Washington Post May 6. The IRS seizure represented a tax assessment to insure payment of back taxes on campaign funds used in the Watergate break-in and later

paid as hush money to defendants in the break-in.

At the end of March, $485,000 remained in the surplus funds account, but claims totaling more than $1 million had been lodged against the money. Claims by the four Cuban-Americans convicted in the break-in had been settled but other suits were unresolved.

Sirica cuts Watergate sentences. Federal district Judge John J. Sirica Oct. 4, 1977 reduced the prison terms of three principal figures in the Watergate cover-up case—former Attorney General John Mitchell and former White House aides H. R. Haldeman and John Ehrlichman. Each had been sentenced to serve terms of 2½ to eight years in prison.

Sirica cut the terms to at least one year but no more than four years. This made Mitchell and Haldeman eligible for parole in June 1978. Ehrlichman, who entered prison earlier, was less than a month from completion of a year's term, but he also was serving a concurrent 20-month-to-five-year sentence imposed by another judge for a separate conviction in the White House "plumbers" case.

Sirica made the ruling after an unusual hearing in which tape-recorded statements of contrition by the three were played in open court.

Mitchell, 64, said he was "truly sorry" and "no set of circumstances" would ever again "lead me to take such actions or to perform such deeds."

Haldeman, 50, expressed "very real remorse" and a desire to make a "constructive contribution" to society to offset "what may have been a destructive contribution."

Ehrlichman, 52, said he had "permitted" himself to be "used." "I abdicated my moral judgments and turned them over to someone else," he said, and making one's own moral judgments was "what a man has to hang onto."

Koreagate

U.S. Congress Members Accused re Korean Bribes

Early in 1976, reports surfaced in Washington about alleged bribes that the South Korean government was said to have paid to members of Congress for their influence in promoting Korean interests with the U.S. government. Little more was heard of the story until much later in 1976. But before the year was over, the reports had grown into a major scandal that soon was called "Koreagate" in obvious reference to the Watergate affair. The principal figure in the scandal was a rich, party-loving Korean named Park Tong Sun but known in the U.S. as Tongsun (or Tong Sun) Park.

2 Representatives face probe. The Washington Post disclosed Feb. 19, 1976 that two House members, Rep. Joseph P. Addabbo (D, N.Y.) and Rep. Robert L. Leggett (D, Calif.), were under investigation by the Justice Department for allegedly taking bribes of under $10,000 each from the government of South Korea. Both members emphatically denied receiving bribes.

The Post report said that government sources outside the Justice Department had informed the newspaper that the investigation had been authorized directly by Attorney General Edward H. Levi in a verbal message to FBI Director Clarence M. Kelley.

The investigation also involved a member of House Speaker Carl Albert's (D, Okla.) staff, Sue Park Thomson. Thomson, a Korean-born U.S. citizen, described her job as serving as Albert's "liaison" with members of the House. She was a frequent hostess of parties for congressmen, congressional aides and lobbyists.

No explanation was reported of the purpose of the alleged bribes.

South Korean lobbying, gifts probed. The Justice Department was engaged in a major investigation of a South Korean scheme to influence U.S. legislators and top executive officials during the 1970s through distribution of cash, gifts and campaign contributions totaling between $500,000 and $1 million annually, the Washington Post reported Oct. 24, 1976.

The Post, citing unnamed government sources, said that there was evidence indicating South Korean President Park Chung Hee had personally approved the plan. South Korean businessman Park Tong Sun was the figure in Washington, D.C., with primary responsibility for dis-

25

tributing the largesse, the Post said. More than 20 past and present congressmen were under investigation, the Post reported, for receiving cash or gifts as part of the Korean effort to "create a favorable legislative climate."

Park Tong Sun, an affluent entrepreneur who entertained many Washington political figures, maintained that his activities had been purely for his own benefit, and were not directed in any way by the South Korean government. The South Korean government, likewise, disclaimed any connection with his activities.

However, according to the initial Post story and subsequent news accounts through November, federal investigators had gathered evidence supporting such a connection and providing the following details:

Park Tong Sun had been arrested in the late 1960s by the Korean Central Intelligence Agency (KCIA) for allegedly claiming to be related to President Chung Hee Park (they were not related). Park Tong Sun was released, and in late 1970 attended a meeting at the South Korean presidential mansion—the Blue House—where he agreed to carry out the lobbying-and-influence-peddling scheme. President Park, high KCIA officials and Pak Bo Hi, who became chief aide to the South Korean evangelist Sun Myung Moon, were at the meeting.

Reportedly, Park Tong Sun was able—with the backing of the Korean government—to become the chief intermediary for Korean imports of American rice. He used, at least in part, the substantial brokerage commissions to finance the influence-peddling scheme. The commission income might have been partly illegal, since some of the rice imports were federally subsidized under the U.S. Food for Peace program, which prohibited commissions for persons officially connected with the importing country.

The financing behind Park Tong Sun's activities, like much else in the case, was the subject of various, conflicting accounts. Park Tong Sun reportedly had told investigators that he received $1 million a month from Gulf Oil Corp. for unspecified services. Gulf said Nov. 2 that it had "never had any financial relationship with Tongsun Park [the English form

of Park's name]." The company acknowledged that it had dealt with two Korean companies owned by Park Tong Sun's brother. Gulf officials called the $1-million-a-month figure "incredibly high."

Agriculture Department sources had expressed doubt that Park Tong Sun could have earned enough from his rice dealings to finance his Capitol Hill lobbying, the New York Times said Nov. 3. The rice commissions at first had been estimated at up to $5 million a year. The Times Nov. 7 reported that investigators had obtained records from a bank account that Park Tong Sun had in the Bahamas showing that he had brought large amounts of cash into the U.S. Whatever the source, investigators agreed that Park Tong Sun's actual expenditures in Washington had been considerable.

One key piece of evidence in the investigation was a list, found on Park Tong Sun's person Dec. 8, 1973 by customs officials at Anchorage, Alaska. On the list were the names of about 90 congressmen and appointed officials. Numbers were noted beside most names. The list was headed by the word "contributions." Park Tong Sun claimed that the figures represented requested contributions, not paid sums. Customs officials had taken notice of Park Tong Sun when he reportedly failed to declare a watch. He had complained about the delay, which, he said, might cause him to miss a dinner engagement with then Vice President Gerald Ford. The officials' attention had been directed to the list when Park Tong Sun reportedly tried to tear it up, along with some other documents.

Bo Hi Pak, reportedly one of those attending the alleged 1970 Blue House meeting, was reportedly at the center of other strands of the investigation that involved a Washington bank and several tax-exempt Korean organizations operating in the U.S. The Post reported Nov. 14 that Pak and various associates owned 36% of the Diplomat National Bank when it opened in 1975. (Pak's associates were reportedly members of Sun Myung Moon's Unification Church, an organization in which Pak had considerable influence.) The Post added that Park Tong Sun owned, through purchases made by three 'front' men, another 10% of the bank when it opened. The Post reported that there was no evidence that Park Tong Sun and Pak had tried to take over the bank, but that federal investigators were curious about their heavy investment in the institution.

(Syndicated columnist Jack Anderson, who was on the board of directors of the bank, announced Nov. 21 that he would resign his position with the bank and liquidate various holdings to avoid the appearance of any conflict of interest with his profession as an investigative journalist.)

Pak was also connected, as an officer and director, with the Korean Cultural and Freedom Foundation, an organization that also figured in the federal probe. According to the Nov. 2 Post, investigators were looking into charges that money raised by the tax-exempt foundation had been used as part of the influence-peddling scheme. (The foundation had been described, in congressional testimony given by a former friend of Pak, as a "front organization" for the South Korean government and Sun Myung Moon's church.)

A New York State official said Oct. 30 that the state would seek to bar the foundation from further fund-raising in New York because, he said, the funds were not going for their stated purposes. The official—head of the State Board of Social Welfare—said that only 8% of the money raised over the past year for the Children's Relief Fund had actually been used to feed hungry children. D. L. Miller, executive director of the foundation, rejected the charge Oct. 30. Miller declined, however, to explain specifically how the foundation's money had been spent. He said that Pak was responsible for that information.

Pak Nov. 1 responded to the charges against him that had surfaced in the press. He read a prepared statement saying that "neither I as an individual, nor the Korean Cultural and Freedom Foundation, nor any of its projects, such as Radio Free Asia, has ever attempted to influence a congressman or official to benefit the Korean Government." Pak said that neither he, nor the foundation "as an organization" had ever contributed money to a political figure, and he specifically denied ever having been "linked with or employed by" the KCIA. He added that the Rev.

Moon had been "mistreated" by the American press.

Pak also denied attending the alleged Blue House meeting where the influence-peddling scheme was planned. He specifically denied a report that said the meeting had taken place in June 1969—a month when, Pak said, he had not been in Korea. (Some press reports gave a different date for the supposed meeting than the one repudiated by Pak. It was not clear how Pak's statement applied to those reports.) Pak said that if tape recordings of the alleged meeting existed—as had been conjectured by some news accounts—they should be made public so that the truth could be known.

However, the Post Nov. 7 reported that the Justice Department probe had unearthed more evidence of links between the KCIA and Pak. According to the Post story, Pak at the request of the KCIA, had arranged in 1974 for Moon's followers to stage demonstrations opposing the impeachment of then President Richard M. Nixon.

The KCIA support for Nixon was motivated by a belief that Nixon was committed to U.S. military and economic support of South Korea, while a succeeding president might not be. Reportedly, the influence-peddling scheme had initially been launched because of South Korean fears that the U.S. might end its military presence there. (The withdrawal by Nixon of 22,000 troops had reportedly contributed to those fears).

The question of troop commitments and the South Korean lobbying effort had surfaced in another area, Donald K. Ranard, a former State Department official, said Nov. 13. Ranard, who had been director of the Office of Korean Affairs from 1970 to 1974, said that the Nixon Administration had been unwilling to take action against the Korean lobbying, despite knowledge of the activities, because Administration officials had feared any action might jeopardize the commitment of 52,000 Korean troups to the U.S. effort in South Vietnam.

Ranard said there had been no official policy guidelines insulating the Korean lobbyists, but "there was always a feeling below the surface that the Korea lobby was to be left alone."

(The New York Times Oct. 29 and 30 reported that there was another federal probe—independent from the influence-peddling one—into KCIA activities in the U.S. Those activities were aimed at stilling criticism of the Korean regime by Korean exiles or Korean Americans, the Times said. The probe was said to be investigating charges of harassment and intimidation—including beatings—of critics of the Seoul government.)

The Justice Department probe was described in November as still in an early stage. The prospects for bringing prosecutions were complicated by the fact that Korean diplomats held legal immunity and by the difficulty in proving that specific legislative votes or executive actions were taken because of a bribe. There were also indications that some of the information obtained by the investigators came from U.S. intelligence electronic surveillance in Korea, and thus might be legally inadmissible as evidence.

Park Tong Sun had claimed to be cooperating fully with the investigation, but he left the U.S. before the end of October. The New York Times reported Nov. 23 that a Korean source had indicated that Park Tong Sun had been told by the Korean government to stay out of the U.S. until the scandal had died. According to the Times source, Park was unwilling to stay abroad and was being detained by KCIA agents in London.

The Times Dec. 1 reported that federal investigators had said that Kim Sang Keun, a Korean Embassy official who was said to be the second highest KCIA official in the U.S., had agreed to aid the investigation and had requested political asylum in the U.S. It had been reported earlier that the Seoul regime, in an attempt to limit the investigation, had ordered Kim to return to Korea.

U.S. figures involved—Among the U.S. political figures named in press accounts in connection with the influence-peddling scheme were:

House Democratic Whip **John J. Mc-Fall** (Calif.), who admitted Nov. 4 that he had received $3,000, in cash from Park Tong Sun in October 1974. On Nov. 25, McFall added that he had received another $1,000 in cash in 1972, also from

Park Tong Sun. The money was all deposited in McFall's office account or put in his office petty cash fund. The office account was used for such purposes as newsletters, lunches for constituents, etc.

Louisiana Gov. **Edwin W. Edwards,** who had been a Democratic representative from 1965 to 1972. He admitted Oct. 25 that Park Tong Sun had given his wife $10,000 in cash in 1971. Edwards said he had not learned of the gift until "late 1973 or early 1974." Edwards admitted receiving other gifts from Park Tong Sun, including a table worth $900. Edwards said that Park Tong Sun had not asked for any favors.

Rep. **John Brademas** (D, Ind.), who said Oct. 26 that he had received $5,150 in campaign contributions from Park since 1972, and that they had all been reported as required by law. A spokesman for Brademas said that the congressman's voting record had been consistently opposed to aid for South Korea.

Rep. **Richard T. Hanna** (D, Calif.), who said Nov. 9 that he had been a silent partner with Park Tong Sun in an import-export business that earned between $60,-000 and $70,000 for Hanna over a three-year period.

Former Rep. **Jerome R. Waldie** (D, Calif. 1966–74), who acknowledged receiving a $2,000 contribution from then South Korean Ambassador Kim Dong Jo for Waldie's unsuccessful 1973 gubernatorial campaign, the Washington Star reported Nov. 4.

Other representatives reported to be under investigation, according to the Oct. 30 and Nov. 13 issues of Congressional Quarterly, were **William S. Broomfield** (R, Mich.), **John M. Murphy** (D, N.Y.), **Lester L. Wolff** (D, N.Y.), **Tennyson Guyer** (R, Ohio), **Robert L. Leggett** (D, Calif.), **Joseph P. Addabbo** (D, N.Y.), **Otto E. Passman** (D, La.). Former Rep. **Cornelius J. Gallagher** (D, N.J., 1959–72) was also said to be under investigation.

The Washington Post Oct. 29 reported that in the last months of the Nixon Administration the South Korean government had attempted to give a cash gift and expensive presents to presidential staff members. The Post story cited a $10,000 gift of cash in May, 1974 to John E. Nidecker, who was then a White House aide. Nidecker gave the money to Philip C. Habib, then U.S. ambassador to Korea, who turned it over to a Central Intelligence Agency official for return to the original donor, identified as Park Chong Kyu, head of the South Korean presidential security forces in Seoul.

General Dynamics wins loan guarantee, Park Tong Sun connection in question. U.S. Commerce Secretary Elliot L. Richardson Jan. 19, 1977 approved a federal loan guarantee of up to $730 million to help General Dynamics Corp. finance the construction of seven supertankers to transport liquefied natural gas (LNG). The ships would be leased by a General Dynamics subsidiary to a subsidiary of the British-based Burmah Oil Co., which had a 20-year contract to transport LNG from Indonesia to utilities in Japan.

Richardson's decision was made during his last full day in office as a member of the outgoing Ford Administration. Jimmy Carter was inaugurated the next day to succeed Gerald R. Ford as President of the United States.

An official of the Office of Management and Budget said Jan. 19 that the loan guarantee apparently was the largest ever granted by the federal government to a single corporation.

British observers believed that without the loan guarantee, Burmah might have lost the LNG contract, which was expected to gross $100–$200 million annually and yield an $8-million annual profit, the Washington Post reported Jan. 17. If the contract had been lost, it was feared, Burmah might have been forced to declare bankruptcy.

Debate over the loan guarantee had centered on Burmah's admission that it had paid $3 million to Park Tong Sun.

The Securities and Exchange Commission was looking into the Burmah payment. Burmah contended the money was Park's fee for negotiating a $56-million settlement in an unrelated shipping dispute that involved Japan Lines Inc., one of Burmah's competitors for the LNG contract.

Several of Burmah's competitors had accused the firm of giving Park $3 million to pay off government officials in the U.S. and abroad. Burmah countered by charging that Park had been working for the competition and had tried recently to obtain hundreds of millions of dollars from General Dynamics in return for not interfering in the loan-guarantee dispute.

In his announcement, Richardson said he was "satisfied" that the $3-million payment "did not relate to" the loan guarantee. However, Richardson also said Burmah had refused to make a full disclosure about the money to the SEC. Burmah had assured the Commerce Department that the withheld material contained no relevant facts, the statement said.

In his announcement, Richardson also said that on Dec. 8, 1976, he had informed the incoming Carter Administration of his plan to make the loan-guarantee decision by Jan. 19. Carter's representatives had "declined to comment," Richardson said.

A Carter Administration official at the Commerce Department said Jan. 21 that the reason there had been no attempt to defer the decision was that "none of us had any legal standing at the time" of Richardson's letter. The incoming administration also had had little time to study the controversial matter, he said. (If the loan guarantee had not been approved by Jan. 31, Japan might have canceled the Burmah contract.)

Inquiry Broadens

Congress probes charges. The House of Representatives opened two inquiries into the "Koreagate" scandal in February 1977.

One of the House probes, being conducted by the International Organizations Subcommittee of the International Relations Committee, was examining the whole range of U.S.-South Korean relations. That inquiry, budgeted at $300,000, had been approved by the full committee Feb. 3. The other House probe was being carried out by Committee on Standards of

Official Conduct (the ethics committee). The ethics committee inquiry, approved 388-0 by the House Feb. 9, was examining allegations of wrongdoing by House members. Its budget was $530,000.

The ethics committee June 8, by a unanimous voice vote, decided to ask every member of the House to fill out a questionnaire covering the legislator's relations with South Korea. The questionnaire included inquiries concerning trips to South Korea, gifts offered or accepted from South Korean officials or "any person now suspected" of representing South Korea, and personal dealings with five persons: Park Tong Sun, Sue Park Thomson, Kim Han Cho, Kim Dong Jo, a former South Korean ambassador to the U.S., and Kim Sang Keun, a KCIA (Korean Central Intelligence Agency) official who reportedly had promised in late 1976 to aid the Justice Department inquiry.

The ethics committee told the full House June 8 it had reached an agreement with the Central Intelligence Agency that gave the committee access to CIA information about Korean attempts to influence the U.S. Congress. It had been reported that the CIA and other executive-branch agencies had gathered considerable information about the Korean effort, but had not acted on it. Reportedly, the failure to take action had stemmed from a desire to protect the sources of the information and to avoid complicating U.S. relations with South Korea. Also, the information reportedly was dispersed among a number of government offices, making it difficult to put together a coherent picture of the South Korean lobbying effort.

Ex-KCIA head describes lobbying effort. Kim Hyung Wook, a former director of the South Korean Central Intelligence Agency (KCIA), asserted in the New York Times June 5, 1977 that Park Tong Sun had served as a KCIA agent.

In addition to the statement about Park, Kim also provided other information about the alleged South Korean lobbying effort.

Kim had become the head of the KCIA in 1963 after taking part in the 1961 coup that brought President Park Chung Hee

into power. Park Tong Sun, Kim said, had worked under him while he was director of the KCIA. Kim said Park continued to work for the KCIA after Kim lost his post as director in 1969.

Park had started in the mid-1960s, Kim said. Kim said Park had told officials of the South Korean government he would use his contacts among American congressmen to work for more U.S. military aid to South Korea if, in return, South Korea designated him sole agent for the purchase of American rice for South Korea.

Park had started off on a small scale, Kim said, and had not at first been considered too successful. However, by the 1970s Park was handling large sums of money, according to Kim. Between 1971 and 1975, Kim said, Park received annually between $500,000 and $1 million from rice sales commissions. Kim said that any money actually given to congressmen came from Park and was always in cash.

By 1975, the KCIA suspected that Park had come under surveillance by U.S. federal investigators, Kim said. Consequently, the Korean agency decided to hand over Park's lobbying operation to another man, according to Kim. Kim said Kim Han Cho (known in the U.S. as Hancho C. Kim) received two payments, of $300,000 each, from the Korean government for lobbying purposes. President Park authorized the payments, Kim said. Kim Han Cho was a businessman and a trustee of American University in Washington, D.C.

Kim, who had left Korea in 1973 because of political differences with President Park and had lived in the U.S. since then, charged President Park with responsibility for the alleged influence-peddling scheme.

Kim also said that Moon Sun Myung (known in the U.S. as Sun Myung Moon), head of the Unification Church, and Pak Bo Hi, a chief aide to Moon, had worked for the KCIA. Kim indicated that Moon's work had not been of much worth to the KCIA, although Moon was considered a valuable source of propaganda for President Park. Moon had denied any connection with the KCIA.

Kim said Han Byung Ki, currently

South Korean ambassador to Canada and formerly a member of South Korea's United Nations observer mission, had worked for the KCIA to stifle opposition to the Park regime by Korean nationals living in the U.S.

Several individuals were named by Kim as "lesser operatives": Alexander Kim, a New York lawyer, and his brother, Charles Kim, former chairman of the Diplomat National Bank in Washington, D.C.; Jhoon Rhee, head of a karate business in Washington, and Sue Park Thomson, former congressional aide to the retired Speaker of the House, Carl Albert (D, Okla.).

The Washington Post June 6 reported that some of the statements made by Kim in the Times article conflicted with confidential information that the Post's sources said Kim had given earlier to U.S. investigators looking into the Korean lobbying effort. Earlier, Kim had maintained that he did not know of any KCIA activities by Jhoon Ree or Sue Park Thomson, the Post reported. Also, Kim had previously told investigators that Park Tong Sun had "no specific relationship" with the KCIA while Kim was head of it, the Post said.

Despite the apparent discrepancies, federal investigators still considered Kim credible, the Post reported.

Kim alternately had made and withdrawn an allegation that the South Korean government had provided cash for the presidential campaigns of former President Lyndon Johnson in 1964 and Sen. Hubert Humphrey (D, Minn.) in 1968, the Post reported.

Kim also claimed, the Post reported, that President Park systematically had channeled into Swiss bank accounts about 5% of the foreign money invested in South Korea. However, the Times June 7 reported that Kim had dismissed the Swiss bank accounts story as "rumors."

The South Korean government June 7 issued a statement sharply criticizing Kim. Kim was accused of "betraying" South Korea and of libeling his country's government by his statements about President Park.

■ Kim Hyung Wook, the former KCIA head, said that Kim Han Cho had given U.S. public officials $200,000 in cash gifts and favors from mid-1975 to mid-1976, the New York Times reported July 26.

GOP proposes special prosecutor. Two Republican Congressional leaders June 9, 1977 urged President Carter to appoint a special prosecutor, as was done for the Watergate scandal, to look into the alleged Korean influence-peddling operation.

Senate Minority Leader Howard H. Baker Jr., (R, Tenn.) said that "fairness and equity" would be served by the appointment of a special prosecutor. House Minority Leader John Rhodes (R, Ariz.) cited news leaks from the Justice Department probe as grounds for the special prosecutor. If the Justice Department probe dragged on with continual leaks to the press, Rhodes said, "it is going to hurt the whole institution of Congress."

White House press spokesman Jody Powell dismissed the proposal as "a fairly adept two-step." Since the Justice Department was vigorously investigating the matter, Powell said, no special prosecutor was needed.

Jaworski enters probe. Leon A. Jaworski, a former Watergate special prosecutor, agreed July 20, 1977 to serve as special counsel to the House ethics committee in its investigation of the South Korean influence-buying scandal.

The probe by the ethics committee—officially known as the Committee on Standards of Official Conduct—had been under fire in recent weeks for progressing too slowly. Criticism of the committee had intensified when Philip Lacovara resigned July 15 from the committee, following a dispute with Committee Chairman John J. Flynt Jr. (D, Ga.).

Lacovara had held the post taken by Jaworski. Lacovara's differences with Flynt surfaced in the press July 12 when it was reported that Lacovara had written to other members of the committee to complain that Flynt was not pressing the investigation forward vigorously. Reportedly, Lacovara had earlier written to Flynt to urge that the committee meet more frequently. Flynt had reportedly replied that it was up to the chairman, not Lacovara, to decide the pace of the committee's investigation.

Flynt July 15 labeled Lacovara's criticisms of him (Flynt) and the committee's work "arrogant, self-serving, misleading and grossly inaccurate."

Despite the criticisms, Flynt said he did not intend to fire Lacovara. However, Lacovara resigned, saying it was "evident that the relationship of mutual trust and confidence that must exist between lawyer and client no longer exists."

Even before the dispute between Flynt and Lacovara, the committee had been accused of foot-dragging, and some observers had questioned how willing the committee was to seriously press an investigation into wrongdoings of fellow House members. Republicans and some of the more junior Democratic House members had charged that the House leadership was reluctant to expose a scandal that might involve large numbers of Democrats.

After Lacovara's resignation, those criticisms were repeated more emphatically. Republican national chairman Bill Brock and Rep. Peter H. Kostmayer (D, Pa.), a leader of the freshmen House Democrats, July 16 reiterated earlier demands that a special prosecutor be appointed. Common Cause, the self-styled citizen's lobby, called for Flynt's resignation as chairman of the committee.

President Carter July 18 rejected the request that he appoint a special prosecutor. Carter said the investigation being conducted by the Justice Department was making "substantial progress." Carter said he had told Attorney General Griffin Bell to "vigorously pursue the matter, without regard to person or party, and to let the chips fall where they may."

House Speaker Thomas P. O'Neill (D, Mass.) admitted July 18 that the House probe had not moved forward quickly enough. Press accounts July 20 noted that O'Neill was vigorously looking for a replacement for Lacovara who would restore credibility to the House investigation.

Jaworski's appointment July 20 as special counsel to the committee was seen by knowledgeable observers as defusing some of the doubts raised about the House probe. Some House members expressed reservations about Jaworski, but House GOP leader John Rhodes (R, Ariz.) greeted Jaworski's appointment approvingly, as did most of the junior Democrats.

The ethics committee July 21 approved a written agreement—devised by O'Neill and Jaworski—guaranteeing Jaworski a large measure of independence in the conduct of the investigation, including decisions over the issuance of subpoenas. Under the agreement, Jaworski could only be fired by vote of the full House, and he would be authorized to bring any problems he faced before the full House.

Jaworski noted that "the charge has been made by some that, after all, we went after a Republican president [a reference to the Watergate investigation]. And now the question is, what are you going to do about the Democratic Congress." He promised that party affiliation would make no difference in his pursuit of the investigation.

House committee active. Sue (Suzy) Park Thomson, former aide to retired House Speaker Carl Albert, met with House Ethics Committee investigators in closed session Aug. 17, 1977 but refused to answer several of their questions. She insisted that she would answer certain questions only in public. She was afraid, she said, that secret testimony would be leaked to the press and reported in a distorted fashion.

Thomson met with committee investigators again August 25. On Aug. 24 the ethics committee had met (a somewhat unusual occurrence since Congress was in recess all but the first week of August) and had let Thomson know that she would probably be cited for contempt of Congress if she did not give private testimony.

Thomson then told reporters Aug. 25 that she had not been party to any attempts to bribe members of Congress and that she had not been an agent of South Korea or of the KCIA.

■ The House ethics committee had attempted to interview Park Tong Sun while he was in London, the August 20 Congressional Quarterly reported. The attempts were apparently unsuccessful.

■ The Justice Department August 3 agreed to share some of its information concerning the lobbying effort with the House ethics committee. According to knowledgeable sources, the information covered by the agreement included a list of about 20 U.S. public officials to whom Park Tong Sun had intended to give money. Attorney General Bell had had some reservations about sharing information with the committee, explaining his reluctance as a concern over not violating grand jury secrecy.

■ Sen. Adlai Stevenson (D, Ill.), chairman of the Select Committee on Ethics, said August 8 he could not hold to his earlier announced belief that no senators were involved in the alleged Korean lobbying effort. Stevenson said he had changed his opinion after reading documents acquired by Justice Department investigators.

■ Congressional investigators claimed to have found documentary evidence showing that former Secretary of State Henry Kissinger had been aware of the lobbying effort in 1972 when he was national security adviser, the New York Times reported Sept. 5. Similar evidence indicated that Gen. Alexander Haig (then Kissinger's deputy, later White House chief of staff and currently head of North Atlantic Treaty Organization forces in Europe) was also aware of the Korean activities. The investigators, the Times said, were attached to the House International Relations subcommittee on international organizations.

■ Stansfield Turner, director of the Central Intelligence Agency, said August 9 that the U.S. had never bugged conversations by high South Korean officials at the South Korean presidential mansion in Seoul. It had been conjectured in news accounts that U.S. bugs at the presidential residence had been the source of some information possessed by U.S. investigators probing the alleged lobbying effort.

Turner refused, however, to explicitly deny that the U.S. had intercepted messages transmitted to or from South Korea.

■ The Defense Department knew about some aspects of the Korean lobbying operation by 1970, the Wall Street Journal reported Oct. 12. According to the Journal, the Pentagon had been reluctant to transmit its information to the Justice Department, and was still reluctant to draw public notice to it, because of the way the information was acquired. The information was gained by secret electronic interception of cable messages, the Journal said. The Pentagon

feared that drawing attention to such electronic surveillance would interrupt existing intelligence gathering practices and possibly create diplomatic complications, according to the Journal.

Indictments Start

Park charged. Attorney General Griffin Bell announced Sept. 6, 1977 that Park Tong Sun, central figure in the "Koreagate" scandal, had been indicted by a federal grand jury on 36 felony counts.

The indictment was the first to emerge from the lengthy investigation. Park (often referred to in U.S. newspapers as Tongsun Park) was charged with conspiracy to bribe a public official and to defraud the U.S.; bribery of a public official; operating a corrupt enterprise; failing to register as an agent of a foreign government; two counts of making illegal campaign contributions, and 29 counts of mail fraud.

The 30-page indictment named three other individuals as unindicted co-conspirators: former California Democratic Rep. Richard T. Hanna, Kim Hyung Wook and Lee Hu Rak. Kim and Lee were former heads of the Korean Central Intelligence Agency (KCIA).

The account of the Korean lobbying effort provided by the indictment generally followed the lines of earlier press reports.

According to the indictment, Park acted "with the knowledge and under the direction of the KCIA." He allegedly used commissions he received as a broker of sales of U.S. rice to South Korea to finance the lobbying effort. Campaign contributions, cash gifts to legislators, trips to Korea and costly parties in Washington D.C. were used to create a favorable climate of opinion in Congress towards South Korea, the indictment said.

The indictment, in listing past and present members of Congress who had allegedly received the Korean largess, added a number of names to those already reported. The indictment also broke new ground by stressing the role of Hanna in the Korean effort.

Park give Hanna "in excess of $75,000" between 1967 and 1974, the indictment charged. The money was given, according to the indictment, on the agreement that Hanna would "make statements in his official capacity which were favorable to the Government of the Republic of Korea" and attempt to "influence other Congressmen" to take positions favorable to South Korea.

Hanna's attorney said Sept. 6 that Hanna flatly denied any suggestion that he had been bribed by Park. Hanna had admitted to having business relations with Park while in Congress, the attorney noted, adding that the business association had been a matter of public knowledge.

Any support of Korea on Hanna's part, his attorney said, came from a "long-standing friendship toward that country."

Park denies charges—At an Aug. 24 news conference in Seoul, South Korea, Park Tong Sun had denied one of the main charges of the indictment—that he was an agent for the KCIA. Park said: "Whatever I have done in Washington has been done on my personal account as a private businessman." He continued: "It has nothing to do with the Korean government."

Park had reportedly arrived in Korea only a few days before the news conference. He had made the trip to visit his mother who was ill, according to Korean sources. Park had been living in London since the fall of 1976.

Before he had gone to London from the U.S., Park reportedly had cooperated to some degree with federal investigators.

The Seoul news conference was the first time Park had publicly responded to the charge that he was a South Korean agent. Park also denied giving money to members of Congress.

Park said he would return to the U.S. to cooperate with the investigation only if he received an "absolute guarantee" that his statements to investigators would be kept strictly secret and not be leaked to the press where they might be distorted.

Bell, at the Sept. 6 news conference, said he would ask President Carter to speak to South Korean President Park Chung Hee and request that Park Tong Sun be returned to the U.S. Bell acknowledged that the U.S. lacked a formal extradition treaty with South Korea but said he was sure the South Korean government could find a way to return Park.

Although the indictment referred to the South Korean government as a foreign "regime," Bell took pains to avoid unfavorably characterizing South Korea. He referred to the country as a "friendly power and an ally."

Park's indictment had been reported in the press several days before it was formally announced. Bell cited that fact, and the "great public concern" attached to the case, in explaining his decision to hold a press conference to announce the indictment. The sealed indictment had been handed up by the grand jury in late August.

The Washington Post reported Sept. 8 that Carter had several times, directly or through diplomatic channels, asked South Korean President Park Chung Hee to return Park to the U.S.

The South Korean foreign minister, Park Tong Jin, said Sept. 8 that his country would not force Park to return to the U.S. against his will. Park Tong Jin said Korea was cooperating with U.S. investigators, but any Korean assistance to the investigation would be given "within the context of Korea's national sovereignty, international practices and diplomatic precedence."

Park Tong Jin noted, in reference to the idea of sending Park to the U.S., that "You can't just arrest a man and put him on the plane."

The foreign minister said he had attempted a number of times to persuade Park to go to the U.S. and talk to investigators, but Park had "strongly opposed the idea."

The lobbying scandal, and the refusal by South Korea to force Park to return to the U.S., had put a strain on relations between the U.S. and Korea. On Sept. 8, as the U.S. House of Representatives was considering the fiscal 1978 budget resolution, an amendment was introduced with the purpose of cutting U.S. aid to South Korea by about $110 million. The amendment lost, but only by the relatively close vote of 205–181.

The indictment listed, in addition to Hanna, the following current and former public officials as having received money or campaign contributions from Park: Louisiana Gov. and former Rep. Edwin Edwards (D); House Majority Whip John Brademas (D, Ind.); Rep. E. de la Garza (D, Tex.); Rep. Thomas Foley (D, Wash.); Rep. William Broomfield (R, Mich.); Rep. John McFall (D, Calif.); Rep. John Murphy (D, N.Y.); Rep. Melvin Price (D, Ill.); Rep. Frank Thompson Jr. (D, N.J.); Rep. Morris Udall (D, Ariz.), and, when he was a member of the House, Sen. Spark Matsunaga (D, Hawaii).

Also listed were former Reps. William Ayres (R, Ohio); Ross Adair (R, Ind.); Lawrence Hogan (R, Md.); Peter Frelinghuysen (R, N.J.); Chester Mize (R, Kans.); Nick Galifianakis (D, N.C.), and Thomas Kleppe (R, N.D.).

Sen. Harry Byrd Jr. (Ind., Va.) was listed as a recipient of a campaign contribution, as were former Sens. Stuart Symington (D, Mo.); Jack Miller (R, Iowa), and Joseph Montoya (D, N.M.).

SEC accuses Park—Park was confronted Sept. 28 with additional accusations of illegality. The Securities & Exchange Commission charged him, several other individuals and the Diplomat National Bank of Washington D.C. with violating federal securities law.

Besides Park, the SEC charged Pak Bo Hi, who had served as a senior aide to the Rev. Sun Myung Moon; Charles C. Kim, a former chairman of the bank, and Spencer E. Robbins, an assistant to Park. The SEC charges, contained in a civil suit filed in federal district court, alleged that the defendants had arranged for Park and Pak to purchase larger amounts of the bank's stock than the 5% limit (on individual holdings of stock) stipulated in the bank's report to the office of the Comptroller of the Currency.

The SEC also charged that the bank had overstated its deposits by $1 million in a 1976 quarterly statement to the government.

Charles Kim and the Diplomat National Bank, without admitting or denying the charges against them, filed consent orders in federal district court in which they promised not to engage in any further violations of federal securities law.

Park, Robbins and Pak took the same course, the SEC announced Oct. 3. Without admitting or denying any wrongdoing, the three men accepted a consent decree barring any future violations.

Park, who was currently residing in South Korea, was represented before the SEC by his U.S. lawyer, William Hundley.

The SEC charges contained no direct reference to the Korean lobbying case. However, there had been allegations that the bank had played a role in handling the money used to finance the alleged lobbying operation.

Federal investigators had urgently sought Park's return to the U.S. from Korea. His knowledge and cooperation were considered essential to a full investigation of the influence-buying operation.

However, Hundley said Sept. 21 that it was unlikely Park would leave Korea soon. Hundley said he had advised Park not to leave Korea until South Korean investigators, who were looking into Park's activities, were finished questioning him.

Hundley Sept. 17 had confirmed reports in the South Korean news media that President Carter had offered immunity to Park if he would return to the U.S. and aid the investigation. According to South Korean press reports, Park had rejected the offer.

■ The Securities and Exchange Commission was investigating an alleged payment of $10,000 by the South Korean Embassy in Washington to a retired U.S. Air Force general living in Seoul, the Washington Post reported Nov. 29. The retired officer was Robert Smith, currently vice president for Far East operations of E-Systems Inc. (E-Systems was a Dallas-headquartered firm that dealt in electronic warfare equipment.)

According to the Post, the money for the alleged payment was thought to have come from a firm called the Korean Research Institute. The Korean Research Institute had received substantial commissions from E-Systems for the sale of equipment to the South Korean government. According to the Post, the SEC was investigating whether the commissions had been used to fund influence-buying efforts.

Park interview bid fails—U.S. Justice Department officials arrived in Seoul, South Korea, Oct. 16 to begin talks with the South Korean government about the possibility of U.S. investigators interrogating Park Tong Sun. However, after four days of negotiations, the U.S. officials left Korea without reaching any agreement on interrogating Park Tong Sun.

The Justice Department Oct. 25 released a statement saying it had sought South Korean agreement to direct questioning of Park Tong Sun by U.S. interrogators. The U.S. had wished to use some kind of check of Park's truthfulness, such as a lie detector or a voice stress analyzer. The U.S. was willing to question Park in the U.S. or any third country (not South Korea) agreeable to Park.

The South Korean position, according to the Justice Department statement, was that the interrogation could only be done in South Korea, and that the questions of U.S. investigators would be given to Korean officials, who would do the actual questioning.

The Justice Department said that Park Tong Sun's information was still sought. In exchange for his testimony, the Justice Department would consider plea bargaining or perhaps even dismissing the indictment against him, the agency's statement said.

■ A State Department spokesman said Nov. 30 that negotiations between the U.S. and South Korea over the return of Park Tong Sun to the U.S. were "progressing."

President Carter Nov. 5 had sent a report to Congress describing the Administration's attempts to obtain testimony from Park Tong Sun. Carter said the U.S. had offered to dismiss a 36-count indictment against Park Tong Sun in return for his testimony. (Leon Jaworski, special counsel to the House Committee on Standards of Official Conduct, was quoted as saying he wanted "no part" of such an agreement for Park's testimony.)

Carter, in his message to Congress,

said, "The Korean government's failure to persuade Mr. Park to return to the United States was not the response expected of a close ally."

Kim Han Cho indicted. Kim Han Cho, a Korean-born naturalized U.S. citizen, was indicted Sept. 27, 1977 on charges related to the alleged Korean influence buying scheme. A federal grand jury in Washington indicted Kim on charges of lying to a grand jury and of conspiracy to defraud the U.S. Another federal grand jury in Baltimore indicated Kim and his wife on income-tax evasion charges. (Kim was convicted on both charges six months later.)

According to the Washington indictment, Kim had received about $600,000 from 1974 to 1976 from the Korean Central Intelligence Agency (KCIA) to finance his lobbying and influence-purchasing efforts. The aim of Kim's alleged scheme—which was code-named "Operation White Snow," according to the indictment—was to create a climate of opinion favorable to the South Korean government and to influence U.S. congressmen and officials to act favorably toward South Korea.

The indictment gave little information about the uses to which Kim put the $600,000 he supposedly received. He was alleged to have purchased two 1975 Cadillacs for his own use (raising the possibility that Kim might have defrauded the South Korean government) and to have made a $10,000 contribution to Findlay College of Findlay, Ohio. Kim had attended Findlay College in the 1950s and was currently a trustee of the college.

The indictment did not specifically name any former or current congressmen as targets of Kim's lobbying. Kim was alleged to have taken two unnamed congressmen and their families to Washington's San Souci restaurant in 1975 and to have provided a catered dinner at his home for two congressmen and their families in 1976.

The indictment indirectly identified two former congressmen as linked to Kim. According to the indictment, Kim twice succeeded in having remarks favorable to South Korea inserted in the Congressional Record. From the dates given, it could be determined that the remarks had been inserted by former Reps. Vernon Thomson (R, Wis., 1961–74), currently chairman of the Federal Election Commission, and Tennyson Guyer (R, Ohio 1973–77). Thomson told the Associated Press Sept. 27 that he did not recall ever having met Kim. He said he thought he had put the statement into the Record at the request of Guyer.

Guyer issued a statement Sept. 27 in which he said the Justice Department had examined his personal and campaign financial records and assured him that "everything is in order." He added that he had known Kim as a fellow student of Findlay College and had always "believed him to be a loyal American citizen."

The indictment apparently was based largely on the testimony of Kim Sang Keun. Kim Sang Keun, a former KCIA officer, had defected from the Korean Embassy to the U.S. in 1976 and had since cooperated with the federal investigation of the alleged Korean lobbying effort.

■ Aides to former President Gerald Ford said Nov. 11 that Guyer had tried to arrange meetings between Ford and Kim. The aides, Vernon Loen and Max Friedersdorf, both congressional lobbyists for the Ford White House—said that Guyer's attempts had not resulted in any meeting between Ford and Kim Han Cho.

The aides said that the requests for the meetings had apparently been rejected, for unknown reasons, by the National Security Council. (The requests were sent to the White House scheduling office and then, because Kim Han Cho was foreign-born, to the NSC.)

Loen said he had never heard Guyer "advance the cause of Korea" while requesting the meetings between the former President and Kim Han Cho. "As far as I know," Loen added, "he [Guyer] was just trying to take care of a constituent."

Kim's conviction—Kim was convicted by a federal jury April 8, 1978 of conspiring to bribe members of Congress and of lying to a federal grand jury about his activities.

The prosecution did not claim that Kim had actually attempted to bribe any

legislators. Kim, according to evidence presented by the prosecution, was in financial difficulties when he received the KCIA money; instead of using the funds for bribery, he decided to keep the money himself, the government said.

The charge against Kim was conspiracy, the government emphasized, not bribery.

Kim denied receiving money from the KCIA.

The government called 65 witnesses to build its case against Kim. The primary witness was Kim Sang Keun, who said he had delivered the conspiracy funds to Kim.

U.S. District Judge Thomas A. Flannery May 19 sentenced Kim to serve a total of six months in prison.

Kim was formally sentenced to a three-year term on each of the counts, but Flannery then suspended all but six months of the sentence.

Hanna indicted. A federal grand jury in Washington Oct. 14, 1977 indicted Richard T. Hanna, a former Democratic representative from California, on 40 felony charges stemming from the Korean lobbying probe. Hanna, who left the House of Representatives in 1974, was the first present or former member of that body to face criminal charges related to the lobbying scandal. (The following year Hanna pleaded guilty to a single count.)

The indictment charged Hanna with 35 mail fraud violations, two counts of bribery, and one count each of conspiracy, acceptance of an illegal gratuity and failure to register as a foreign agent.

Hanna, according to the indictment, had used his position as a congressman to urge the government of South Korea to make Park Tong Sun the agent for Korean purchases of U.S. rice. Park Tong Sun would then, the indictment alleged, "corruptly provide monies derived from the commissions on the sale of rice" to Hanna.

The indictment listed over $100,000 in checks that Hanna received from business controlled by Park Tong Sun.

Hanna advised Park Tong Sun on how to conduct his influence-peddling operation, according to the indictment. Hanna suggested the names of individual congressmen who might be influenced by financial payments, the indictment charged.

Most of the allegations in the Hanna indictment had been heard previously. The indictment did contain new allegations to the effect that Reps. Melvin Price (D, Ill.) and Edward Patten (D, N.J.) had been persuaded to write letters to South Korean President Park Chung Hee praising Park Tong Sun. Also, the indictment said that Hanna had successfully urged both Price and Patten to speak favorably of South Korea at 1974 congressional hearings on South Korean violations of human rights.

Two former heads of the Korean Central Intelligence Agency (KCIA) were named as unindicted co-conspirators in the Hanna indictment: Kim Hyung Wook and Lee Hu Rak. Kim Hyung Wook had given testimony about the Korean lobbying effort to a House subcommittee in June.

Investigators at Work

Ethics committee hearings. The House Committee on Standards of Official Conduct (the ethics committee) held public hearings Oct. 19-21, 1977. The Korean lobbying effort was outlined and specific incidents of illicit or unethical nature were described.

In his opening statement, committee counsel Leon Jaworski asserted: "In the spring of 1973, representatives of the Korean embassy here in Washington were told of a plan to 'buy off' American congressmen. . . . The plan was to be implemented personally by the Ambassador, Kim Dong Jo, and by the KCIA station chief, Yang Doo Wan."

Jaworski continued: "The plan was shrouded in extreme secrecy. . . . Nevertheless, the evidence we have been able to gather indicates that a plan was made and, at least in part, carried out."

The hearings, which were the first round planned by the committee, focused on the activities of South Korean nationals.

Among the testimony heard by the committee:

■ Kim Sang Keun, a former KCIA agent who defected to the U.S. in 1976, recounted his involvement in a secret project called "Operation Snow White." The scheme funneled hundreds of thousands of KCIA dollars to Kim Han Cho, a naturalized U.S. citizen, who was supposed to use it to further the Korean lobbying effort. Kim Sang Keun said he had received a letter from a KCIA official in Seoul saying "The patriarch has expressed his satisfaction" with the operation. The "patriarch" referred to in the letter was South Korean President Park Chung Hee, according to Kim Sang Keun.

■ Nan Elder, a staff employe of Rep. Larry Winn Jr. (R, Kan.), said that at some time near September 1972, a man had visited Winn's office and left on his desk an envelope stuffed with $100 bills. Elder said she later learned the man was the South Korean Ambassador, Kim Dong Jo. The money was promptly returned to Kim Dong Jo, Elder testified.

■ A former high official in the Korean embassy in Washington, Jai Hyon Lee, testified that he had seen Kim Dong Jo filling about two dozen plain white enveloped with $100 bills in the spring of 1973 for delivery to "the Capitol." Jai Hyon Lee had defected in June 1973.

■ The wives of Reps. E. de la Garza (D, Texas) and John Myers (R, Ind.) testified that during an August 1975 trip to South Korea they were given envelopes with large amounts of cash. Both said the money had been promptly returned.

■ Cheryl Holmes, a staff analyst for the committee, testified that Park Tong Sun was paid about $9.2 million in commissions on rice sales from 1969 to 1976. She had traced the funds, which were payments from the Rice Growers Association of California and the Connell Rice and Sugar Company, through banks in Washington and Bermuda to Park Tong Sun, she said.

Holmes said she had found evidence indicating Park Tong Sun had changed about $1.6 million of the commission payments into cash. She also testified she had seen perhaps fifty checks written by Park to congressmen, but she had not added up the amount of the checks.

At the conclusion of the three days of hearings, Peter White, deputy special counsel for the committee, said the evidence proved beyond doubt the reality of the Korean lobbying effort. "There was an official plan, and it was executed," White said. He added, "The question of whether these things took place is, very simply, a dead issue."

House vote asks Korean cooperation—The House of Representatives Oct. 31 adopted, 407–0, a resolution calling on the government of South Korea to "cooperate fully and without reservation with the Committee on Standards of Official Conduct and with its special counsel...."

Although no one voted against the resolution, several representatives cautioned that the issue of South Korea's cooperation with the ethics committee probe should be considered separately from the question of South Korea's need for U.S. military aid.

Passman named. In London, friends and associates of Park Tong Sun said Park Tong Sun had given $190,000 to former Rep. Otto Passman (D, La.), the New York Times reported Nov. 2. According to the sources cited by the Times, it was the largest amount given by Park Tong Sun to any congressman.

Passman, defeated in 1976 in a bid for a 16th term, denied the Times report. He was quoted in the Times as saying, "I have never received a dime from Mr. Park or any other foreign national."

While in the House, Passman had been chairman of the House Appropriations Committee subcommittee on foreign operations, a position that gave him considerable influence over foreign aid legislation.

The Washington Post Dec. 2 reported that the House Committee on Standards of Official Conduct had issued a subpoena for Passman's papers. The subpoena was served Nov. 30 upon the president of Northeast Louisiana University, where Passman's papers were stored, the Post reported.

■ The House Committee on Standards of Official Conduct had subpoenaed former House Speaker Carl Albert and some of his records, it was reported Dec.

1. The subpoenaed records, the Washington Post reported, had been lodged at the University of Oklahoma, but Albert with two aides retrieved some of his records before the university sealed them for delivery to the committee.

Lois Butler, an Albert aide, confirmed that Albert had taken some of his records back from the university but said that the records in question did not relate to the Korean inquiry, the Post reported. However, the Post reported that an unnamed source said that the records retrieved by Albert did in fact concern trips he had made to Korea.

KCIA influence plan. A House International Relations subcommittee Nov. 29, 1977 made public what it described as a translation of a plan drafted by the South Korean Central Intelligence Agency in 1976 for influencing the U.S. government and American public opinion. The plan called for placing an intelligence network in the White House. Other goals were to influence congressional groups and to "co-opt and utilize reporters of influential U.S. papers."

The plan also called for efforts to block North Korean attempts at improving relations with the U.S. Another aspect of the plan involved South Koreans living in the U.S. Supporters of the Seoul regime were to be supported, while critics of the regime were to be the targets of KCIA operations.

The House subcommittee on international organizations (of the International Relations Committee) did not reveal how it obtained the document. Subcommittee Chairman Donald Fraser (D, Minn.) said, "It's legitimate, that's all I can say."

The document was released as the subcommittee resumed hearings on the Korean influence-purchasing effort. (The panel had held hearings in the summer. Sohn Ho Young, a former KCIA agent who had defected, testified Nov. 29 that the document was genuine. (U.S. and Korean sources had identified Sohn as KCIA officer in charge of the New York area. State Department officials said Sept. 27 that he had requested and been granted U.S. protection Sept. 16. The Wall St. Journal reported Oct. 28 that the Justice Department suspected Rep. Edward

Derwinski [R, Ill.] of having informed the South Korean government of Sohn's plan to defect.)

Sohn said it was "unthinkable" that the KCIA was continuing its covert influence-buying activities in the U.S. at present, citing the "negative publicity" that had recently come to bear on those activities.

The 1976 plan, the New York Times reported Nov. 30, was apparently the latest in a series of yearly plans going back to the early 1970s. The 1976 plan was formulated in Washington D.C. and then approved by KCIA headquarters in Seoul in late 1975, the Times reported.

The 1976 plan called for expenditures totalling $750,000 on about 140 different operations.

Gifts and free trips to Korea were proposed as means of influencing journalists, academics and executive and congressional branch officials to take a friendly attitude toward the South Korean government.

The plan named specific individuals as targets for KCIA attempts at influence-buying, including two White House aides and a specialist on Far Eastern affairs on the staff of the National Security Council. The subcommittee, however, deleted the names of the individuals before releasing the document.

It was not indicated at the Nov. 29 hearing to what extent the KCIA actually carried out the 1976 plan.

Korean bid to block testimony charged—Subcommittee Chairman Fraser Nov. 30, at the second day of hearings, charged that the South Korean government had attempted to prevent Kim Hyung Wook from testifying before the subcommittee in June.

Sohn Ho Young testified Nov. 30 that while he was still a KCIA agent he had been ordered to see Kim Hyung Wook and try to persuade him not to testify before the Fraser subcommittee. Another witness, Yoo Yung Soo, a supermarket owner in New Jersey who had been present with Sohn Ho Young at the interview with Kim Hyung Wook, also described the episode to the subcommittee.

The subcommittee released 18 cables and messages between KCIA head-quarters in Seoul and the KCIA offices in Washington D.C. and New York. The cables revealed that a South Korean cabinet minister, Min Byung Kwon, had also attempted to persuade Kim Hyung Wook to refrain from testifying, or at least to testify in such a way that South Korean President Park Chung Hee would not be faced with any embarrassment.

The South Korean importuning did not apparently have any effect on Kim Hyung Wook's testimony. Kim Hyung Wook said he had changed "nothing at all" because of the Korean requests. Fraser, meanwhile, observed that there were no indications that the former KCIA chief's testimony was inaccurate.

Fraser characterized the alleged South Korean actions as an "attempt to suborn a witness . . . . [that was] contrary to the laws of this country."

Park testimony accord reached. The Department of Justice Dec. 30, 1977 announced an agreement with Park Tong Sun and the South Korean government whereby Park Tong Sun promised to testify in the U.S. in criminal trials stemming from the Korean lobbying investigation. In return for the testimony, the Justice Department would give Park Tong Sun immunity from prosecution for past criminal acts.

Park Tong Sun also agreed to submit to questioning with a lie detector by U.S. and Korean officials in Korea, where he was currently residing.

The agreement was the product of several months of negotiations between the Justice Department and South Korea.

Leon Jaworski, special counsel to the House Committee on Standards of Official Conduct (the ethics committee), Dec. 30 assailed the Justice Department agreement as "inadequate and unacceptable."

Jaworski complained that under the terms of the Justice Department agreement, Park Tong Sun would only be required to testify in the U.S. about statements he made during questioning in Korea, where he would be, Jaworski noted, under the "watchful eye of the Korean government." Also, Jaworski objected that the agreement dealing with Park Tong Sun would reduce pressure on the Korean government to make other Korean citizens who might be involved in the lobbying scandal available to U.S. investigators and prosecutors.

The Justice Department agreement specified that Park Tong Sun would "assume no obligation to appear before congressional committees." However, a Justice Department spokesman said nothing in the agreement was intended to block a congressional subpoena, and he added that the department would not seek to "abridge, impede or prohibit" the ethics committee from seeking Park Tong Sun's testimony.

South Korea's Justice Ministry and the U.S. Justice Department Jan. 10, 1978 signed an agreement stating the rules that would govern the interrogation; the next day, Park signed a formal agreement with the Justice Department.

In return for his promise to give truthful information concerning his lobbying efforts and to testify at any Korean lobbying prosecutions, the 36-count indictment against Park would be dropped and he would receive immunity from prosecution for any past criminal acts.

(The New York Times reported Jan. 13 that the agreement between the U.S. and South Korea, which was kept secret, was framed so as to bar U.S. investigators from pressing for information about Korean officials. One section of the agreement, the Times reported, read as follows: "The questioning shall not concern actions or statements of any officials of the Republic of Korea or any third country, except any which may have occurred in the U.S. or in the presence of U.S. officials." The main concern of the Justice Department, the Times said, was to uncover wrongdoing by U.S. citizens and public officials, not the mounting of the lobbying effort by the Koreans.)

House Speaker Thomas P. O'Neill, interviewed Jan. 22 on the CBS TV program "Face the Nation," said he had told the South Korean Ambassador, Kim Yong Shik, Jan. 18 that U.S. military and economic aid to South Korea would be jeopardized unless Park testified before House investigators.

Rep. Allen Ertel (D, Pa.) Jan. 23 submitted a strongly worded resolution to the House. The resolution "insists" that the Korean government "take all steps within its power to insure that Tongsun Park [the anglicized form of Park Tong Sun's name], Kim Dong Jo [a former South Korean ambassador to the U.S.], and such other individuals" as the House ethics committee required appear before committee investigators.

The confrontation apparently was defused Jan. 31 when Ambassador Shik met with O'Neill and told him South Korea had no objection to Park testifying before the House committee.

O'Neill said South Korea would not allow Kim Dong Jo to appear before the committee, however. O'Neill quoted Ambassador Shik as saying "we cannot do anything at variance with international practice"—apparently a reference to the diplomatic immunity that Kim Dong Jo enjoyed as a former ambassador.

Park questioned in Korea. Park Tong Sun underwent his first questioning by Justice Department investigators Jan. 13, 1978 in Seoul, South Korea. Park was questioned in English, and at times a polygraph, or lie detector, was used.

In his first interrogation session, Park told U.S. investigators that he had handed out a total of $750,000 in covert gifts and political payments to U.S. public officials and to political campaigns from 1970 to 1975, according to sources cited in the New York Times Jan. 14.

According to the Times, Park claimed to have given more than $100,000 to former Reps. Cornelius Gallagher (D, N.J.), Richard Hanna (D, Calif.) and Otto Passman (D, La.). He also said he had given $60,000 to former Rep. William Minshall (R, Ohio), the Times reported. All of the alleged recipients had denied any wrongdoing.

Park also confirmed reports that he had given Louisiana Gov. Edwin Edwards (D) about $20,000 while Edwards was serving in the House, the Times said. Edwards had acknowledged those gifts.

According to the Times, Park said he had given Rep. Thomas P. O'Neill a set of golf clubs and some hurricane lamps at a birthday party, but denied ever handing O'Neill any cash.

Park also admitted to giving dozens of campaign contributions on the order of $500 to $2,000 in the 1972 and 1974 elections, the Times reported.

Rep. Bruce Caputo (R, N.Y.), a member of the House ethics committee, sat in on the questioning as an observer. After the Jan. 13 session, he said Park's testimony left him "embarrassed, alarmed and disgraced." Caputo said that, according to Park's testimony, a wide range of U.S. political figures had received "substantial" amounts of money. Park was questioned in Seoul throughout January. U.S. and South Korean officials issued a statement Feb. 1 saying the interrogation was completed. U.S. Justice Department official Paul Michel called the interviews "useful." The joint statement said the 2,000-page transcript of Park's testimony would be turned over to the House and Senate committees that were investigating the lobbying scandal.

Park testifies to House probers. Park Tong Sun testified at closed sessions of the House ethics committee Feb. 28–March 9, 1978.

Park's credibility was a question mark to committee members, according to news reports. Some committee members found his answers evasive on certain subjects. Also, Park had steadfastly denied that he had acted as an agent of the South Korean government—a claim that conflicted with other evidence generated by the Korean lobbying investigations.

Park had testified to the Justice Department that he had made friends of three consecutive directors of the KCIA only for the purpose of safeguarding his business interests, in particular his position as rice broker to Korea, the New York Times reported March 1.

Leon Jaworski, special counsel to the ethics committee, said March 9 that the committee wanted to question other Koreans in addition to Park. Of particular interest to the committee was former South Korean Ambassador Kim Dong Jo. A committee source cited in the Feb. 28 Wall Street Journal said there were "indications" that "Kim was a much bigger fish" than Park Tong Sun in the lobbying operation.

In his first public testimony, Park said at an open session of the House ethics committee April 3 that he had given a total of $850,000 in gifts and campaign contributions to U.S. politicians.

He had made the gifts and contributions to 30 present and former members of Congress, two unsuccessful candidates for the House of Representatives, and to former President Nixon's reelection committee, Park said.

Much of what Park told the committee had already been reported in the press.

Park insisted, as he had before, that his lobbying activities had not been directed by the South Korean government. "Whatever I did in this country, I did on my own," he said.

Park's claim did not pass unchallenged. John Nields, the committee's chief of staff for the investigation, produced numerous documents intended to show that Park had acted as an agent of the Korean government, with the aim of making secure the U.S. political and military commitment to South Korea.

But Park was unmoved by the interrogation. He said, "I have denied that [being an agent] a thousand times. Nothing is going to make me change something I didn't do."

Two members of the ethics panel, quoted in the New York Times April 4, indicated they had doubts about Park's testimony. Rep. Millicent Fenwick (R, N.J.) said, "There's no question in my mind that high Korean officials knew what he [Tong Sun Park] was doing, approved what he was doing and supported what he was doing." Park, Fenwick continued, had "a warm and close relationship" with the Korean Central Intelligence Agency.

Rep. Bruce F. Caputo (R, N.Y.) observed that Park "testifies to the limit of our knowledge, but then his amnesia sets in."

Park said he had made his biggest payments to three former House members —Otto Passman (D, La.), Richard Hanna (D, Calif.) and Cornelius Gallagher (D, N.J.)—because they had helped him keep his job as the exclusive broker of sales of U.S. rice to South Korea.

Park reportedly had received $9 million in commissions from those sales from 1970 to 1975.

Park described his life in the U.S., which had combined his rice business with an active social life that included elegant parties attended by high government officials, as an "American success story on a small scale."

Jaworski differed with Park over the

amount given to Passman. Park said the total was around $250,000. Jaworski's questioning indicated the committee had evidence of payments totaling almost $500,000.

Most of the present and former members of Congress who had taken money from Park said they had treated it as campaign contributions, according to a UPI report April 3.

On April 4, the second day of Park's public testimony, the ethics committee released a document described as a Korean intelligence report that said House Speaker Thomas P. O'Neill Jr. (D, Mass.) had sought Korean contributions for his congressional supporters. The unsigned report had been found in Park's house.

Park, however, testified that O'Neill had never made such a request for funds. Park said he did not know where the document had come from.

(Park had previously admitted giving two birthday parties for O'Neill that had cost several thousand dollars and had also acknowledged giving O'Neill gifts of golf clubs and hurricane lamps. But he had never given money to O'Neill, Park said.)

O'Neill April 4 termed the allegation in the document "self-serving and a total fabrication." O'Neill told reporters he had "never had a discussion covering Korea with Tong Sun Park in my life."

■ Park's testimony that he had made several payments to Louisiana businessman Gordon Dore was disputed by Dore April 5 in testimony before the House ethics committee. Park had testified that he had given Dore a check for $5,000 after Dore requested a campaign contribution for Rep. John Breaux (D, La.). Dore told the committee he had "absolutely no recollection" of the check.

Park and Dore also differed on two other payments. Jaworski told reporters April 5 that one of the two witnesses was "bound not to be telling the facts."

Aid to Korea endangered. Sen. Adlai Stevenson 3rd (D, Ill.) Feb 22 said that he would block a proposed $500 million Export-Import Bank loan to South Korea if that country did not cooperate more fully with the Senate Select Ethics Committee inquiry into the lobbying operation.

Stevenson was chairman of the ethics panel. He was also chairman of the Senate Banking Committee subcommittee on international finance, which reviewed large loans by the Export-Import Bank. The loan in question was for the purchase of two nuclear reactors by the Koreans.

The ethics committee wanted to question Kim Dong Jo and four other senior Korean officials. Unless the Korean government cooperated, Stevenson said, he would not bring up the loan for approval by the international finance subcommittee.

The same day, Feb. 22, Clement Zablocki (D, Wis.) had told Defense Secretary Harold Brown that an Administration plan to transfer $800 million in military equipment to South Korea was unlikely to get through Congress because of the climate of opinion created by the lobbying scandal. Zablocki was chairman of the House International Relations Committee. The transfer of equipment was seen by the Administration as an essential part of its plan to reduce U.S. ground forces in that country.

The Carter Administration, while insisting that it wanted the Korean government to cooperate more fully with the lobbying probes, had argued against congressional attempts to link aid to Korea with cooperation in the lobbying investigation. Brown Feb. 22 told Zablocki's committee that "to look at Korea solely in terms of this scandal without regard to our security interests and responsibilities would endanger not only South Korea and its people, but the stability of northeast Asia and the security of this country as well."

Intelligence agency findings. The House International Organizations Subcommittee, at a March 14, 1978 hearing, released summaries of reports in which U.S. intelligence agencies had indicated that South Korean President Park Chung Hee was personally involved in the scandal.

The panel—chaired by Rep. Donald M. Fraser (D, Minn.)—also released intelligence reports that claimed the Unification Church of Rev. Sun Myung Moon had been organized by Kim Chong Pil, a former KCIA director, to serve the political ends of the South Korean government.

At a subcommittee hearing March 22, Pak Bo Hi, a chief aid to Rev. Moon, testified that he had received $3,000 in cash from the KCIA. But the money had been intended merely to reimburse a Unification Church member who went on an anti-communist speaking tour in Korea, Pak Bo Hi said.

At the March 15 hearing, Fraser said that the intelligence reports indicated that Park Chung Hee had been present at at least one meeting in which strategy for the lobbying operation was discussed. Former U.S. Ambassador to South Korea William Porter warned the subcommittee, however, that the intelligence reports might be unreliable.

A spokesman for Park Chung Hee March 17 said that "there never were any such 'secret strategy meetings,' " as Fraser had described. "Naturally President Park could not be present at a meeting that never took place," the spokesman continued.

Summaries of intelligence reports released the second day of the hearings, March 16, described Park Tong Sun as "receiving assistance from the KCIA." Park Tong Sun was "under the KCIA's control, but was not an 'agent' as such," according to the summaries of the reports.

The House subcommittee March 21 released documents that seemed to indicate that high officials of the Nixon Administration had been made aware of Korean lobbying efforts.

The documents were dated 1971 and 1972. One asserted that Park Chung Hee was "directly involved in directing the contribution of several hundred thousand dollars to the Democratic Party."

(The Washington Post March 22 reported that, according to other sources, the contribution was $400,000, and was made for the 1968 elections. The Post said that it was believed that the subcommittee had reports of a smaller, but still "six figure," Korean contribution to the Republican Party.)

Robert Short, who was treasurer of the Democratic Party in 1968, denied March 21 that the party had received such a gift.

The allegation about the contribution to the Democratic Party was made in three memoranda prepared by former Federal Bureau of Investigation Director J. Edgar Hoover.

Hoover apparently sent the memoranda in late 1971 and early 1972 to John Mitchell, then Attorney General, and to Henry Kissinger, then national security advisor to President Nixon.

Mitchell testified to the subcommittee March 21 that he had received the first of the three memoranda. But he could not recall ever having seen the other two memoranda, he said.

"The files down here are filled with memoranda that were never sent," Mitchell said, offering a possible explanation of why he might not have seen Hoover's memoranda.

The memorandum that Mitchell acknowledged seeing said that two congressional staff aides had links to the KCIA. According to subcommittee sources, the aides were Suzi Park Thomson, a Korean-born aide to former House Speaker Carl Albert (D, Okla.), and Kim Kwang, who had been on the staff of former Rep. Cornelius Gallagher (D, N.J.).

Mitchell said that, after receiving the memorandum, he had brought the matter up with Albert. Albert, however, had seen no reason to dismiss Thomson, Mitchell said. Albert had referred to Thomson as a "nice young lady with a fine American education" and had observed that her work did not involve sensitive information, Mitchell said.

Mitchell said he had not approached Gallagher in regard to the memorandum because Gallagher was then under investigation about a tax matter.

The intelligence report summaries also alleged that the South Korean government was spending large sums of money to influence U.S. and Korean journalists.

The assertions in Hoover's memoranda, according to the March 22 Wall Street Journal, were based on information the National Security Agency had obtained by intercepting cable communications between the South Korean embassy in Washington and the South Korean government.

The subcommittee released copies of an FBI report concluding that "while criminal activities are strongly indicated warranting Bureau investigation, we are stopped from conducting such investigation" because of restrictions imposed by the intelligence agency that gathered the information.

William McDonnell, the FBI agent who prepared the memoranda for Hoover, told the subcommittee that the bureau had refrained from launching a criminal investigation in order to avoid jeopardizing the "sensitive source" that obtained the information.

However, subcommittee deputy staff director Michael Hershman asserted at the March 21 hearing that the NSA had not imposed such restrictions when it transmitted its information to the FBI. Hershman said his conclusion was based on a review of classified papers.

Kissinger testifies—Henry Kissinger told the House subcommittee April 20 that he had first learned of Korean attempts to bribe U.S. officials in early 1975.

Evidence he received then was not strong, Kissinger said. Later in 1975 he received firmer information, Kissinger testified, and he notified then-President Ford. Ford told him to give his information to the Justice Department for investigation, Kissinger said, and "This whole investigation was started because I turned over to the attorney general a list of names we had."

Kissinger said he had learned of the allegations from former Assistant Secretary of State Philip C. Habib. The allegations, Kissinger said, referred "not to lobbying but to bribery."

Kissinger testified that he had "no recollection" of three memos describing the Korean activities that had been addressed to him by FBI Director Hoover in 1971 and 1972. Kissinger said he remembered one allegation of bribery, but he could not recall the source of the allegation.

One of the Hoover memos described an alleged South Korean contribution of several hundred thousand dollars to the Democratic Party. Kissinger said it was "inconceivable" that he could have seen the memo and subsequently forgotten the allegation.

The Hoover memos had also been addressed to former Attorney General John Mitchell.

Kissinger told the subcommittee that he found it "even more inconceivable" that Mitchell could have learned of the allegation and "done nothing about it."

Focus on Congress Members

Current House Members implicated. Leon Jaworski, special counsel to the House ethics committee, said Jan. 20, 1978 at a meeting he with junior House Democrats that committee investigators had found evidence of wrongdoing on the part of some current members of Congress. Some members were "possibly criminally culpable," Jaworski asserted.

Another staff member of the committee asserted that the evidence of wrongdoing would "at the appropriate time be turned over to the Justice Department." The Justice Department was conducting a separate investigation of the Korean lobbying effort.

Jaworski's comments appeared at variance with earlier reports by Justice Department investigators. Benjamin Civiletti, acting deputy attorney general, had told reporters Jan. 18 that Park Tong Sun, in his first questioning sessions with department investigators, had not provided information that would lead to the indictment of present members of Congress.

However, on Jan. 26 Civiletti spoke to junior House Democrats and said Park Tong Sun's information suggested that 15 to 18 current members of Congress might have violated ethical standards. Civiletti indicated, however, that indictments of those incumbents would not be sought, in some cases because the statute of limitations had expired.

(Civiletti's remarks came at a private meeting, but several congressmen told reporters what he had said.)

The Justice Department also was investigating, Civiletti said, whether there had been a cover-up of the Korean lobbying effort by the Justice Department during John Mitchell's tenure as attorney general in the Nixon Administration.

Civiletti did not give the names of any of the former or current members of Congress implicated in the lobbying scandal. He said both Democrats and Republicans were involved.

Hanna pleads guilty. Ex-Rep. Richard T. Hanna pleaded guilty March 17, 1978 to a single count of conspiring to defraud the U.S. The plea came as the result of an agreement between Hanna and the Justice Department; in exchange, the Justice Department dropped 39 other counts upon which Hanna had been indicted, including bribery, accepting illegal gifts and failure to register as a foreign agent.

Hanna made his plea before U.S. District Judge William B. Bryant. The Justice Department submitted an "offer of proof" to the court that said Hanna had received $246,640 from 1970 to 1975 from Park Tong Sun.

The Justice Department document noted that Hanna had written many times to South Korean government officials, including successive heads of the South Korean Central Intelligence Agency (KCIA). One of Hanna's letters, the Justice Department said, referred to a "rivalry between Park [Tong Sun] and [former] Ambassador Kim Dong Jo as to whether Park or Kim should direct the Korean lobbying activities in Congress." That statement and others in the Justice Department document appeared to conflict with Park Tong Sun's claim that he had not been an agent of the Korean government.

The Justice Department said it did not have any evidence indicating "that Hanna transmitted or aided anyone else to transmit" money to members of Congress. In order to maintain a good standing with officials in Seoul, Hanna had "exaggerated or even fabricated" claims to have influenced other members of Congress, the Justice Department said.

The Justice Department said the conspiracy to which Hanna pleaded guilty began in August 1968 with a meeting of Hanna, Park Tong Sun and Kim Hyung Wook, then director of the KCIA.

Rice transactions were used to fund the lobbying effort, the Justice Department said. Lavish entertainments in Washington and trips for congressmen to South Korea were used to create a favorable climate of opinion towards South Korea, the Justice Department said.

Prison sentence—U.S. District Judge William B. Bryant April 24, 1978 sentenced Hanna to serve six to 30 months in prison. He was the first person imprisoned in the Koreagate scandal.

At the sentencing hearing, Hanna apologized "as a person who held public office and who has had to plead to a count that brings me here." He told reporters later that he thought "the law has been served."

Hanna also commented that "overzealous people" in the Justice Department were trying to blow up the Korean scandal into another Watergate.

Passman indicted. Ex-Rep. Otto Passman was indicted by a federal grand jury in Washington March 31, 1978 on charges of taking $98,000 in bribes or illegal gratuities from Park Tong Sun. Passman had also conspired to obtain more than $200,000 from Park, the indictment alleged.

Passman, 77, was staying in a New Orleans hospital because of "mental and physical exhaustion" when the indictment was handed up. He had consistently denied taking any illegal payments from Park.

In return for the money from Park, Passman used his position in Congress to influence federal agencies to increase loans to South Korea for the purchase of U.S. rice, the indictment alleged. Passman also exerted his influence to pressure South Korean officials to insist that U.S. rice dealers use Park as their agent, according to the indictment.

Park Tong Sun had used money received from commissions on rice sales to pay Passman, the indictment said.

The conspiracy began when Passman and Park Tong Sun met in Hong Kong and Seoul in early 1972, according to the indictment. In March 1972, the two met in the Korean Embassy in Washington, together with Kim Dong Jo (then the South Korean ambassador to the U.S.), Edwin W. Edwards, at the time the governor-elect of Louisiana, congressional candidate John Breaux (D, La., elected in 1972) and Gordon Dore, a major rice miller in Louisiana, according to the indictment.

Passman was specifically charged with three counts of accepting bribes, three counts of accepting illegal gratuities and one count of conspiracy to defraud the U.S. of the proper performance of government officials.

Passman was only the second person who had been in Congress to be indicted in connection with the Korean lobbying scandal.

Passman was also indicted April 28 on charges of evading taxes.

The indictment, handed up by a federal grand jury in Washington, D.C., charged the former representative with failing to report $143,000 in income in 1972 and 1973. Passman concealed the money through currency dealings and false statements to government officials, according to the indictment.

The tax indictment did not specifically link its charges to the earlier bribery charges. However, the amount of income Passman was charged with concealing in 1973 was $98,000, which was the size of the bribe he was accused of taking that year.

Other Congress members seen as involved. Leon Jaworski told the House International Relations Committee May 22, 1978 that the House ethics committee had information indicating that Kim Dong Jo, ex-South Korean ambassador to the U.S., had made cash payments to a number of members of Congress. Jaworski had been speaking in support of a resolution calling upon Korea to make Kim Dong Jo available to House investigators.

The Washington Post May 23 reported that House probers had evidence indicating that as many as 10 current House members had taken cash payments from Kim Dong Jo.

Rep. Bruce Caputo (R, N.Y.), a member of the House ethics panel, said May 25 that cables intercepted and decoded by U.S. intelligence, together with other evidence, indicated a "pattern of suspicious involvement" of eight current members of the House with Kim Dong Jo.

But Deputy Attorney General Benjamin Civiletti told reporters June 1 that he did not expect any more indictments of current or former Congress members on Koreagate charges. He said that the House ethics committee had not furnished him with evidence supporting further prosecution of members of Congress.

Civiletti also noted that, in deciding whether to prosecute, Justice Department

criterion was not whether there was "an allegation that someone was paid money." The question was whether there was "evidence of a crime in receiving the money," Civiletti said.

Civiletti said the Justice Department had "about exhausted the amount of heavy information we have had from Tong Sun Park" and other witnesses and documents.

Civiletti said there might be one additional indictment in the case, but it would not be of a public official.

■ John Nidecker, an aide to former President Richard Nixon, told the international organizations subcommittee of the House International Relations Committee June 1 that a South Korean government official had given him $10,000 while he was on an official visit to South Korea in 1974. Nidecker said he had had the U.S. Embassy return the money. The Korean official was Park Chong Kyu, protection chief to South Korean President Park Chung Hee, Nidecker said.

A little later, when he had returned to Washington, Nidecker said, a South Korean assemblyman named Row Chin Hwan approached him to ask for the names of members of Congress to whom the assemblyman could give large contributions.

Nidecker said he gave Row no names and told him that such contributions would be illegal. Nidecker said he reported the incident to a National Security Council aide and to Alexander Haig Jr., then chief of staff to Nixon.

■ The Senate Ethics Committee, in the first formal report on its investigation, said June 19 that the late Sen. John L. McClellan had admitted before his death in 1977 that he had received an unreported campaign contribution from Park.

The Senate panel also said that spokesmen for three present or former senators had denied claims by Park that he had made campaign contributions to the senators. The senators were Birch Bayh (D, Ind.), the late Hubert Humphrey (D, Minn.) and former senator Jack Miller (R, Iowa). A Miller aide said that Park had made a contribution, but that it had been returned.

House panel cites 4 in Congress. The House Committee on Standards of Official Conduct (the ethics committee) July 13 cited four House members, all Democrats, for misconduct connected with the Korean lobbying effort.

The four, all of whom had previously denied wrongdoing, were:

John J. McFall (D, Calif.)—The former majority whip was charged with accepting a $4,000 contribution from Tong Sun Park and putting it to personal use under circumstances that, according to the committee, "might be construed by reasonable persons as influencing the performance of his government duties." McFall had acknowledged receiving the money.

Edward J. Patten (D, N.J.)—Patten was charged with giving money he had received from Park to a New Jersey Democratic organization, without telling the group that Park was the source of the contribution. Patten July 12 said that a former administrative assistant of his had accepted responsibility for not informing the New Jersey group that the funds came from Park.

Edward Roybal (D, Calif.)—The ethics panel charged that Roybal had made personal use of a $1,000 contribution from Park and then told committee investigators under oath that he had not taken the money.

Charles H. Wilson (D, Calif.)—Wilson, the committee said, had received a $1,000 wedding gift from Park, but had not told committee investigators of it. Wilson was quoted in the Washington Post July 14 as saying that he had "completely forgotten some of the events surrounding the hectic week I married Mrs. Wilson." He said he had told the committee of the gift later. Mrs. Wilson was of Korean descent.

Rep. John Breaux (D, La.) and two other witnesses seen by committee investigators gave conflicting accounts of Breaux's alleged links with Park. The committee report said that the evidence was "compelling that one of the three has committed perjury."

The conflict centered around a $5,000 check from Park. The evidence, however, was not sufficient to proceed against Breaux, the panel decided, because the bank where the check was cashed had lost the relevant records and no one at the bank remembered who had cashed the check.

The committee exonerated six House members who had been investigated as part of a group of about 30 representatives who had received money gifts from Park. The six were: E. de la Garza (D, Tex.): Thomas S. Foley (D, Wash.); John M. Murphy (D, N.Y.); Melvin Price (D, Ill.), Frank Thompson Jr. (D, N.J.) and Morris K. Udall (D, Ariz.).

Panel clears O'Neill—House Speaker Thomas P. O'Neill (D, Mass.) had been the subject of a number of allegations, but the committee concluded that "the only thing the evidence shows Mr. O'Neill to have done of questionable propriety is to accept two parties in his honor paid for by Tong Sun Park."

The panel said that "by today's standards it may be unwise for an important Congressman to permit either a foreigner or a suspected lobbyist to give him a party," but there did not appear to be any basis for disciplinary proceedings.

The committee noted that Rep. John Brademas (D, Ind.), the House majority whip, had accepted $2,950 from Park at the same time that he was preparing legislation that would outlaw such gifts. Brademas, the committee said, "defended his acceptance of cash from a foreign national at the very time he was advocating making such a contribution illegal by pointing out that he, nevertheless, had acted within the law."

Other Developments

Connell indicted. Grover Connell, president of a big rice trading company, was indicted by a federal grand jury in Washington May 26, 1978 on charges that he had illegally used Park Tong Sun as an agent for rice deals with Korea and had lied about his activities to a grand jury.

The indictment said that Tong Sun Park was an "ineligible selling agent" for rice sales to Korea under the Food for Peace program, because Park was "connected directly and indirectly with the government of the Republic of Korea and its agencies."

Connell had paid commissions to Park through a bank account set up in the name of a South Korean firm, Daiban Nongsan Co. Ltd., the indictment said. Connell was charged with paying over $600,000 in commissions from 1972 to 1975.

Connell was president of Connell Rice and Sugar Company Inc., which was based in Westfield, N.J. Connell's lawyer, Joseph Alioto said, "The facts will show clearly that Tong Sun Park was foisted upon the American rice industry by top officials of the Nixon Administration."

Halt to Korean food aid voted. The U.S. House of Representatives June 22, 1978 voted, 273–125, to halt $56 million to aid Korea under the Food for Peace program.

The vote was in retaliation for South Korea's refusal to cooperate with an American investigation of the Koreagate scandal by requiring ex-Ambassador Kim Dong Jo to testify to the House Committee on Standards of Official Conduct (the ethics committee).

The cutoff in food aid was added as an amendment to an $18-billion agricultural appropriations bill.

Majority Leader James Wright (D, Tex.) sponsored the aid cutoff amendment. Wright said that Kim Dong Jo's testimony was "vital and essential."

The Korean refusal to make Kim Dong Jo available, Wright said, left "no other alternatives. A cloud of suspicion hangs over the House and that cloud must be dispelled."

Opponents of the cutoff argued that it would hurt American farmers and the Korean people without putting any great pressure on the Korean government. Rep. Andrew Jacobs (D, Ind.) noted that there was "a question as to whether a dictator cares if we cut off aid to his people so long as we send him guns to keep them in line."

(The House had indicated earlier that it would not end military assistance—which was much more sizable—along with the food aid.)

Rep. B. F. Sisk (D, Calif.) observed that the U.S. might respond in the same fashion as Korea if it were put in the same position. Referring to charges that the U.S. had given money to Italian legislators, Sisk said, "If Italy decided to hold hearings on the American money and they decided to subpoena our ambassador and the head of the CIA [the Central Intelligence Agency], I don't think there is any question but that we would raise up in holy horror at such a request."

The Wright amendment was supported strongly by Democrats: 205 voted for it and 58 opposed it. Republicans split almost evenly: 68 favored the cutoff and 67 voted against it.

A spokesman for the Korean Embassy called the approval of the cutoff "regrettable." He added that it ignored "the cooperation that the Republic of Korea already has extended" to the influence-buying probe.

Congressional Ethics & Morality

Both Houses Adopt Codes

During the two centuries of Congress' existence, its members have frequently been attacked on various ethics charges.

The Constitution (Article I, Section 5, Clause 2) gives each house of Congress the right to "punish its Members for disorderly Behaviour, and, with the Concurrence of two thirds, expel a Member." Neither house, however, has ever displayed excessive eagerness in exercising this right in matters involving lapses in ethics.

In 200 years, the two houses have censured a total of seven senators, 18 representatives and a territorial delegate. They have expelled 15 senators and three representatives; of these, all but one (a senator ousted in 1979) were expelled during the Civil War. Since the Civil War, the Senate has acted on 12 motions for expulsion and the House on three, but in no case was a member expelled.

For most of its life, Congress left the judgment of the behavior of its members to the courts or to the voters as much as possible. The scandals of the 1960s, however, convinced many Congress members that they must occasionally act against gross misconduct by their colleagues or Congressional employes.

The Senate created a Select Committee on Standards & Conduct (the Senate ethics committee) in 1964, and the first members of the panel were appointed in July 1965. Four rules of ethical conduct for senators and Senate employes were adopted by the Senate March 22, 1968 as what Sen. John C. Stennis (D, Miss.), ethics committee chairman, indicated were supplements to "that great body of unwritten but generally accepted standards that will, of course, continue in effect."

Two years earlier (in 1966) the House had appointed a committee to draft an ethics code, but it went out of existence two months later before it could take substantial action. A new House Committee on Standards of Official Conduct was appointed in 1967, and its proposed code of conduct was adopted in 1968.

The fresh scandals of the mid-1970s demonstrated the need for further action, and both houses of Congress approved codes of ethics in 1977.

House adopts code. The House March 2, 1977 approved, 402–22, a new code of ethics for members that contained a strong financial disclosure requirement and set a limit on outside earnings. The earnings limit—15% of a member's current salary of $57,500, or $8,625—was the

51

most controversial feature of the code, but after a sharp debate the limit was approved, 344–79, in a vote especially on it.

The drive for ethics reform had built over the previous year as Congress was troubled with sex-payroll scandals and allegations that members had received gifts from South Koreans in exchange for sympathetic legislative treatment of that country. Also, the Congressional leadership had recently prevailed upon Congress to accept a pay raise on the understanding that the increase would be linked to a firm code of ethics.

Apart from the limit on outside earnings, the other major sections of the code:

■ Required disclosure of the source and amount of all income and gifts totaling more than $100 in one year from a single source. (If the gifts took the form of transportation, food, lodging or entertainment, the minimum for required disclosure was $250. Gifts from relatives, gifts of "personal hospitality" and gifts with a value of $35 or less were exempt from disclosure.)

■ Required that the source and amount of any reimbursements totalling $250 or more from a single source other than the federal government be disclosed.

■ Required disclosure of the identity and category of value (i.e., less than $5,000, between $5,000 and $15,000, etc.) of any financial holdings of $1,000 or more. Similar disclosure requirements covered debts of more than $2,500 (except mortgages on a member's homes), financial transactions, and real estate purchases or sales (except of personal residences).

■ Banned "unofficial office accounts," which reportedly had been used as slush funds by some members. However, the official expense allowance for members was increased to $7,000 from $2,000.

■ Barred travel abroad at government expense by lame-duck members.

■ Imposed some restrictions on franking (free mailing) privileges. Members were barred from using the frank for a mass mailing sent less than 60 days prior to a primary or general election in which the member was a candidate.

■ Barred members and House employes from accepting gifts totaling $100 or more in one year from lobbyists or foreign nationals.

The ethics code in the form it was adopted was largely the work of a special House commission chaired by Rep. David R. Obey (D, Wis.). A few elements of the code were voted on individually on the floor, but an effort by Republicans to open the whole package to floor amendments was turned back, 267–153, on a key procedural vote.

The limit on outside earnings applied to honoraria—payments for speeches, appearances or articles—as well as to job income. It did not apply to unearned income, such as stock or bond dividends, or to income from a family business to which the member did not make a significant contribution.

Critics of the limit charged that it amounted to discrimination against middle-income members—who supplemented their congressional salary by outside work—in favor of rich members, who could continue to draw income from investments. Supporters of the limit—among whom were numbered the Democratic House leadership—argued that congressional service was a full-time job and should be treated as such, that the recent pay raise for members of Congress largely removed the need for earning additional income and that the limit would help eliminate potential conflict-of-interests.

Rep. James H. Quillen (R, Tenn.) argued March 2 (according to his statement in the Congressional Record) that "the much-needed elimination of official corruption and conflicts of interest must not be deflected into a misguided assault on the right of members to earn money by hard work and honest effort in enterprises which have no conflict of interest with their official responsibilities."

Quillen continued: " ... I have read and reread Madison and Hamilton in the Federalist Papers regarding the qualifications of Members of the House and I am convinced that this limitation on outside income is unconstitutional. The qualifications for membership in the House are fixed in this Constitution, and as Hamilton wrote in Federalist Paper No. 60, these qualifications 'are unalterable by the Legislature.'

"Madison in Federalist Paper No. 52 wrote:

The qualifications of the elected ... have been very properly considered and regulated by the convention.

A Representative of the United States must be of the age of 25; must have been 7 years a citizen of the United States; must, at the time of his election, be an inhabitant of the State he is to represent; and during the time of his service, must be in no office under the United States.

"And listen:

Under these reasonable limitations, the door of this part of the Federal Government is open to merit of every description, whether native or adoptive, whether young or old, and without regard to poverty or wealth, or to any particular profession of religious faith.

"What this income limitation really amounts to is an amendment to the Constitution. This new amendment says that no person may serve as a U.S. Representative unless he or she meets an earned income test and earns less than 15 percent of the congressional salary, or $15,000, if the amendment is adopted. "The implications of this income limitation are so odious as to remind me of the ancient suggestion that a person must own property to vote. Both notions are dangerous and do violence to the Constitution and to the democratic process, because they stand in the way of the people and their choice to serve as their elected Representatives.

"In Federalist Paper No. 57, Madison addressed this very point when he wrote:

The electors are to be the great body of the people of the United States. Who are to be the objects of popular choice? Every citizen whose merit may recommend him to the esteem and confidence of his country. No qualification of wealth, of birth, of religious faith, or of civil profession is permitted to fetter the judgment or disappoint the inclination of the people.

"I am convinced that beyond what qualifications for membership of the House are fixed in this Constitution, this House dare not go, for that path is closed to us by the Founding Fathers.

"I further suggest that this income limitation is riddled with loopholes. Unearned income from investments of, say, $100,000 a year, is ethical and proper, but making 15 percent of the congressional salary annually or $15,000 a year at honest work involving no conflict of interest is deemed unethical and improper.... "

Rep. Robert W. Kastenmeier (D, Wis.) had explained March 2 that the disclosure requirement covered the following:

Income.—The source and amount of all income, including honoraria from a single source aggregating $100 or more during the preceding calendar year;

Gifts.—The source and value of gifts aggregating $100 or more during the preceding calendar year from a single source, excluding relatives or $250 for gifts of transportation, lodging, food or entertainment;

Reimbursements.—The source and amount aggregating $250 or more from a single source during the preceding calendar year;

Financial holdings.—The identity and category of value of any property held, directly or indirectly, in a trade or business or for investment or the production of income which has a fair market value of at least $1,000 as of the close of the preceding calendar year;

Liabilities.—The identity and category of value of each liability owed, directly or indirectly, which exceeds $2,500 as of the close of the preceding calendar year, excluding mortgages on personal residences;

Securities Transactions.—The identity, category of value and date of any transaction, directly or indirectly, in securities or commodities futures during the preceding calendar year which exceeds $1,000, except for transactions donating such securities to charitable or tax-exempt organizations; and

Real Estate.—The identity and category of value of any purchase or sale, directly or indirectly, of real property during the preceding calendar year and which exceeds $1,000 in value as of the date of such purchase or sale, excluding personal residences.

Rep. Clarence J. Brown (R, Ohio), also objecting March 2 to the limitation on outside earned income, said:

"There was a day in this Congress when the Congressmen served from January to July, even from March to July, and then went home and practiced some kind of normal business activity such as farming, newspapering, law, medicine, or the like. They then had some contact with the real world in which their constituents are obliged to operate all the time within the rules and the regulations which this body imposes upon them. At that time the Members understood how it was to operate in the real world.

"Mr. Chairman, we are creating by this

legislation, it seems to me, a separate ruling class that will be removed from the real world, that will be well compensated for the responsibility of ruling, but but will not be directly involved in the day-to-day activities by which our constituents earn their livings...."

Rep. Robert E. Bauman (R, Md.) discussed the same issue. He said:

"If we go down the list, we find that in 8 years 15 Members of Congress were convicted of criminal conduct and 2 acquitted. In every instance we find convictions on income tax and election laws. There is not one crime committed that involved or in any way relates to earned income or part-time or outside jobs. Reading down the list, we find accepting a gratuity, income tax violations, perjury, tax evasion, bribery, conspiracy to take bribes, mail fraud and obstruction of justice, bribery, mail fraud and filing false statements dealing with clerk hire. None of this wrongdoing involved outside income...

"I would suggest that there is no real need for this kind of limitation to make sure that we are all full-time Congressmen. The second session of the 93d Congress met only 173 days. That is not even one-half of the year.

"We were out of session 192 days; 27 weeks; more than 6 months....

"So, if it is a full-time job, why are we not in Washington the full time? What really is the problem? Is it abuse of honoraria? That could have been dealt with appropriate restrictions.

"There are many Members—some of them on the floor at this moment—who have written books and have copyrights, who are completely exempted under this bill. If writing a book about the House and becoming a well-known expert and having a best seller is not cashing in on the job, what is?

"So, the Members should see the double and triple standards that are being imposed. I suggest to the Members that the fundamental problem we are facing is not earned income. The fundamental problems can be addressed by full disclosure.

"But the real threat in this bill is the loss of our political independence...."

Will we create two classes of Members; one, clipping coupons and living off the inherited income; the other group of Members, afraid to make a misstep lest their congressional livelihood be taken away with nothing to go back to. This entire plan is part and parcel of reducing Members of Congress to glorified Government employees afraid to speak their minds. We are soon going to see the suggestion for taxes financing election campaigns for the House and the Senate; all a part of one grand plan financed out of the taxpayers' pockets."

Rep. Lee H. Hamilton (D, Ind.) had written about the problem in the Feb. 28 issue of the Washington Post:

The issue, as the commission viewed it, is not one of equity, but rather how to eliminate avoidable conflicts of interest in a reasonable and effective way.

Perhaps the single most difficult problem for a member of Congress is the effective use of his time—how to decide which among the thousands of competing concerns and demands merit his time and attention. Unlike earned income, investment income raises no problem as the best use of time. It does not create the same type of subtle influence on a member's judgment about the use of his time as does, for example, an offer to speak for $1,000.

Furthermore, investment income creates less of a risk of a financial conflict of interest than does earned income. A member does not need to "cash in" on his position as an elected official to receive investment income. He often does to receive earned income. Also, as we said in our report, there is far less of a potential conflict if a member receives stock dividends from a company than if the company pays the member for services rendered. A member can always change his investment if there is even the appearance of a conflict. On the other hand, if the company arbitrarily cuts him off, he is out of luck.

The goal of the commission was not to figure out how to maximize the income of a member of Congress, but how best to increase his effectiveness as a member and to remove potential conflicts of interest.

Our recommendations attempt to deal with clear and major abuses. No one seriously suggested before the commission that there is either a financial or time conflict in income from investments. Furthermore, it must be acknowledged that the remedies often suggested for dealing with investment income—divestment, disqualification from voting and blind trusts—are either too extreme or ineffective. About the best we can require is strict financial disclosure—which the commission has proposed—and the discipline of the electoral process.

Disclosure alone, however, will not work for outside earned income. I do not think we can have an effective ethics code without a limit on outside earned income. Earned income creates a variety of serious potential conflicts of interest for a member of Congress, ranging from the payment of large fees to gain his support for legislation to subtle distortions in the use of his time by offering him payment for a speech. The acceptance of a large honorarium from a group interested in legislation is troublesome to most members of Congress and to the public. ...''

Rep. Mario Biaggi (D, N.Y.) objected to the earnings limitation. He said:

"Mr. Chairman, the resolution we are considering has as its admirable goal the establishing of strict ethical standards for Members of Congress. The public is concerned over the recent scandals of a few Congressmen and want to eliminate even the hint of suspicion. While this resolution has many good features, the limitation on outside earned income is wrong, immoral, and just possibly unconstitutional.

" If the genuine concern here is for integrity, then all outside income regardless of source should be eliminated. But no, this resolution sacrifices integrity on the altar of hypocrisy. The millionaires or gentleman farmers, those with inherited wealth or vast holdings of stocks and bonds can continue to enjoy their incomes and get wealthier still. Those who work for a living are the only ones affected by this bill. It is a rich man's code of ethics designed to help the rich get richer and to keep the poor in their place.

"A few years ago we passed a tough election reform law which contained a limitation on the amount a millionaire can spend to get elected. Our objective was to end the buying of congressional seats by individuals with vast sums of money to spend. That provision was declared unconstitutional. The millionaires won again.

" Let us face it, while some of our membership have been around here for a long time, this job is not permanent. It is not civil service. There are no guarantees that we will be back in 2 years. In fact, over 60 percent of our membership has been elected since 1970. Yet for the workingman elected to Congress he must give up all his outside connections with employment that might be necessary 2, or 4, or 6 years down the road.

It is the same old story we see every day—a form of selective morality. We have it in the judicial system. There are two standards of justice—one for the rich fellow who usually gets off scot-free or with a fine, another for the poor- and middle-income individual, who ends up in the penitentiary.

"We have it in the tax laws. The richer you get, the easier it is to find the loopholes to avoid paying taxes. Yet, if you just work for a living and make your money from "earned income," you pay and pay till there is nothing left to take home.

"Look what is going to happen if this resolution with its earned income limitation is approved.

"One of our colleagues who draws $21,-000 in salary and $18,000 in dividends from a family-owned business told the press he will simply change the salary to dividends.

"Another colleague who supports the resolution said he had no problem with the proposal despite the fact that he gets $122,000 from a business he holds the majority stock in. He will have no problem converting that salary to dividends and adding it to the $300,000 in dividends he already receives.

"Another colleague says he will put his wife in the two positions on bank boards that he now holds and she can draw the salary.

"Large financial holdings create as much a conflict of interest as outside earned income. How can a Member vote to cut capital gains taxes, which only the millionaires really benefit from, if he is going to cut his own income. What Member is going to vote for tougher regulations of banks and corporations if he derives a great portion of his income from these sources? Unfortunately, no one is concerned about that.

"The tough financial disclosure provisions are the only things necessary to prevent abuse of power. If a Member is taking income from sources that present a conflict of interest, the members of the press, I am sure, will quickly bring that to the attention of the public. Then let his constituency decide whether they want such a man to continue to represent them in Congress. If, as some suggest, the people cannot be relied upon to vote out a scoundrel, then we here in Congress can censure and suspend from various privileges any Member violating general standards of morality and ethics.

"You cannot set arbitrary limits on outside earned income. Who is to say what an individual's time is worth. Two senators got $25,000 a piece for a few hours work on television during the national political conventions. I doubt if anyone can argue that such a fee compromised their positions as Senators, created a conflict of interest or deprived their constituency of representation. Yet, that type of income will be closed to Members of Congress if this resolution is passed.

"Let us get everything on the record. The financial disclosure sections do that. If a Member received a $25,000 fee from some industry that he is responsible for in the legislative field, that fee and its consequences will be well publicized. No one in his right mind—even a criminal mind—is going to risk that.

" If the disclosure route does not work, I will be among the first to suggest limitations on income—but on all income regardless of source. If the argument is true that an individual can live quite well on his congressional salary and should not need anything else, then let us apply that policy across the board. It might have the salutary effect of making this body more representative of all people instead of limiting it more and more to only the wealthy."

In the March 2 debate, Rep. Charles Thone (R, Neb.) objected to what he called a "bribe" to House members to give up their "office accounts." He said:

" May I remind the Members of the events that caused the Commission on Ethical Review to come into being. There were scandals about abuse of office allowances by Members and by committee chairmen. We in the minority asked for an audit of every fund. The leadership, however, said we should forgive and forget past sins. We should only promise to be good in the future.

"I favor ethical conduct. I also favor exposure of past unethical conduct.

" In general, I strongly support the proposed resolution on ethics for Members of this body....

"Title III of the resolution is concerned with 'Unofficial Office Accounts and Official Expense Allowances.' The so-called office accounts are an evil, in my view. Under present law, there is no requirement for the reporting of them. There is no regulation of them. Some Members accept both corporate and labor union money for these accounts, despite the fact that such contributions are illegal to Federal campaign funds.

" Title III proposes to end these accounts. The price that is enacted in this resolution is unnecessary and unwise. The majority is offering a bribe to those who have had these office accounts. The leadership is saying, 'Give up these office ac-

counts and we will give you another $5,000 a year in Federal funds for operation of your office.' The price is too high. We can abolish office accounts. Or, we could tightly regulate them. We do not have to dip once more into the taxpayers' pocket. Therefore, I strongly favor striking title III of this resolution. ... "

Rep. Timothy E. Wirth (D, Colo.) also commented March 2 on the special office accounts. "I have had to maintain such an account since elected in 1974," he said. He explained:

" ... Under existing laws, there simply was not enough money available to run my office adequately. The account has never exceeded $3,000 and was funded primarily out of my own pocket. It has been used for such things as subscriptions to newspapers and magazines relevant to my committee assignments, dues to official House organizations that study legislation, and other assorted office-related expenditures, all of which I publicly disclosed. House Resolution 287 will provide additional office funds and will remove any need for maintaining such a private account.

"As is always the case, the questionable and secret use of such funds by a few Members of Congress has resulted in much understandable public concern about all such accounts. The proposed funding increase for official expenses is the correct solution to this problem. An important thing to note here is that the added cost of the increase in office accounts will be more than offset by the savings realized by making all postal patron mailings third-class mail instead of first class, as is the current practice.

" Mr. Chairman, the issue here is one of trying to end any special influence with a Member that money could buy for an individual, corporation, or special-interest group. ... "

Rep. Bill Frenzel (R, Minn.) objected March 2 to the code's failure to require audits and to other flaws. He said it contained "many worthwhile and long overdue recommendations" but added:

" The new ethics code, alone, however, merely defines some new standards of conduct for Members. It is still imcomplete, and surely imperfect. Obfuscations and ommissions in the reform package have clearly underscored its imperfections. Absence of a creditable mechanism for enforcement of the code emphasizes its weaknesses, but there are even more egregious ommissions.

"The first major ommission is the lack of any audits. An ethics package without audit is like a sprinter with one leg. A systematic audit procedure for all House expenses and liberal public access to disclosure records should be fundamental components of any stringent congressional reform package. Yet the necessity and merit of such procedures were neither addressed by the Commission on Administrative Review nor included in the Obey reform package.

"If the recent past has taught us anything, it is that the public demands the right to know how public money is managed and spent by its elected officials. As I understand it, the people are far more interested in how we spend their money than in our willingness to disclose our own personal finances. ... "

Rep. J. Kenneth Robinson (R, Va.) March 2 assailed the Obey Commission's ethics package as a "sham." He said:

"As debate begins on the so-called ethics package, my real complaints center on those important matters of ethics that are left out and ignored altogether, as well as with certain serious flaws within the package of recommendations itself—such as the wholly unjustified $5,000 increase in each Members' office expense allowances.

"For example, most if not all conservatives believe a recorded vote should be required for any salary increase that applies to Members of Congress and that any such increases should be deferred until the next Congress is seated as the best means to avoid conflict-of-interest questions. Permitting the voters to know how a Congressman actually votes on a salary increase that benefits himself is an elementary matter of ethical practice, in my judgment. I also share the view of many conservatives that all congressional expenses should be regularly audited as a safeguard against the misappropriation of public funds or their misuse. We believe the personnel system should be broadly reformed in the House of Representatives so that there can be no chance that political cronies or personal, but unskilled, friends of Members can be put on the public payroll improperly, as has happened in the recent past.

"Yet unbelievably, not one single one of these matters is included in the ethics package to be voted upon today. That is why, in important respects, this ethics package can be termed a sham.

"As to the serious flaws I mentioned, one of the most serious certainly is the Obey Commission's recommendation, as provided in House Resolution 287, to increase the allowance for official expenses from $2,000 to $7,000. As a member of the House Republican Policy Committee, I take the liberty of quoting from our committee's policy statement about this matter:

It requires the American taxpayer to pay the extra $5,000 for each Member as the trade-off for the abolishing of unofficial office accounts known as "slush funds." This is legislative bribery at its worst.

" The truth is less than one-half or some 40 percent of the House Members have been maintaining these slush funds in the first place. But increasing the expense allowance by $5,000 per Member would mean another $2.2 bill to be picked up by taxpayers. "

Most of the rest of the code conformed to proposals made earlier by the House Republican. Task Force on Reform. The GOP task force, however, had proposed a $15,000 ceiling on outside earned income. In its statement on reforms, the GOP panel said:

The Task Force earnestly believes that the most effective remedy against unethical or financially questionable activities is the requirement of public disclosure. It also believes that the major thrust of public concern is accountability for public funds. ...

Authentic reform goes beyond simple alterations in the law or a rewriting of the ethics code. The Task Force therefore recommends that accompanying any new regulations will be the adoption of effective enforcement mechanisms coupled with nonpartisan, systematic, and independent auditing procedures. If the Congress refuses to implement the necessary means to ensure compliance with the new standards, there will be no reform—only a futile exercise. ...

House Rule 44 governs the disclosure of financial interests by Members. Two reports are required—the first, which is available for public review, provides limited information concerning the sources of income and the identity of certain categories of liabilities and assets; the second, which is kept confidential, discloses the amounts of income from each source listed on the public report and the fair market value of business holdings, This second report is filed with the House Ethics Committee and can only be opened if examination of the information is deemed essential to an official investigation of the committee.

Such restricted disclosure merely reinforces public cynicsim and fosters the misperception of extensive conflicts of interests in the dispatch of legislative business. The

Task Force believes that a Member's constituents have the right to be given a more honest appraisal of their representative's financial situation.

The Task Force supports the adoption of disclosure rules which would indicate:

1. the source and amount of each item of income which exceeds $100 in a calendar year.

2. the identity and category of value of each asset which has a value of over $1,000.

3. the identity of each liability owed.

4. the identity of any position as an officer, director, partner, advisor, or consultant of any business enterprise or partnership.

5. the transfer of assets from an officeholder to a spouse or dependents which have a value in excess of $1,000.

Whether an officeholder's disclosure requirements should be interpreted to include the financial activities of the spouse and dependents is a matter of serious debate. This extension is often justified as a means to prevent the improper transfer of assets, controlled by the officeholder, to the spouse and dependents, in order to avoid public disclosure. However, to require the reporting of items which are the sole property of the spouse and dependents and are in no way connected with the income of the officeholder is an invasion of privacy and may equally violate the confidentiality provisions of the Internal Revenue Code. In order to balance these conflicting concerns, the Task Force recommends that the financial disclosure requirements imposed on an officeholder not include the independent financial activities of a spouse and dependents, with the provision that any transfer of assets from an officeholder to a spouse or dependents in excess of $1,000 must be reported (proposal #5 above).

The Task Force supports the concept of requiring assets and liabilities to be reported in ranges: under $5,000; between $5,000 and $15,000; between $15,000 and $50,000; between $50,000 and $100,000; and greater than $100,000. The Task Force would additionally require a description of any contract or understanding regarding post-government employment. Finally, all disclosure reports should be filed with the Clerk of the House and be available for public inspection. . . .

Obey told the House March 2 that his committee had engaged pollster Louis Harris to survey public opinion on the Congressional ethics question because "we did not want to rely upon the views of any self-annointed organizations, be they labor, business, Common Cause, anybody. . . ." Obey continued:

" We found some interesting things. We found, first of all, that the public wants financial disclosure from Members of Congress. By a margin of 63 to 23 the public indicated that they thought both Members of Congress and their opponents at election time ought to have to disclose their financial affairs.

" Interestingly enough, Members felt much more strongly. The membership by 87 percent was in favor of disclosure and 13 percent against.

"The Commissioin felt we ought to be guided by two principles on disclosure: first, that the items to be disclosed would be items which would be relevant, which would help measure the potential conflict of interest, and second, that we should also establish a system to avoid purposeless recordkeeping and to protect, whenever possible, a Member's privacy rights.

" We specifically rejected, for instance, the requirement that a Member file an income tax return. We were told by people who administer the toughest State ethics codes in the country that, No. 1, they very often do not pick up relevant information on an income tax return; that is, if someone owns municipal bonds which are tax exempt.

" We were also told that, in fact, there was no public interest to be served by spelling out what a Member's medical payments were or his alimony payments, or things of that nature.

" So, we rejected the income tax requirement. Second, we rejected the requirement that Members file a net worth statement, because we thought that it is not necessary for the public to know whether a Member is worth $126,000 or $124,000 so long as they can measure within a reasonable range what our potential conflicts might be. So, we rely, in the main, on categories of value when we require disclosure of holdings and other items.

"The second thing that the survey showed us was that the public wants Members of Congress to be full time. We laid out 20 potential conflict-of-interest situations. We asked the public to respond to all of them and tell us which ones bothered them the most. Interestingly enough, the item which bothered them the most, more than any other, was the example of the Member of Congress who gave a large number of speeches to organizations for pay, and received large speaking fees for those speeches. That bothered the public the most, and that was the situation about which the public was least satisfied by the mechanism of disclosure alone.

"That is what we tried to do. We tried to reflect the public's concerns in that area as best we could, given our own judgments in the matter, by limiting outside income to 15 percent and putting an honorarium limitation of $750 per speech on a Member's outside income. The Rules Committee changed that to $1,000, and we think that is a reasonable change and we can live with it.

"The third clear message that showed up in that public opinion poll is especially relevant, I think, to titles III and IV. That poll showed that above all else, the public wants more contact with their Members of Congress. In fact, the biggest gap—the biggest gap in all the activities we measured—the biggest gap between what the public saw Members of Congress doing versus what they wanted them to do was to get back home to communicate with them, whether it was by newsletter or by personal consultation, and we tried to reflect that....

"Fourth, the public showed very clearly that they want public duties paid for out of public funds, and not private funds and not personal funds. I think that is essential. So, the Commission responded to that desire by trying to build a well between official expenses on the one hand and personal and political expenses on the other. So, we recommended the elimination of artificial office accounts, or slush funds, depending upon one's literary style. We recommended the elimination of the ability to convert political funds to personal use in titles III and IV, and recommended a limitation on the use of the frank.

"On the frank, very frankly, we had two considerations which were expressed by the different political parties in the House. Republicans expressed to me their concern about the fact that we had a Democratic-controlled Congress, a 2-to-1, Democratic-controlled Congress, which could pour newsletters into districts very shortly before the election, thereby resulting in a very heavy partisan advantage for the Democratic Party. So, we corrected that. We also heard from a good many Democrats who were unhappy with published reports that the Republican Congressional Campaign Committee contributed over $220,-000 for the printing of newsletters in the last election year, which were then franked at a public cost of $2.5 million.

"And so we tried to deal with both of those concerns. What we said was that we could not send out a postal paper mailing or, for that matter, a mass mailing of any kind, if it were paid for by anything other than public funds, so that we could not lever the expenditure of $1,500 of our own money into the expenditure of $15,000 to $25,000 of taxpayers' money. ...

"We also recommended that if we wipe out those unofficial office accounts, that we then ought to increase the official allowance by $5,000. Some people will ask why. Again I return to the public opinion poll conducted by Lou Harris. The public believes we are not getting home enough and the public believes we are not communicating enough with them. They are desperate for communication of almost any kind from us. They also indicated that they want that communication paid for not by United States Steel, not by Joe Blow down at the corner grocery store who may contribute to a voluntary fund for any of us, but they, rather, want that official business conducted in an official way.

"That is the straightest way to do it, and the public is smart enough to understand that. In fact, when we asked them whether they wanted weekly trips for Members of Congress to be paid for out of private funds or out of public funds, by a margin of 54 to 30 they said they wanted that done above board, in a public way, out of public funds, not private funds. When we asked them whether they would rather see all travel within a Member's district paid for out of private funds or out of public funds, by a 76 to 19 margin they said they wanted those funds paid for in a public way, not in a private way.

"We asked them whether they wanted newsletters sent out by using private funds or using public funds, and by a 57 to 33 margin they said they wanted them paid out of public funds.

"What it amounts to is that, up to now, Members of Congress have accurately perceived that the public wants communication from us but they have paid for those items out of unofficial accounts and campaign funds.

"We have approximately 40 percent of the Members of this House right now who have unofficial office allowances. In addition to that, I would venture to say that we have close to another 100 Members of the House who pay for official expenses directly out of their campaign funds. ...

' On travel, we asked the public a number of questions, and to make it short, the public response was very clear. They responded by something like 86 to 11 percent, I believe, to this question: The question was asked whether they minded Members of Congress traveling abroad, so long as they were real trips and not disguised vacations and so long as the expenses were adequately vouched for, and they said by a margin of 86 to 11 percent that they did not mind those trips provided those requirements were met. They did indicate that they do not believe that lame ducks have any business traveling.

"So we have simply spelled out two requirements under travel: No. 1, that there shall be no double-dipping. In other words, if a Member is reimbursed from some other source for travel abroad, he cannot also collect a per diem so that he is in effect collecting twice. We have also said that a Member of Congress who is defeated in a general election or who is no longer a candidate may not travel abroad after either sine die adjournment or the election, whichever comes first. ...

" Let me just say this in closing: I think it should be understood that what we are not doing here today is drafting a set or a code of ethics which will raise the Members of Congress up to the pure ethics of everybody else in society. That is not what we are doing. What we are trying to do here is to recognize that the ethics of the marketplace are not sufficient for public life in the conduct of our official duties and our public responsibilities, and we are simply trying to draft a code which will reflect that.

"I have served in the Wisconsin Legislature for over 6 years, I have served in this House for almost 8 years, and I can truthfully say that I believe the ethical behavior exhibited by members both in the legislature in which I served before and here is quite a bit higher than in almost any other group with which I have ever dealt in any other walk of life.

" I think I can also say that the members I served with in the Wisconsin Legislature and in this House worry more about the country and care more about what happens to the country and worry more about public problems than does any other group in society.

"I think it is important that we understand that what we are trying to do here is to draft a code of ethics today which simply reflects what our public responsibilities are so that we can have public confidence in at least the integrity of the processes around here.

" Mr. Chairman, I just want to close by making one further statement. In that public opinion poll we asked the question: How many of you believe that the leadership of the House is right in making ethics reform a top order of business? Seventy-eight percent of them said, yes, they agreed with that. When we asked them how many people agreed or how many people thought that we would in fact get significant ethics reform in this session of Congress, only 35 percent indicated their belief that we would get it.

"What I think is essential for this House to do today is to show that 65 percent that they are wrong."

Rep. Christopher J. Dodd (D, Conn.) indorsed the Obey Commission's proposals March 2 but urged further "ethics reform." Dodd said:

" ... I must agree with many of my colleagues who fail to see the actual distinctions between earned and unearned outside income—between salaries and investment income. I believe that both forms of income can lead to potential conflicts of interest and should be included under some sort of outside income limitation.

"I fail to see how it is any less of a possible conflict when a Member knows a vote might indirectly help a firm in which he holds stock, as opposed to those Members who work a certain amount of time earning money through outside personal services.

"Granted the latter is an active, possible conflict; the former might be a passive, possible conflict. However, I think the fact remains that the potential conflict of interest in either case could be equally corrupting.

"Now I know how difficult finding a solution to the outside income problem will be, but I think more study must be done. I also know that there are legitimate questions about the efficacy of possible solutions to these problems, especially the one known as "blind trusts."

"But the subject must be further deliberated because I do not believe the present distinctions remove as much of the potential conflicts of interest as possible.

"In that area, I also think that further study should be made of whether, by simple legal means, any Member can convert his outside salary into dividends on stock, thereby circumventing the spirit of the outside income limitations. This procedure has received quite a bit of press coverage, and I think the public should be convinced that we in Congress are aware of it and will not allow it to become a loophole in our carefully drawn ethics package...."

Obey rejected what he considered implications that the $5,000 increase in the official expense allowance was an effort "to buy out members of Congress and that the only way we can make them end unethical behavior is to provide this $5,000 addition." Obey said:

"It is not unethical for Members who have exceeded their official allowance to try to meet official expenses. It is not unethical for Members of Congress who feel it is necessary for them to go home to their districts every weekend in order to service their constituents, to try to find a way to do it. It is not unethical for Members of Congress to try to provide additional newsletters which tell people back home what we are trying to do in Washington.

"The fact is that we interviewed over 150 Members of this House and we found out that approximately 40 percent of the Members of this House already have unofficial office accounts. They expend out of those unofficial office accounts anywhere from $360 to $60,000 a year. We found the average expenditure out of those accounts is $6,800. We found out the median is approximately $5,000.

"In addition to that we also found out that we have approaching 100 other Members of this House who pay for these official kinds of expenses right out of their own campaign funds, right out of their political funds...."

House forms ethics panel—The House March 9, 1977 created, by 410–1 vote, a Select Committee on Ethics to write the recently adopted House ethics code into law.

Currently, the ethics code was only embodied in House rules. That meant suspected violations could only be investi-

gated through House channels—such as the Committee on Standards of Official Conduct (the House committee normally referred to as the Ethics Committee)—and that violations could only be punished by internal House sanctions, such as censure.

If the code were enacted into law, suspected violations could be investigated by federal law enforcement agencies. Also, criminal penalties could be attached to various violations.

In writing the legislation, the select committee would have the task of giving specific interpretations to the sometimes general provisions of the ethics code adopted March 2. The committee would also have to consider making the ethics legislation applicable to the executive branch as well as Congress.

Rep. Richardson Preyer (D, N.C.) was appointed March 10 to head the select committee. Twelve other Democrats and 6 Republicans were named to the panel.

Members disclose finances—The first reports on the personal finances of House members were made public May 4, 1978. The reports, required under the new code, showed that at least five House members were millionaires, and at least 153 had investments worth more than $100,000.

Only 22 of the more than 400 House members who filed reports said they had received no income in addition to the $57,500 congressional salary. (Members who announced before April 30 that they intended to retire from Congress were not required to file reports.)

The reports—in which the representatives were obliged to give information on outside income for only the last three months of 1977—showed that lobbying groups frequently paid House members substantial fees for speaking engagements.

Senate forms panel. The Senate Jan. 18, 1977 had formed by voice vote a special committee to formulate a code of ethics for the Senate. The 15-member committee was directed to report back to the Senate with its proposals by March 1. It was agreed that the Senate would give expedited consideration to the proposals. Sen. Gaylord Nelson (D, Wis.) was appointed chairman of the panel, made up of eight Democrats and seven Republicans.

The resolution setting up the committee was sponsored by the two top party leaders in the Senate, Majority Leader Robert C. Byrd (D, W.Va.) and Minority Leader Howard Baker Jr. (R, Tenn.). The reason for mandating speedy action on the ethics question lay in the then pending pay increase for members of Congress.

Byrd Jan. 18 said it was "imperative" that the pay raise be tied to a "code of conduct." On Jan. 10, Byrd had expressed support for the raise—to $57,500 from $44,600 for members of Congress—provided that it was linked to a requirement of complete financial disclosure by members of Congress and to a ban on outside earnings from speaking fees or business activity.

The pay increase had been proposed Jan. 17 by President Ford in his budget message and would take effect 30 days later unless vetoed by Congress. Ford also had urged Congress to adopt a code of ethics and had forwarded the ethics proposals of the Commission on Executive, Legislative and Judicial Salaries. That group—known as the Peterson commission after its chairman, Peter G. Peterson—Dec. 6, 1976 had urged Congress to adopt a code barring certain kinds of outside income and requiring members of Congress to make full public financial disclosures.

Reasons for the proposal to impose an ethics code and comments on some of the specific rules proposed were presented by Sen. William D. Hathaway (D, Me.) Feb. 1 in testimony before the Senate's new Special Committee on Official conduct:

If the polls are to be believed, the level of trust our constituents place in Congress, and in government in general, is unfortunately low.

The reasons for this are no doubt complex, and I won't speculate on all of them. But one reason is that some voters and, more tragically, non-voters seem to feel that those in political life are solely interested in lining their own pockets or taking ·junkets to the exclusion of helping those who elected them.

These sentiments are difficult to understand since the vast majority of the men and women in public life whom I have come to know are extraordinarily dedicated and hardworking, and scrupulously honest.

There have unfortunately been an infamous few who have abused and debased public office. And these individuals, with the assistance of vigilant and persistent press, have managed to shape and dominate public perceptions, and thereby obscure the positive examples and clean records of so many others.

This sort of feeling on the part of a significant portion of the electorate represents a cancer on our Democracy which we must take every step to eliminate.

We have various Senate rules, the Federal Election Campaign Act, and provisions of the criminal code already in place, but it is appropriate that we reexamine all of these standards on a comprehensive basis and draft a code of conduct.

But at the outset we should realize that no matter what system we devise there will continue to be a few who will attempt to abuse public office—we cannot alter human nature.

Among 535 members of Congress, and many times more top-level Presidential appointees, civil servants, and federal judges, there will always be some who will try to put personal gain above public service.

After all, ethics are ultimately a matter or personal standards and self-examination— any institutionalized set of rules cannot possibly be expansive enough to yield answers to all of the ethical dilemmas and problems which might arise.

But this should not preclude us from institutionalizing basic standards to apply to all and seting up mechanisms for enforcing those standards upon those who might otherwise ignore and resist them.

In fact, if the public is going to continue to denigrate the vast majority on the basis of a small unscrupulous minority, then we must set up such standards and do all we can to enforce them. . . .

Office funds, comprised of contributions received by an office holder in addition to campaign contributions, along with excèss contributions from prior campaigns put into such funds, are utilized for expenses arising out of his job that are not otherwise covered by Senate allowances. The Senate already has reporting provisions as contained in Rule 42 of the Standing Rules of the Senate.

This Rule requires that these contributions be reported, if more than $50, and that such reports are to be made available to the public.

It is my understanding that a number of Senators maintain such funds, and use them for reprints of speeches, for television taping, and for excess stationery costs.

While the existence of these funds has always in the past been recognized by the Rules as being proper, and I maintained one myself until a year ago, I think that on balance they ought to be banned and specifically prohibited by a new Senate rule.

This is in no way to criticize those who maintain such funds, but I have found that some voters consider such funds to be improper and inappropriate, that they feel no Senator should accept any kind of contribution other than a campaign contribution.

They view these contributions, if received throughout the Senator's six year term, as being motivated by a desire on the part of the contributor to influence the day to day voting decisions of the Senator or otherwise curry his favor.

Though most of us would disagree with this analysis, it seems simpler, and more likely to engender trust on the part of the electorate to ban these funds altogether and thereby avoid any improper appearances.

At the same time we are eliminating office funds, we ought to insure that the legitimate expenses which arise out of official duties of Senators are fully addressed and compensated by expense accounts, subject to verification and strict accounting.

Particularly necessary in this, regard are sufficient funds for travel, lodging, and meals within the Senator's home state. Direct transportation costs such as plane fare are covered already, but the latter two items are not. and should be.

If office funds are eliminated, there remains the problem of what are permissible uses of excess campaign funds. I do not think that Senators should in any way be able to convert such funds to personal use, except to cover personal campaign debts incurred prior to the contributions being received. Otherwise, Senators would directly and personally benefit from contributions.

If there are excess funds, these should be restricted to use in future campaigns, donated to charitable causes, or returned to the donors.

There are other problems associated with the issue of Senate travel. Some believe that committee trips overseas and elsewhere are by and large junkets, with no valid purpose except the enjoyment of the Members. There have been occasional abuses in this area to in part justify this impression.

But in general the trips of which I am aware have fulfilled a legitimate function of making the Members more knowledgeable of problems in all parts of the country and the world on a direct basis, and haev been far more work than pleasure.

However, since the perception of misbehavior is present, we must institute firm procedures to require that these trips be specifically considered and justified prior to approval and, except where necessary for security reasons, be reported publicly during and subsequent to their occurrence. ...

It is my understanding that this panel is particularly interested in ideas on how a code of conduct might be enforced, or more properly, how violations of that code ought to be punished.

I approve of the basic philosophy behind the restructuring of the Select Committee on Standards and Conduct into the Committee on Ethics as contained in S. Res. 4.

The "new" Ethics Committee would be different from the Select Committee on Standards in one basic and fundamental fashion—its members would serve for a maximum of six years in order to insure that new ideas and new approaches are brought to bear on the complex problems of conflict of interest. Also, the Committee would be composed of Senators with differing lengths of service in the Senate—some having served less than six years, some having served between 6 and 12 years, and some, more than twelve.

This Committee should be empowered to investigate any allegation of conflict of interest, self-dealing, or other improper or illegal activity on the part of any Senator.

It ought to be empowered to report resolutions to the full Senate imposing a wide range of sanctions, from reprimand to censure, to expulsion.

The exact procedures and the appropriate penalty for each offense, if substantiated, should be left to the Ethics Committee to determine on a case-by-case basis.

In addition, it should be available for advice and consultation with individual Senators on whether and how to divest themselves of particular assets which might present a conflict of interest, how to set up blind trusts when appropriate, and for advisory opinions on all of these matters.

Beyond this, it is my belief that any criminal allegations which might arise and appear to be substantiated ought to be referred to the Department of Justice, or the Special Prosecutor. We are not in the business of deciding criminal guilt or innocence and we should quickly turn such matters over to those who are.

Senate approves code. The Senate April 1, 1977 followed the example of the House by adopting, 86–9, a code of ethics that required full financial disclosure and set a limit on the income a senator could earn in addition to his salary.

Final approval came after two weeks of debate and action on 64 amendments. At times the debate grew acrimonious, especially on the issue of a limit on outside earned income. That limit was upheld March 22, when the Senate voted 62–35 to reject an amendment by Sen. Edmund S. Muskie (D, Me.) that would have deleted the limit from the code. (On the same day but prior to the vote, the Senate rejected, 67–29, another amendment by Muskie that would have extended the limit to unearned income—i.e., investment, etc.)

The question of public trust in Congress

figured prominently in the debate on both the code as a whole and the income limit. Senate Majority Leader Robert Byrd (D, W.Va.), a staunch supporter of the code, April 1 said it was "absurd that the Senate has to demean itself by enacting a code of conduct, but in a climate of public distrust it is a necessity." Muskie viewed the matter in a different light. "Public dissatisfaction with congressional ethics," when combined with Byrd's advocacy, had created "a sort of lynch mob environment in which people will just vote anything in the name of ethics," Muskie said.

Byrd also cited the recent salary increase for members of Congress as a reason for enacting the code. Congress would only be right in accepting that increase, Byrd maintained, if it also accepted the limit on outside earnings. An ethics code had been recommended by Presidents Ford and Carter as part of the pay-increase package.

In its main provisions, the code adopted by the Senate April 1:

■ Limited outside earnings for a member or employe of the Senate making over $35,000 a year to 15% of his official salary—$8,625 a year, based on the current senatorial salary of $57,500. The limit—which would not go into effect until 1979—did not apply to income from investments or from family farms or businesses, provided the family farm or business did not require "significant amounts" of a senator's time while the Senate was in session.

■ Barred senators, senate employes and their spouses and dependents from accepting gifts totaling more than $100 in value from an individual or organization with a direct interest in legislation before Congress. Gifts from relatives and gifts of personal hospitality were exempt from the prohibition.

■ Required annual disclosure of the source and amount of earned income exceeding $100.

■ For unearned income over $100, disclosure of the source and category of value was required (i.e., not more than $1,000, between $1,000 and $2,500, etc.). There were also disclosure requirements for gifts, real estate, liabilities and transac-tions in securities or commodities. The first disclosure statement would apply to financial activities and holdings for the last three months of 1977.

■ Barred unofficial office accounts (allegedly used as slush funds by some members of Congress). No expenditures could be made from existing accounts after Dec. 31, 1977 (no contributions to them could be made after adoption of the code).

■ Barred lame-duck senators from making trips abroad on federal funds. Senators and Senate employes could take foreign trips paid for by foreign educational or charitable organizations, provided the trips were approved by the ethics committee.

■ Barred senators from using franked (government-paid) mass mailing less than 60 days prior to a primary or general election. Required that franked mass-mailings be printed with official funds—a provision designed to end the practice of using the frank to mail privately printed material that was labeled "Not Printed at Government Expense." (The franking rules went into effect Aug. 1, 1977.)

■ Prohibited, effective Jan. 3, 1979, senators and Senate employes from discriminating in hiring, firing or promoting on the basis of sex, race, color, national origin, age or physical handicap.

The code would be enforced by the Select Committee on Ethics. Chaired by Sen. Adlai E. Stevenson 3rd (D, Ill.), the committee had three Democratic and three Republican members. Two of the Republican members—Sen. Lowell P. Weicker Jr. (Conn.) and Sen. Harrison H. Schmitt (N.M.)—voted against the code; the third GOP member—Sen. John G. Tower (Tex.)—was absent when the final vote was taken, but had attacked the code in debate, terming it a "hoax." (A majority vote was needed for the committee to begin an investigation of a member's conduct or to recommend sanctions for a member. The sanctions the committee could recommend included censure, expulsion and loss of seniority.)

Commenting on passage of the legislation, Weicker said, "In a knee-jerk effort to quiet some criticism over a pay raise, we have done fundamental institutional harm to the Senate." Others who voted against the bill beside Weicker and Schmitt were Sens. Carl T. Curtis (R,. Neb.), Barry Goldwater (R, Ariz.), Clifford T. Hansen (R, Wyo.), S. I. Hayakawa (R, Calif.), Paul Laxalt (R, Nev.), William V. Roth Jr. (R, Dela.) and Malcolm Wallop (R, Wyo.).

Arguing against the limitation on outside income, Muskie March 18 had given the Senate details of his own situation: "When I was elected Governor of my State in 1954, I had a one-man law office. We struggled, my wife and I, to make a living. We got by—not much more, because I was a young lawyer just starting out.

"A year before I ran for Governor, I had broken my back, been hospitalized for weeks, and been without an income for months. So when I was elected, I had thousands of dollars of medical and hospital bills, a law office which I had to decide to keep open or close, and I had to look forward to a salary of $10,000 a year as Governor of my State.

"I closed my law office. The option was to do that—or take on some young lawyer and hopefully to stimulate business because of the fact that I was Governor—to attract business because of the fact that I was Governor, and build up a practice in that fashion. I chose not to do it, notwithstanding the bills and notwithstanding the limited salary.

"I sold my home, because there was a Governor's mansion in Maine. I do not know how long the non-Indians are going to keep it, but there is a Governor's mansion in Maine. So I sold my home. It would have been hard to maintain it on the Governor's salary, given the ordinary pressures on a Governor's income, so I sold it. The equity brought me $5,000. It was not enough to pay my bills, if I had paid all my bills at that point, but I invested that money in mutual funds as the most ethical kind of investment that I could conceive of from a conflict of interest point of view.

" Then I deliberately said to myself, I have made these two decisions because there is a way for me to augment my income as Governor.' There was fresh in my mind the experience of such public figures as Winston Churchill, Eleanor Roosevelt, and others like them who, in a very public way, traveled the lecture circuit, and I was well aware from my own reading of history that the lecture circuit—as a way of enlightening the public, of disseminating information and understanding on the issues—was as old as the Republic.

"So I said:

Muskie, there is your answer. You can perform a public service, you can augment your income, and it will be clean, so you can stay in public life and be economically viable.

"That was my decision, and I have been on the lecture circuit ever since. My salary as Governor never rose above $10,-000. When I came down here to the Senate, my salary was $22,000. Then it rose to $30,000, and I say to you gentlemen that if it had not been for the lecture circuit, ED MUSKIE would not be here today. I would have quit long ago, because I would have had no choice; none whatsoever. ...

" Now I come down to the year 1977. The committee report says I used my time as a Senator to become wealthy, to enrich myself, because I have gone on the lecture circuit. ...

"Mind you, nobody on the committee or committee staff has gone over my record to determine whether or not I neglected my duties. ...

"What is the second judgment they made? That because I was on the lecture circuit, obviously I enriched myself and became wealthy.

"What is the third judgment they made? That because I was on the lecture circuit, obviously I must have been involved in conflicts of interest.

"They say these three consequences are endemic to the lecture circuit and if I took that route, if I relied on that source of income, I am guilty of neglecting my public duty, of exposing myself to conflicts of interest, and of enriching myself because of my office.

"That is the judgment that this committee report makes with respect to my 22 years as Governor and as U.S. Senator. If it says, as it does, that all such activity in the future would have those unavoidable implications, then, obviously, all those implications are unavoidably to be drawn from those who practiced this in the past. How else do you judge it? How else?

" There has been an attempt to confuse this. There was an editorial in the New York Times on March 17. ...

Let me quote:

Just imagine the appearances if the ceil-

ing is scrapped. A Senator now earns $57,-
500 a year. Under the proposed ceiling he
could also earn up to 15 percent of that in
outside activities, another $8,625. If the
Senate eliminates that ceiling, as Senator
Muskie proposes, it will, in effect, be pro-
claiming to the public that the new raise is
not enough, not even $66,125 is enough. 'We
want more.'....

"The gentleman who wrote the editorial
did not even focus on the issue. What I
have said is that if $66,125 is enough for
some Senators, it ought to be enough for
all Senators. I personally do not think
income limitations are the answer to this
problem. But if it is the committee's
judgment, and if it is the Senate's judgment, that income limitations are the
answer, then let us apply them across
the board.

" I have read everything I could find
which has been said in public print by
the sponsors of this resolution to find
out why they did not do that. The reason is that it is too difficult to do.

"What does that mean, may I ask? All
it means is that no matter the source of
income, once converted to assets that
are in place—though by way of investments in securities, in real estate or in
any other way—there is something re-
pugnant to the thought of divesting people of it. There is no way of separating
the income from the asset. I suppose that
is what they mean.

"But it is easy to divest someone on the
lecture circuit. You just prohibit him
from going on it. You divest him of his
income just as surely, but it is so invis-
ible, it is so clean. You have not forced
anybody to sell assets or to give them
away. It is so surgical.

"It reminds me of the novel 'Call of
the wild,' ... Remember when the dog
teams went through wolf country and
one dog faltered? Rather than jeopardize the whole team they threw the
weakened dog to the wolves, hoping that
would appease the wolves and the team
could get away, without jeopardizing any
others.

"Well, so it is with those of us on the
lecture circuit. We are being thrown to
the wolves.

"Because we are so visible. Why are we
so visible, may I ask? Because we are
the only form of income which has been
subject to any form of discipline for 10
years. We have had to report and disclose, and not in categories, I might say.
Would not it be nice to report in cate-

gories of zero to $5,000? Then people
would not know whether we had $500
for an honorarium or $5,000.

"We had to report everything, and I
had no reluctance to do so. But having
reported, then we become the visible
target, and since there were a few honoraria that carried an aura of conflict,
the public record spread it out and tarnished all the others. But the conflicts
in other forms of income that did not
have to be disclosed—that did not have
to be reported—did not become visible
so they did not become targets.

"But, having become visible, what is
the committee's solution? The committee's solution is to punish us all, whether
or not we ever accept an honorarium
that involved a conflict of interest.

"The ridiculous thing about this resolution is this: If I were to go to a college campus on the invitation of a student lecture group and were offered an
honorarium of $1,500 to discuss the is-
sues of the day, that is forbidden. But
if I had used ... $5,000 from the sale
of my house, with the advice of all that
expert opinion that is available around
this town, to invest in speculative real
estate, oil ventures, stocks of any kind
of companies regulated by Congress or
by executive agencies—if I got $50,000
a year from those kinds of investments—
that is all right. But that $1,500 lecture
to a college student group on the subject of any public issue you want to
name, that is forbidden.

" That may seem like justice to my colleagues. It does not to me and it never
will. There has to be some kind of judgment on the part of the committee that
lecture fees are so prone to conflicts, so
much more prone to conflicts than any
other form of outside income, that they
need to be prohibited...

"Then it is argued that this takes time
from the full-time job of a Senator, the
lecture circuit. The committee did not
even attempt to define what a full-time
Senator is. There are 168 hours in every
week. Do we owe that whole 168 hours to
the Senate? Is it permissible to take one
day, 24 hours, out of that week for my
own personal purposes? Is it? If it is, is it
any of the Senate's business how I use
that one day, whether it is used for giving that college lecture I described a
moment ago or playing golf, or spending
the time with my family? ...

"Last year, I did 19 lectures. That is one
every 19 days. Do you really believe that

cut into the time I should be devoting to Senate duties? Nineteen days. "I shall tell you how I devoted time last year to my committees. In 1975, on Budget Committee meetings, I attended 44 of 48 meetings; in 1976, 28 of 33 meetings. Most of those I missed because I was attending other meetings of other committees.

"The Environmental and Pollution Subcommittee: in 1975, 54 of 58 meetings; in 1976, 16 of 24 meetings.

"The Intergovernmental Relations Subcommittee: in 1975, 18 of 19 meetings; in 1976, 10 of 11 meetings.

"My voting attendance record for the 4 years: 90.4 percent as compared to a Senate average of 86 percent. During those 2 years, I was campaigning for reelection and spent 1 out of 3 days in my State doing that and attending to the public business there.

"Have I been neglecting my duties? I am not going to try to judge anyone else's use of his time. I made 19 lectures; I did my duty. In addition to this, I monitored this floor for 2 solid years in connection with my duties as chairman of the Senate Committee on the Budget, and I think most of you are aware, in a general way at least, of the time I devoted to that responsibility. Now I am told that, because I was on the lecture circuit, I neglected my duties as a Senator. . . ."

Sen. Gaylord Nelson (D, Wis.) replied that the code was not a "code of ethics" but a "code of conduct for members, officers and employes of the Senate." He indicated that Muskie's ethics were not under attack. "Nevertheless," he said, "the public does perceive there is potential for conflict [of interests]," and "we have addressed ourselves to it in the best way we know how."

Sen. Strom Thurmond (R, S.C.), discussing the same point March 21, recalled that his father had told him when he started out in public life, "You have got to appear right as well as be right." Thurmond continued:

"I think if you give the appearance that you are spending a lot of time away from Washington, even though you may not be busy on your particular duties at that time, if you are spending a large amount of time earning excessive speaking fees, which a great many Senators, or some, are earning, it gives the appearance that you are using your office for your personal gain.

"I think Senator BYRD expressed that pretty well a few days ago when he made this statement . . . :

I don't think any group of citizens would pay me $2,000 to play my fiddle for 15 minutes if I were a meatcutter, or working in a shipyard, or practicing law.

"In other words, probably most of the invitations that are received here by Members of the Senate—and we have to admit this—are received because we are United States Senators."

Sen. Dick Clark (D, Ia.), commenting on the limit being placed on honoraria for lecturing, noted March 22 that "many groups who have very direct interests in legislation are paying very large sums of money" as honoraria for speeches by senators. Clark said:

"It is true that more money for honoraria comes from colleges and universities than from many other single source. But who else is prominent in the honoraria business? Here are some of the figures for honoraria sources, according to Congressional Quarterly:

"For 1972, banks, bankers' groups, savings and loan associations, and similar organizations paid $49,650 to 18 Senators.

For 1973—$49,850 to 27 Senators;

For 1974—$70,388 to 28 Senators;

For 1975—$16,300 to 16 Senators.

For 1972, labor groups paid $21,390 to 17 Senators;

For 1973—$23,850 to 13 Senators;

For 1974—$32,046 to 23 Senators;

For 1975—$22,380 to 19 Senators.

For 1972, homebuilders, construction materials organizations and contractors paid $15,550 to 12 Senators;

For 1973—$21,850 to 12 Senators;

For 1974—$36,900 to 23 Senators;

For 1975—$10,000 to 8 Senators.

For 1973, medical, dental, and pharamaceutical associations paid $48,750 to 28 Senators;

For 1974—$38,610 to 22 Senators;

For 1975—$30,612 to 26 Senators.

"One could go on and on with a list of special interest groups, what they paid, year after year, to Member after Member of the Senate.

"I am sure that when the figures for 1976 become available we will be able to add to that list. And, as we move to limit the amounts that special interest groups can contribute to our political campaigns, I have no doubt that we will be able to add to that list even more; because the more we shut out the special interests in campaigns the more they will be looking for other ways to gain influence, unless we adopt the limitation propose in this code. It seems to me that will inevitably happen. . . .

"Mr. President, there is a potential for conflict in unearned income, as I mentioned earlier. But, in my judgment, the potential is truly of a greater magnitude where earned income is involved. Much investment income is derived from assets accumulated by a Member before he comes to the Senate. Earned income, obviously, is derived only when a Member is already in the Senate. A member will receive his stock dividends no matter how he votes on legislation affecting the stock of a particular corporation. He will receive those dividends whether or not he is in the Senate. That is not necessarily the case with honoraria. There is a big difference. . . . ''

Sen. Robert Dole (R, Kan.) March 22 suggested that there were complex reasons for the ethics debate. He said:
"We have talked about perceptions, we have talked about time, we have talked about everything but the test of leadership. This one issue has become a test of leadership.

"How many arms have been twisted to vote against the Muskie amendment? This is a debate between the generals and the privates. This is also a contest between the House of Representatives leadership and the leadership in the Senate to see who can push through the so-called toughest ethics code.

"Somehow, there is a feeling that you can impress the American people if we take a bird bath in the Senate, and we probably will take a bird bath in the Senate.

"We can talk about being full-time Senators, and we can talk about our own personal situation; but before we address these points, it should be emphasized that the standards which these rules are meant to enforce are accepted by all of us.

"I do not know of anyone in this body who wants to lower ethical standards, whether he be in a leadership position or not. . . .

"No Senator seeks anything less than the very highest standards of ethical conduct from Members of this body, and I would suppose that the public interest must be our sole guide. Whatever rules we adopt will guide our conduct. . . .

"Why should this be a contest of Senate leadership? Why should the leaders be arrayed on one side against some of us in this body unless there is some good reason? Why is it necessary that we have an ethics code with 23 major items that the House ethics code does not contain? Is there a contest between the House leadership and the Senate leadership? Why are we concerned about public impressions? Are we concerned about a tradeoff for the pay raise? What is the concern of the leadership? . . .

"It just seems to me we talk about confidence and we talk about polls, and we talk about the impression we are making on the American public, and that is what this is all about. It is perception—how will the leadership in the Senate be perceived if we do not have the same limitation that the Speaker achieved in the House? Will that mean our leadership is weak in the eyes of the public? That is what this is all about.

"The Senator from Wisconsin told us on Friday that the necessity for the outside income limitation was, in fact, related to how the public perceives its Congress. But are we to legislate based on what the opinion polls tell us may be a public misperception of our outside income? Are we to abdicate our responsibility based on what the polls say? Are we to prescribe regulatory medicine without any more definite diagnosis than that?

"Votes in this body are not sold. Voting commitments are not made in exchange for honorarium. Nor am I aware of any evidence of violations of the public trust associated with the earning of outside income. . . . "

In his attack on the code March 23, Weicker said:
' Ethics need not be achieved at the expense of constitutional principle. Yet, this legislation does just that.

"The proponents of this legislation know full well that if it were presented as law, it would fall constitutionally.

"I might add, I think it can fall constitutionally also, even though presented as a rule.

"There is no question in my mind that what the legislation does is to superimpose additional requirements upon those who serve as Senators and Representatives, or who are candidates for the Senate and for the House.

"I think this point was very well covered in the Adam Clayton Powell case which, in effect, prohibited our rule-making authority as among ourselves from being used to place additional requirements above and beyond those set forth in the Constitution of the United States.

"So make no mistake about it, whether we win or lose in the debate on this, I predict now that should this be taken into the courts and tested, it will clearly fall on constitutional grounds....

"For years I have been accused by the law enforcement intelligence community of weakening their pursuit of evil by insisting such pursuit take place within the bounds of the Nation's laws and ideals.

"After today, I know there are those who will say that I am against senatorial ethics and weakening the cause of them because of my insistence that whatever is propounded in the way of standards be associated with those same laws and ideals.

"The problem is not rooted in philosophy.

"It is simply that the word and spirit of the Constitution of the United States does not lend itself to expediency. The word and spirit of the Constitution of the United States does not lend itself to shortcuts. The word and spirit of the Constitution of the United States does not lend itself to intellectual lynchings.

"Unfortunately, some or all of those traits have been evident in recently enacted or proposed 'wildcat' Watergate reform legislation. More on that later.

"First of all, let me comment upon the ploy of linking pay raises to ethics because, very frankly, it has been suggested that is the only way to direct it.

"Where the dickens was the Democratic leadership of the Congress, and Common Cause when people were being paid $42,500 and when people were being paid $30,000.

"Why is the 1977 model Senator, costing $57,000, supposed to be more ethical than the 1877 model, costing $5,000?

"As far as I am concerned, when you get paid 1 cent, or if it is a nonpaid political trust, when you have one ounce of trust put in you, when you serve in that capacity as representative for your fellow citizens, you do it right or you get out. It is not a matter of $57,500 as being the magic level.

"Second, the recent pay raise was not—repeat, not—recommended by Congress but by an independent commission, which, interestingly enough, was constituted to reform the rather nasty habit of Congress giving itself its own pay raises. That is a point that everybody likes to skip over. It is a fact, and it raises the question whether any reform is going to satisfy those who chronically want to tinker with the democratic process.

"Third, the Senate did not accept the raise sub rosa but accepted it by a record vote of 56 to 42. That is a fact. It is not the theory of the pay raise.

"If anyone is suffering from a guilt complex, induced either by visions of political gain or by editorial chastisement, then may I make one simple request: Please do your flagellation act in private and leave the Constitution of the United States and the dignity of the U.S. Senate alone.

"Speaking for myself, I was not born again on February 20, 1977, in exchange for $13,000. I think I am a good Senator, worth more than a nickel of my pay, and before I would dishonor my oath of office to uphold the Constitution of the United States, I would walk away from the job.

"Now, to the business of reform. I am sure that most Senators are familiar with the saying, 'Once shame on you, twice shame on me.' Well, if I let this smelly piece of legislation go through without a fight, the shame would be on me; because more than a year ago I did just that with the Federal financing of presidential campaigns. Frankly, I have been disappointed with myself ever since.

"Remember how that was sold on the basis of being Watergate reform? That is the way it was sold. It is true that it was passed during the era of Watergate, but have any Senators read the Watergate Committee's report on that subject? Let me quote from the report, to see just how far afield this body can go in an exercise of demagoguery.

"Recommendation No. 7, found on page 572 of that report:

7. The committee recommends against the adoption of any form of public financing in which tax moneys are collected and allocated to political candidates by the Federal Government.

The Select Committee opposes the various proposals which have been offered in the Congress to provide mandatory public financing of campaigns for Federal office. While recognizing the basis of support for the concept of public financing and the potential difficulty in adequately funding campaigns in the midst of strict limitations on the form and amount of contributions, the committee takes issue with the contention that public financing affords either an effective or appropriate solution. Thomas Jefferson believed 'to compel a man to furnish contributions of money for the propagation of opinions which he disbelieves and abhors, is sinful and tyrannical.'

The committee's opposition is based like Jefferson's upon the fundamental need to protect the voluntary right of individual citizens to express themselves politically as guaranteed by the first amendment. Furthermore, we find inherent dangers in authorizing the Federal bureaucracy to fund and excessively regulate political campaigns.

The abuses experienced during the 1972 campaign and unearthed by the Select Committee were perpetrated in the absence of any effective regulation of the source, form, or amount of campaign contributions. In fact, despite the progress made by the Federal Elections Campaign Act of 1971, in requiring full public disclosure of contributions, the 1972 campaign still was funded through a system of essentially unrestricted, private financing.

What now seems appropriate is not the abandonment of private financing, but rather the reform of that system in an effort to vastly expand the voluntary participation of individual citizens while avoiding the abuses of earlier campaigns.

"Yet, that is termed Watergate reform, even though, in black and white, the committee which was charged with the responsibility of unearthing those abuses and then making whatever recommendations it deemed appropriate clearly recommended against Federal financing. "So, what followed was not Watergate reform but, rather, certain activists, certain reformers, certain Senators, and certain philosophers using an atmosphere of tragedy and apprehension to attain a legislative end that, standing alone, in more deliberative times, would not have gotten a hearing, much less a final passage vote....

"Let me be very specific. I have no problems with the dollar limits on contributions or full disclosure and reporting or eliminating multiple committees. Those truly were reforms of problems discovered by the Watergate Committee. But I saw nothing in the fact of Watergate that indicated that the people of this Nation deserve the punishment of a Federal election financing act....

"I cite the Federal financing experience as an example of reform that was not. It was the first step in nationalizing and neutralizing the individual response factor in American politics.

"The second step in that nationalization is before us today. Whereas Federal financing set the criteria of eligibility for political contributions, at the common level of being a warm body, this ethics code places the criteria of who should be a Senator in the hands of the Senate.

"People used to worry about Nixon perpetuating himself. If we keep legislating as we have in the past year, the American people will have deeded their resources, their judgment, and, yes, eventually their vote, to those whose incompetence, whose insensitivity, and whose intransigence created the need for reform in the first place.

"What makes this whole exercise on the floor so redundant is that a system to achieve appropriate senatorial ethics already is in place. It is known as the democratic process, the election process.

"The people who run that system are in place and are known as the American citizens.

"Do we have a contribution to make as Senators? Yes. The truth. All of it.

"If you put those three elements together—elections, the voters, and the facts—the job will be handled better outside this Chamber than ever could be possible for 100 men, each of whom, on this measure or its interpretation, will have at least one conflict of interest.

"What is the monumental conceit that exists in this Chamber, that exists in the editorial pages of newspapers, that exist in Common Cause, that places them above the American people or the capacity of the American people to judge? The only ones who will be accountable for actions here today are the Members of this body. It certainly will not be the other entities or individuals to whom I have referred.

"Seventy-four years ago, the British philosopher George Edward Moore wrote of the 'difficulties and disagreements' that arise over the subject of ethics. These problems, he wrote. 'are mainly due to a very simply cause: Namely, the attempt to answer questions without first discovering precisely what question it is which you desire to answer.'

"The U.S. Senate, now considering a new code of ethics, provides living proof of Moore's thesis. Members know full well that they must answer the public cry for stringent rules of conduct. But let us not be fooled. There are not stringent rules of conduct that we have before us. It is some disclosure and some illogical limitations.

"The committee plan before us is an amalgam of editorial restrictions and incomplete regulations whose only claim to the title of reform stems from its public relations value....

"Senators should be required to make public every financial detail they possess through yearly publications of individual income tax returns and an itemized statement of net worth, detailing assets, liabilities, and gifts received. Every share of stock, every holding in trust, every interest payment on every loan should be offered to the voters for consideration.

"The financial status of Senators' spouses and dependent children should also go public, with all the records being published in a single, easily accessible public document. If voters from a Midwestern State feel that the ownership of a farm by their Senator helps him to better understand their rural problems, why should I, from the urban Northeast, say no? Likewise, if another State's voters are outraged by their Senator's earning one nickel from a law firm, why should I say 15 percent is all right?

"The wealthy already dominate the Senate's membership. Inequitable regulations based on mythical standards of financial right and wrong can only serve to increase that fact.

"A no-exceptions policy of financial disclosure will insure accountable ethics rather than a muddle of self-regulation. Replacing the people's freedom to elect, and the Senators to associate, with a how-to book on honesty simply will not work.

"Lay it on the table and let the people decide. Their decisions on who should serve, rather than those of Common Cause, the U.S. Senate, or the news media are still good enough for me...."

Sen. James A. McClure (R, Ida.), speaking the day before the Senate code was passed, assailed the code as a "fraud." He said March 31:

"During the entire debate about the question of outside income—and sometimes it got muddied in the discussions between earned and unearned income—it seems to me that the entire basis for trying to limit outside income from whatever sources boiled down to about three particular areas.

"One was the conflict or possible conflicts because of the source of the income, whether it be honorarium, or income from property, or income from stocks, or income that might be affected by the actions of the Congress of the United States.

"The second question was in regard to conflicts because of the time it might take from a Senator's busy schedule to earn the money or to manage the portfolio of stock or manage the real estate that might be involved.

"The third reason given by proponents of this bill was because of political activities, because they indicate that sometimes the time it took to earn honorariums also involved political activities.

"Indeed, they are right in every instance. Whether it is earned or unearned income, there can be conflicts because of the source of that income. There can be conflicts because of the time that it takes. There can be conflicts because of the political activity that is involved.

"Yet, this bill, which is bound to pass tomorrow, does not really address any one of those problems.

"If the Congress were to subject itself to the same test that we have required in the truth in packaging and truth in labeling, this Congress would be guilty of a criminal violation of the law because this bill is a fraud.

"We say that we are acting in behalf of the American people by raising the ethical standards of this Congress, and I say that this resolution does not really do that and only does a little of it. It allows more to be concealed than is required to be revealed. We do that in the name of ethics. We do it because we are told the public demands it. Well, if we are really concerned about the conflict of time, then I should have offered an amendment which I had prepared but which I will not offer because the pattern has been very abundantly demonstrated that there will be no serious consideration of many of the amendments that have been offered. The amendment I had prepared, which I will not offer, simply says that it shall be against the rules of the Senate for any sitting Member of the Senate to be a candidate for the office of President or Vice President of the United States.

"If we are concerned about a conflict of time and the demand upon the time of a Senator, I ask the Members of the

Senate, or anyone else who cares, to look at the time that has been taken away from this body by Members of this body who, within the last 2 years, have been candidate for the office of President or Vice President of the United States. "The record is adequate, I am certain, that far more time has been devoted by Members of the Senate to seeking other political office—Vice President or President of the United States—than has been taken away from this body by those who earned large honorariums. Yet, nothing is said about that conflict of interest. "It is said that we must adopt a code of ethics that confines the areas of political activity because we are servants of the public and not political officers, not seeking political office. Yet, what greater conflict is there than the abuse of this office and the time that we take to seek other office? How many Members of the Senate, within the last 2 years, sought other office at the time they were supposed to be discharging duties in this office? "If we are really concerned about the conflict of time, if we are really concerned about the conflict of political activity, then this body would be interested in purging itself of that apparent conflict by adopting an amendment which would prohibit any Member from running for the office of President of the United States or Vice President of the United States. ... "The resolution before us does not meet the demands of the public so far as the elimination of the appearance or the reality of conflicts of interest are concerned. It does not require disclosure in kind and form that would allow the public to judge whether or not there is a conflict of interest. It very carefully avoids doing that. Yet, we tell the public that we have done something about disclosure when precisely the opposite is the case. ... "If any political activity ever were conducted by a Member of the U.S. Senate that is higher than the political activity in which we are engaged right now, I would like to know what it is; because all this debate on ethics is being done in the name of giving politics a better name. It is done in the name of giving us a better image to the American people. It is done to enhance the reputations of individual Members of the Senate. That is a political activity. Yet, we are told that we must have an ethics measure that carefully separates political

and nonpolitical activities. But I think that is obviously impossible. ... "

Senate rules take effect—Sen. Stevenson announced April 1, after the new Senate Code of Official Conduct was adopted, that a number of the code's rules would take effect that midnight. His announcement said:

IMMEDIATELY EFFECTIVE PORTIONS OF THE SENATE CODE OF OFFICIAL CONDUCT

A. RULE 43—GIFTS

New rule 43 takes effect at midnight tonight. It states prohibitions against a Member, officer, or employee, or a spouse or dependent, accepting gifts with aggregate value exceeding $100 during the calendar year from a person, organization, or corporation having direct interest in legislation before the Congress; or from a foreign national, with certain exceptions relating to gifts which are private and personal and gifts of educational travel to a foreign country.

B. RULE 45—CONFLICT OF INTEREST

Paragraphs 1 through 5 of rule 45 take effect at midnight tonight.

Paragraph 1 prohibits the taking of a bribe.

Paragraph 2 prohibits outside employment which is inconsistent or in conflict with the conscientious performance of official duties.

Paragraph 3 continues the requirement, previously stated in old Senate rule 41, that officers and employees must report to supervisors in writing any outside employment for compensation immediately upon taking such employment and on May 15 of each year. This paragraph further imposes on the supervising Senator the full responsibility to see that such activities by his employee do not represent a conflict of interest or interference with the employee's duties to the Senate.

Paragraph 4 prohibits Members, officers, or employees from knowingly using their official position to advance legislation which furthers their pecuniary interests.

Paragraph 5 permits a Senator to decline to vote, in committee or on the floor, when he believes his voting would be a conflict of interest.

C. RULE 46—PROHIBITION OF UNOFFICIAL OFFICE ACCOUNTS

Under provisions of Rule 46 which are effective at midnight tonight, no contribution henceforth may be received into an "unofficial office account," but otherwise approved expenditures from present funds in existing unofficial office accounts may continue until December 31, 1977.

Further, this rule provides that expenses incurrd by a Member in connection with his official duties shall be defrayed only from personal funds of the Member; official funds specifically appropriated for that purpose; funds derived from a political committee—as defined in section 301(d) of the Federal Election Campaign Act of 1971 (2 U.S.C. 431)); and funds received as reasonable reimbursements for expenses incurred by a Member in connection with personal services provided by the Member to the organization making the reimbursement.

Further, the rule states that, effective midnight tonight, no contribution shall be converted to the personal use of any Member or any former Member.

"Old" rule 42, paragraph 1, may still remain in effect with respect to the source of contributions which legally may be expended from an unofficial office account during the remainder of this year. This "old" rule 42 may also qualify the Federal Election Commission's regulations or IRS regulations regarding purposes for which such funds may be spent during the remainder of this year.

D. RULE 47—FOREIGN TRAVEL

Under rule 47, effective immediately, no Member of the Senate whose term will expire at the end of the Congress may use Government funds for foreign travel after the date of the general election in which his successor is elected, or in the case of a Senator who is not a candidate in the general election, the earlier of the date of such general election or the adjournment sine die of the second regular session of the Congress.

Second, rule 47 prohibits, effective immediately, the practice commonly known as "double dipping." That is, those accepting Govenrment funds for foreign travel may not receive reimbursement for any expense both from the Government and from another source.

Similarly, it prohibits such persons engaged in foreign travel from receiving reimbursement for the same expense more than once from the Government. And, further, it requires that Government funds to defray expenses for foreign travel can be used for no other purpose.

Also, rule 47 requires that a per diem allowance for foreign travel must be used for lodging, food, and related expenses and the portion not actually used must be returned.

E. RULE 49—POLITICAL FUND ACTIVITY: DEFINITIONS

Paragraph 1 of new rule 49, which limits staff political fund activity, takes effect in 30 days, but similar provisions of "old" rule 43 remain in effect: Only an employee in the personal office of a Senator, receiving an annual salary of $10,000 or more who is designated by the employing Senator in writing for the purpose, and who files a public financial disclosure statement regarding contributions, may "receive, solicit, be the custodian of, or distribute" campaign funds. When paragraph 1 of rule 49 takes effect on May 1, a restricted number of employees may be so qualified and "solicitation" will not be permitted even by the qualified staff persons.

Paragraphs 2, 3, and 4 take effect at midnight tonight. They change the definition of a Senate employee covered for the purposes of compliance with some parts of the Senate Code of Official Conduct. Under these new definitions, employees detailed for Senate service from Government agencies on a reimbursable basis, educational fellows, and other temporary assistants paid from non-Government funds, and reemployed annuitants may be required to publicly disclose contributions and honoraria received or handled, submit confidential statements of their financial interests, and report to supervisors in writing their outside business and professional activities.

F. DISCLOSURE OF FINANCIAL INTERESTS UNDER PRESENT RULE 44

The Senate's approval of Senate Resolution 110 does not relieve Senators, officers, employees, and candidates of their obligations under present rule 44 to submit to the GAO before May 15, a sealed disclosure of financial interests. Nor does Senate Resolution 110 change existing requirements for the public reporting, by May 15, of contributions received, contributions expended, and honoraria received. Forms and instructions for these reports are available in the office of the Ethics Committee. ...

Rules for Senate employees—Additional and more detailed interpretations of the rules, as they affected Senate employes, were explained by Sens. Stevenson and Schmitt later in a letter to some 6,600 Senate employes. The letter said:

SELECT COMMITTEE ON ETHICS,
Washington, D.C., April 26, 1977.

DEAR SENATE EMPLOYEE: On April 1, the Senate agreed to Senate Resolution 110 which provides nine new "ethics" Rules for the official conduct of Senate members and employees. It also strengthens the enforcement responsibilities of the Select Committee on Ethics.

In January of this year, the Senate also passed S. Res. 4 which created an entirely new Ethics Committee to enforce both the new Code of Official Conduct subsequently approved in S. Res. 110 and the portions of the previous ethics Rules which continue in effect.

Some of the provisions of the new Code of Official Conduct take effect immediately. Others take effect later this year, next year, and in January, 1979. Some present ethics Rules remains in effect until they are replaced by the new Rules. Some aspects of ethical conduct subject to the review of the Ethics Committee, which are in law or part of Senate Rules and Standing Orders and not stated as part of the Code of Official Conduct, were unaffected by S. Res. 110. These include the unauthorized disclosure of intelligence information in the possession of the Select Committee on Intelligence as provided for in S. Res. 400, 94th Congress, and franked mail as provided for in Public Law 93-191. Most of the new Ethics Rules apply to all Members and officers of the Senate. Some apply to their spouses and dependents, and to candidates for election to the Senate as well.

EMPLOYEES COVERED

If you are a senior Senate employee, paid for more than 90 days at an annual rate exceeding $35,000, you must comply with all the ethics Rules applicable to staff. If your compensation is at a rate exceeding $25,000, you are covered by all the rules applicable to staff except Rule 44 which regulates outside earned income. If your compensation is at a rate of $25,000 or less, you must comply with all the new Rules applicable to staff except Rule 44, Rule 42 which requires public financial disclosure, and paragraphs 6, 7 and 8 of Rule 45 which forbid certain business and professional activities and may require (of committee staff only) divestiture of financial holdings. Some of the rules may also apply to your spouse and other relatives. For example, if you meet the income test for public financial disclosure ($25,000 under Rule 42), you must report interests of your spouse (unless you are living separate and apart) and dependents if such interests are within your constructive control. Spouses also are covered under the gifts section (Rule 43).

You are subject to the Code of Official Conduct and other ethics Rules even if your sal-

ary is not paid by the Senate and you are, for example, an employee of an agency detailed to work in a Senate office, or serving in a Senate office under an educational program. Moreover, retired federal annuitants working on Senate staffs now must add the amount of their annuity to their salary to determine if they are covered by Rules affecting employees with salaries above $25,000 and $35,000.

Staffs of joint committees and other Congressional offices are covered by Senate or House ethics Rules, although staff of independent offices may not be subject to either set of ethics Rules. Those joint staffs paid by the Senate and hence subject to the Senate Code include: the staffs of the Joint Committees on: Atomic Energy, Economics and Printing; the American Indian Policy Review Commission; and the Capitol Guide Service. Staffs subject to House Rules include those of the Joint Committees on Taxation, Defense Production and Congressional Operations, and of the Congressional Budget Office. Staffs apparently not covered under Senate or House ethics Rules include those of the Architect of the Capitol, the Office of the Attending Physician, and the Office of Technology Assessment.

These groups may adopt Senate or House ethics rules, or be brought under similar coverage by legislation now before the Governmental Affairs Committee.

EMPLOYEES STILL COVERED BY SOME "OLD"
CONDUCT RULES

The new Code of Official Conduct also continues the present requirement under "old" Rules, if your rate of salary exceeded $15,000 and you were employed by the Senate for 90 days or more in 1976, that you make public disclosure before May 15 of the contributions you received and expended and the honoraria you received during 1976 and file, also before May 15, in a sealed envelope (to be opened only in the case of an investigation), your income tax returns and other information about gifts and financial interests. Forms and instructions for these reports may be ordered from the Select Committee on Ethics.

NEW RULES FOR ALL EMPLOYEES IN EFFECT ON
APRIL 2, 1977

The new Rules now in effect prohibit you from:

Accepting a gift from anyone with an interest in legislation before the Congress or from a foreign national, with certain exceptions subject to the approval of the Ethics Committee (as described in Rule 43).

Taking a bribe or using your official position to advance legislation which furthers your own pecuniary interest;

Engaging in outside paid employment which is in conflict with official duties;

Engaging in outside employment unless you report your outside employment to the Senator you work for immediately upon taking such employment and on May 15 of each year (you may secure forms for this report from the Select Committee on Ethics);

Receiving contributions in so-called unofficial office accounts (after the end of this year, the Rules forbid the use of such accounts altogether, although an account may be maintained by a political committee if it is disclosed under F.E.C. regulations and its funds are spent for approved purposes);

Securing reimbursement from two sources for the same foreign travel expense;

Assisting a Senator or former Senator in converting campaign funds to their personal use;

Assisting a lame duck Senator to travel at government expense after certain "cut-off" dates;

Performing services for any Member, committee, or office of the Senate for a period in excess of four weeks (and for more than eight hours a week)—if you receive compensation therefor from any source other than the U.S. Government—unless your supervisor reports to the Ethics Committee how your services are used: (a) when you begin; (b) at the end of each quarter; and (c) when you stop;

Using travel funds for other than actual travel expenses (and require unused balances to be returned to the government).

NEW RULES FOR ALL EMPLOYEES WHICH TAKE EFFECT AFTER APRIL 2

Other major provisions of the Code of Official Conduct will have these effects on and after the dates shown:

On May 1, 1977, you may not:

Solicit campaign funds;

Receive, be custodian of, or distribute any campaign funds unless you are one of no more than two employees (in the personal office) of a Senator, who receives an annual salary of $10,000 or more and who files a comprehensive financial disclosure statement each year, whom the Senator formally has designated with the Secretary of the Senate to do so.

On October 1, 1977 (with the first filing on May 15, 1978, or on any date immediately after October 1 if you leave Senate employment) you must, if your compensation is $25,000 or more:

Publicly disclose the details of your earned income, honoraria, gifts, real and personal property, personal liabilities, transactions in securities or commodities futures and purchase or sale of real property;

File your income tax returns with the General Accounting Office in a sealed envelope to be opened only in the case of an investigation.

On January 1, 1978, you may not assist a Senator to:

Use the frank for mass mailing 60 days before the date of a primary or general election in which the Senator is a candidate (and Senators must register mass mailings, newsletters, for example, periodically with

the Secretary of the Senate so that the public may inspect them);

Use campaign or personal funds to buy paper for mass mailings;

Use the Senate computer facilities to store, maintain, or otherwise process lists of names and addresses identifying individuals as campaign workers or contributors, as members of a political party or by any other partisan political designation; nor to produce mailing labels or computer tapes except for use in Senate facilities;

Use the radio and TV facilities in the Capitol for 60 days preceding a primary or general election in which he is a candidate.

On April 1, 1978, you:

May not, if your Senate salary exceeds $25,000, provide professional services for compensation, such as engaging in the practice of law, in affiliation with a firm, partnership, association or corporation; permit the use of your name by a law firm or other business; practice a profession for compensation during regular working hours; or serve as an officer or director of a publicly-held business, with minor exceptions (as stated in Rule 45, paragraph 7);

May be required, if a committee employee with a salary exceeding $25,000, to divest yourself of financial holdings which may be affected by the actions of the committee for which you work, unless the Ethics Committee and your supervisor approve otherwise (as stated in Rule 45, paragraph 8);

May not, for a period of one year after leaving your position, lobby certain members and employees of the Senate (as stated in Rule 45, paragraph 10).

On May 15, 1978:

Your public financial disclosure statements are subject to audit.

On January 1, 1979, if your Senate salary exceeds $35,000:

Your outside earned income may not exceed 15 percent of your Senate salary, with exceptions for income from advances and royalties on books and from the sale of creative or artistic works, and for income from buyout arrangements, family enterprises, and distributive shares of partnership income if certain tests are met (as stated in Rule 45, paragraph 3).

After January 3, 1979:

You may not, as a supervisor, engage in (and as an employee you may seek Ethics Committee investigation and other action regarding) discrimination in Senate employment on the grounds of race, religion, sex, national origin, age or state of physical handicap. ...

Interpretive rulings—Sen. Stevenson Oct. 7, 1977 inserted in the Congressional Record various interpretive rulings of the Senate Ethics committee on the new ethics code. Among the rulings:

RULE 44: OUTSIDE EARNED INCOME

Interpretative ruling No. 7: Date issued: June 7, 1977

Question considered: May a Senator accept honoraria in excess of $25,000 in a calendar year, so long as the excess is donated to charity?

Ruling: Acceptance of honoraria in excess of $25,000 in any calendar year is prohibited by Sec. 441(i) of the Federal Election Campaign Act. That section, entitled "Acceptance of Excessive Honorariums" provides that:

No person while an elected or appointed officer or employee of any branch of the Federal Government shall accept—

(1) any honorarium of more than $2,000 (excluding amounts accepted for actual travel and subsistence expenses for such person and his spouse or an aide to such person, and excluding amounts paid or incurred for any agents' fees or commissions) for any appearance, speech, or article; or (2) honoraria (not prohibited by paragraph (1) of this section) aggregating more than $25,000 in any calendar year.

Regulation 110.12(b)(5), issued pursuant to the Federal Election Campaign Act, provides:

(5) Accepted.—"Accepted" means that there has been actual or constructive receipt of the honorarium and the Federal officeholder or employee exercises dominion or control over it. A Federal officeholder or employee is considered to have accepted an honorarium (i) if he or she actually receives it and determines its subsequent use, or (ii) he or she directs that the organization offering the honorarium give the honorarium to a charity or other beneficiary which he or she names, (iii) an honorarium is not accepted if he or she makes a suggestion that the honorarium be given to a charity or other like beneficiary of the organization's own choosing. Nothing in this paragraph shall be construed as an interpretation of relevant provisions of the Internal Revenue Code.

With respect to (i) and (ii) above, these honoraria are includable in gross income for federal (and most state) income tax purposes if the taxable year payment is received, and are also deductible from gross income under section 170 of the Internal Revenue Code in the taxable year during which the charitable contribution is paid, provided the donee organization is one described in section 501(c)(3) of the Internal Revenue Code as being exempt under section 501(a). If the above procedure is followed there is no tax benefit; it is a wash transaction. If the receipt and the gift did not both fall within the same taxable year tax planning with respect to the timing of income and deductions could result in tax benefits, perfectly proper when so arranged by private citizens.

RULE 45: CONFLICT OF INTEREST

Interpretative ruling No. 20: Date issued: May 26, 1977

Question Considered: May the staff director of a Senate Committee accept appointment to the advisory board of a college interested in establishing a center which may be eligible for partial federal funding, pursuant to legislation now under consideration by the Committee of which he is staff director?

Ruling: The appointment in question creates the appearance of conflict with the subject's responsibilities as staff director of the committee despite the fact that Rule 45 appears to permit Members, officers and employees to serve in such appointments if they do not receive compensation therefor.

The Committee therefore recommends that the appointment not be accepted.

Interpretative ruling No. 39. Date issued: June 27, 1977

Question Considered: What provisions of the Code of Official Conduct must a full-time S. Res. 60 aide to a Senator with a salary between $15,000 and $25,000 consider in determining whether or not outside employment is proper?

Ruling: An employee compensated at an annual rate of $25,000 or less is not subject to the financial disclosure requirements of new Rule 42. But an employee compensated at an annual rate of $15,000 or more must file on May 15, 1978 or upon leaving the Senate a sealed financial statement with the Comptroller General and a statement of contributions and honoraria with the Secretary of the Senate under old Rules 42 and 44.

The propriety of outside employment is governed by Rule 45. No employee, regardless of salary level, may receive compensation by virtue of influence improperly exerted. Nor may any employee engage in any outside business or professional activity or employment for compensation which is inconsistent or in conflict with the conscientious performance of official duties. Any outside employment for compensation must be reported in writing to the supervising Senator when the employment commences and thereafter on May 15 of each year. That report must describe the nature of the employment. The supervising Senator must then take whatever action is appropriate for the avoidance of conflict of interest or interference with duties to the Senate. That action could, of course, be a denial of permission to undertake or continue the outside employment. After April 1, 1978, employees compensated at more than $25,000 per year will also be subject to restrictions on providing professional services for compensation and on serving as officers or on boards of publicly held or regulated corporations, financial institutions or business entities.

Interpretative ruling No. 43: Date issued: August 5, 1977

Question Considered: Whether a subcommittee may employ as consultant to it, and later its chief counsel, an attorney who plans later in the year temporarily to leave the Senate payroll to return to association with his former law firm, and to argue a case pending before an appellate court on a subject which is a direct and principal concern of the subcommittee, and then severe his ties with the firm following the appeal proceedings.

Ruling: The employee's continuing association with the firm for purposes of preparing the appeal while also acting as consultant to the subcommittee (even though he would terminate that association when he becomes chief counsel), and his continuing obligations to the firm's client in connection with the appeal, create both the appearance of a conflict of interest and too great a potential for an actual conflict.

Accordingly, the subcommittee should not employ the person in question in either capacity until his association with the law firm is terminated and his obligations to the firm's client have been discharged.

RULE 46: PROHIBITION OF UNOFFICIAL OFFICE ACCOUNTS

Interpretative ruling No. 11: Date issued:
May 16, 1977

Question Considered: May a Member continue to use contributions from private sources to defray official expenses?

Ruling: Rule 46 prohibits the receipt of contributions to an unofficial office account for the purpose, at least in part, of defraying otherwise unreimbursed expenses allowable in connection with the operation of a Member's office. Expenditures from unofficial office accounts must terminate by the end of 1977.

Accounts may be maintained for personal funds and for funds received as reasonable reimbursements for expenses incurred by a Member in connection with personal services provided by a Member to the reimbursing organization, and those funds may be used to defray otherwise unreimbursed expenses of official duties. Funds derived from a political committee may also be used for those purposes. Those funds should not be commingled with other funds, and the political committee should pay directly those official expenses it chooses to defray.

The Committee expresses no opinion as to the tax consequences of using political committee funds to defray official expenses.

RULE 49: POLITICAL FUND ACTIVITY

Interpretative ruling No. 3: Date issued:
May 5, 1977

Question Considered: May Senate staff attend and participate as hostesses, while on leave, in a fundraising event to be held in behalf of a Senator in his state?

Ruling: No provision of the Code of Official Conduct prohibits staff from attending a campaign fundraising event outside office hours or while on recorded vacation leave. Under Rule 49, paragraph (1), however, a Senate staff member may not receive, solicit, be the custodian of or distribute campaign funds unless he or she is one of the two assistants specifically designated for those pur-

poses. In order to stay well within the spirit and letter of the Rule, staff who are not so designated and who attend such an event should not collect funds or sell tickets or otherwise participate in the fundraising aspects of the event.

Since 18 USC 602 prohibits staff from making a monetary campaign contribution to a Member of Congress, the participating staff should not attend as paying guests.

The Committee on Rules and Administration and this Committee will provide guidelines in due course with respect to campaign participation by staff after hours or while on annual leave. The interim position of this Committee is that Senators should encourage staff to remove themselves from the payroll for periods during which they expect to be heavily involved in campaign activities. Routine participation after hours or on an annual leave time is not now prohibited by the Code of Conduct.

Interpretative ruling No. 5: Date issued:
May 11, 1977

Question Considered: To what extent may Senate employees volunteer time after office hours or while on annual leave to assist in political fund raising events for Members and candidates for election to the Senate?

Ruling: Sections 307 and 308 of S. Res. 110 direct the Committee on Rules and Administration to consider matters closely related to this question and report to the Senate by October, 1977. In the interim Members should remove staff from the Senate payroll to participate for any extended period in such activities. The Code of Official Conduct, however, was not intended to prohibit routine matters performed outside of working hours such as preparing for mailing (e.g. typing, addressing, and stuffing envelopes) invitations and letters signed by others; making follow-up telephone calls on behalf of the sponsoring organization to determine projected attendance at the event; helping the sponsoring organization make arrangements for flowers, food, and entertainment; and serving on a committee of hosts or hostesses at the time of the event, not as a sponsor, but simply to mingle with the guests on behalf of the sponsoring group.

Unless the employee is one of the two assistants specifically so designated, he or she may not receive, solicit, be the custodian of, or distribute any campaign funds. Accordingly, care must be taken to avoid involvement in those functions.

Interpretative ruling No. 8: Date issued:
May 11, 1977

Question Considered: Under the Code of Official Conduct, to what extent may staff engage in campaign activities?

Ruling: Sections 307 and 309 of S. Res. 110 direct the Committee on Rules and Administration to consider and report back within 180 days on this question.

In the interim, Members must use their

best judgment in taking staff off the Senate payroll to devote substantial portions of their time or to participate for any extended period in such activities. The Committee on Ethics recognizes staff frequently will be reinstated after campaign activities.

Interpretative ruling No. 19: Date issued: May 26, 1977

Question Considered: May Senate staff persons solicit, receive or distribute funds for a campaign organization, and during off hours, participate in party activities which may include fund-raising efforts.

Ruling: Rule 49 provides that two staff persons may be designated by a Senator to be the custodians of or to distribute funds in connection with a campaign, but no officer or employee of the Senate may solicit funds, (or solicit others to solicit funds in behalf of a Senator) while on the Senate payroll. Staff may be removed temporarily from the Senate payroll to engage in such campaign type activities.

It is not intended that Senate employees be barred completely from all participation in political activity. Outside of Senate office hours staff may assist in planning and making arrangements for fund raisers so long as they do not become involved with solicitation of funds.

The difficulties in drawing the line between these two types of activity led to the mandate in Title II section 206 of S. Res. 110 which directs the Committee on Rules and Administration to study and report within 180 days on the misuse of staff by incumbents in reelection campaigns.

Note: On June 13, 1977, the Senate agreed to S. Res. 136 which amended Rule 49 to remove the prohibition on solicitation applying to employees designated for political fund activity.

Interpretative ruling No. 21: Date issued May 26, 1977

Question Considered: May a Senator store political documents, such as records and financial statements of past campaigns, in his Washington office and in federal space provided in his state?

Ruling: The Committee is not aware of any Senate rule or law on these points. Counsel for GSA advises that he knows of no law or regulation with respect to what may be stored in space under its jurisdiction.

Storage of substantial quantities of such personal and political materials, i.e., bulk storage of materials unrelated to one's official duties, would be an improper use of public property. Members are, however, entitled to some latitude with respect to documents needed for reference purposes or public disclosure. Campaign materials used by Members for gifts and all such materials that are incidental to the normal business of a Senate office and require no substantial storage space may be maintained in a Senator's offices.

Interpretative ruling No. 30: Date issued: June 28, 1977

Question Considered: May a newspaper reporter have access to the files, records and opinions of the former Select Committee on Standards and Conduct now in the custody of the Select Committee on Ethics?

Ruling: This Committee will fully respect the public's right to know. It is required to, and will, make available to complainants, as well as to persons charged, its findings in investigations involving violations of the franking privilege and the Code of Official Conduct. If it decides not to investigate complaints, the complainant will be advised with an explanation. Furthermore, the Committee has kept nearly all its proceedings open to the public and will continue to do so to the extent individual rights and national security permit. It will make public all of its interpretations of the Code.

The files of this Committee and its predecessor, not unlike those of a grand jury, from time to time receive unsupported complaints, highly personal information and information affecting the national security which would harm individual rights or national interests if revealed. Disclosure of such information would contravene law and time-honored standards of Anglo-Saxon justice, as well as severely handicap the Committee in its educational, investigative and judgemental duties. The Committee cannot, therefore, open all its files in response to such requests. It will make its opinions and advisory rulings public in due course.

Ketchum scores Senate ethics breach. Rep. William M. Ketchum (R, Calif.), in a statement printed in the Congressional Record April 6, 1977, only five days after the Senate had adopted its ethics code, denounced a Senate Ethics Committee action as "one of the most underhanded and unethical tactics I have ever witnessed in this Congress."

Ketchum referred to a report that the Senate Ethics Committee had just "waived a provision in its new ethics code." He said "At its initial meeting, the very first, mind you, committee members waived the rule prohibiting members from accepting gifts of over $100 in the aggregate per year so that Senators may visit Communist China as guests of the government-sponsored Chinese People's Institute of Foreign Affairs. This sleight-of-hand maneuver was accomplished in order to relieve the fear of our esteemed colleagues who would knowingly violate their rules because the Chinese insist on paying for all arrangements when an official delegation visits their country. In other words, either find a way around the rules or stay at home. . . ."

Political Funds

Prior to the adoption of the Congressional "ethics codes" in 1977, various moves had been made to reform criticized practices in regard to political funds.

Laundering of gifts barred. Common Cause had won agreement from two Congressional officials to end the practice of concealing contributions earmarked for specific candidates by laundering the money through committees, the New York Times reported May 20, 1974.

W. Patrick Jennings, clerk of the House, and Francis Valeo, secretary of the Senate, agreed to end the system, which Common Cause lawyers, termed "using a third party as a false front."

The system, which enabled donors to funnel money to candidates without being specifically associated with their campaigns by making contributions through committees, such as the Congressional and Senatorial campaign committees, was widely practiced by both parties, organized labor and other groups.

Senate rejects campaign fund curb. The Senate Oct. 8, 1975 had rejected a plan to make the "office accounts" of members of Congress subject to campaign fund regulations while they were seeking re-election.

The vote was 48–47, but opposition to the proposal was considered much more substantial than the one-vote margin formally killing the plan would indicate.

The plan had been proposed by the Federal Election Commission. Proposed regulations of the commission, which was established under the 1974 campaign

reform law, were subject to veto by a vote of either house of Congress. During the two-hour debate in the Senate, only one member, Sen. Dick Clark (D, Ia.), rose in defense of the commission's proposal, the first one from the panel to be voted on by either house.

The private office accounts maintained by members of Congress, popularly known as "slush funds," customarily could be spent for political purposes without being reported as campaign spending, which was subject to ceilings under the 1974 legislation.

These "slush funds" could be financed from outside contributions. Nominally, they were to be used for constituent services, such as Christmas cards, in the day-to-day operations of the members' offices.

The commission's proposal was to have these funds treated as political funds under the law, and thus counted as part of the campaign funds subject to the mandated ceilings, during the last two years of a senator's term and the last year of a representative's term.

The proposal was a less stringent one than the commission had approved originally. The first version, adopted by the panel July 29, construed the "slush funds" as political expenses throughout a member's term to be deducted from the amount an incumbent could spend on his or her next campaign.

The commission also adopted a companion ruling to require members of Congress to file campaign finance reports with the commission itself, which would send them in turn to the regular filing offices of each house.

The House Administration Committee rejected the companion filing-procedure regulation Sept. 11 and a Senate Rules Committee panel disapproved the "slush fund" regulation Sept. 12.

The opposition to the "slush fund" regulation in Congress, which had created the commission and funded it, was widespread. It included the Senate's majority and minority leaders, Mike Mansfield (D, Mont.), and Hugh Scott (R, Pa.).

House rejects reports proposal—The House Oct. 22 rejected by 257–148 vote a proposed regulation of the Federal

Election Commission to require members of Congress to file campaign financial reports with the agency.

The House move against the commission's second proposal was organized by Rep. Wayne L. Hays (D, Ohio), chairman of the House Administration Committee, who wanted the campaign fund reports filed first with the clerk of the House.

The House decision was by a regular majority vote after Hays had lost an earlier vote requiring a two-thirds majority because of the procedural aspect of its introduction on the floor—without clearance by the Rules Committee. That vote, on Oct. 20, was 220–169, or 40 less than the two-thirds needed to carry the resolution of disapproval.

Special interest contributions soared in '76. Special interest groups contributed a record $22.5 million to 1976 Congressional candidates, nearly double the $12.5 million donated for 1974 races, according to Common Cause Feb. 15, 1977.

The self-described citizen's lobby based its report on financial records filed with the Federal Election Commission. The study showed that labor groups had contributed $8.2 million to the 1976 congressional compaigns, up from $6.3 million in 1974. Although contributions by corporate and business-trade association political committees trailed labor's gifts, their donations rose 300% from 1974 to $7.1 million.

The American Medical Association, which had been the top contributor in 1974, led the list again in 1976 with contributions of $1.8 million, about $300,-000 more than in 1974.

Dairy groups ranked second with donations of $1.4 million. That represented more than a six-fold increase over 1972 contributions of $225,000. Contributions had been sharply reduced in the 1974 campaign because dairy groups, particularly Associated Milk Producers Inc., a major dairy cooperative, were tarnished by Watergate-related scandals.

Labor groups ranked third, fourth and fifth on the list of major contributors. The AFL-CIO's political committee contributed $1 million, maritime-related unions gave $980,000 and the United Auto Workers donated $846,000.

Two groups that showed a sharp increase in 1976 campaign contributions from 1974 were the National Education Association, whose contributions increased 88% to $752,000, and the National Association of Realtors, whose contributions rose 132% to $606,000.

Former Sen. Vance Hartke (D, Ind.), who was defeated for reelection in 1976, led all 1976 congressional candidates in total donations from special interest groups. Hartke's $245,000 in contributions was closely followed by the $244,000 accepted by Sen. Harrison Williams (D, N.J.).

Among House candidates, Minority Leaders John Rhodes (R, Ariz.) received the largest contributions—$99,000 from business, professional and agricultural groups. Two members of the Democratic leadership also accepted large contributions from business, professional and agricultural interests. Majority Leader Jim Wright (D, Tex.) received $40,500 in donations, and Deputy Majority Whip Daniel Rostenkowski (D, Ill.) received $44,400. Rep. John J. Flynt Jr. (D, Ga.), chairman of the House Committee on Standards of Official Conduct (the ethics committee), accepted $40,700.

Eleven senatorial candidates, all Democrats, accepted more than $100,000 from labor groups for the 1976 campaign, compared with five in 1974 races. They were former Sen. John V. Tunney (Calif.) $164,000; former Rep. William J. Green (Pa.), $154,000; Williams (N.J.), $149,000; Hartke (Ind.), $144,000; Sen. Daniel P. Moynihan (N.Y.), $133,000; Sen. Paul S. Sarbanes (Md.), $122,000; Sen. Hubert H. Humphrey (Minn.), $121,000; Sen. Howard Metzenbaum (Ohio), $112,000; former Sen. Frank E. Moss (Utah), $107,000; former Rep. James G. O'Hara (Mich.), $106,200, and Elmo Zumwalt of Virginia, $100,100. (Five of the candidates were not elected.)

Eight senatorial candidates accepted more than $100,000 from business, professional and agricultural interests for the 1976 campaign, compared with one in 1974. They were: former Sen. Robert Taft Jr. (R, Ohio), $187,000; Sen. Lloyd M. Bentsen (D, Tex.), $174,000; former

Sen. Bill Brock (R, Tenn.), $155,000; former Rep. Marvin Esch (R, Mich.), $121,000; former Sen. James Buckley (R, N.Y.), $120,000; Sen. Richard Lugar (R, Ind.), $116,000; Sen. S.I. Hayakawa (R, Calif.), $107,000, and Hartke (Ind.), $102,000. (Five were not elected.)

House members who accepted largest contributions from labor interests were: Rep. Jim Mattox (D, Tex.), $59,000; Rep. Lloyd Meeds (D, Wash.), $56,000; Rep. Martin A. Russo (D, Ill.), $48,250; Rep. John H. Dent (D, Pa.), $48,250; Rep. Thomas L. Ashley (D, Ohio), $45,700; Rep. Michael T. Blouin (D, Iowa), $41,250; and Rep. Floyd J. Fithian (D, Ind.), $40,300.

Business, professional and agricutural groups concentrated their donations on these members of the House: Rhodes (Ariz.), $98,300; Rep. John J. Duncan (R, Tenn.), $64,400; former Rep. Ron Paul (R, Tex.), $59,900; Rep. Samuel L. Devine (R, Ohio), $57,600, and Rep. Olin E. Teague (D, Tex.), $54,500.

Analysts attributed the sharp increase in contributions by special interest groups to changes mandated in the 1974 Campaign Reform Act, which provided for the financing of presidential elections through tax revenues.

With direct private contributions limited in presidential primary campaigns and barred in the general election, special interest groups were able to channel more money to congressional campaigns.

Common Cause also noted that about 370 corporations had established political committees since 1974, when the new law formally recognized the groups for the first time. A total of 468 corporations currently had registered committees that were authorized to collect and disburse voluntary contributions on behalf of company executives and stockholders.

Analysts said the formation of the new committees reflected the business community's anxiety about making illegal corporate contributions and its desire to compete with unions, which had been making voluntary donations on behalf of their members for years.

Special interest contributions to chairmen of Senate, House committees. Special interest groups, representing busi-ness and professional associations and labor, contributed heavily to the reelection campaigns of the chairmen of major committees in the Senate and House, according to the New York Times.

The Times reported Jan. 15, 1977 that 14 Senate chairmen had taken $896,000 in contributions from lobbying groups during the last campaigns in which the senators had sought reelection. The contributions made up nearly 20% of the $5.1 million they collected for their campaigns.

Donations from business and labor groups were about equal—$457,700 from committees representing business and professional groups and $440,900 from labor's political committees.

In the House, the Times reported Feb. 4, 15 chairman had accepted $326,000 from special interest groups, or about 60% of their overall campaign expenses, which totaled $547,800.

Business groups donated far more for House races than did labor committees—$196,800, or 60% of the contributions from special interest groups, came from business, while $129,200, or 40%, came from labor groups.

The Times reports were based on financial statements filed by House and Senate members with the Federal Election Commission and supplemented by information from Common Cause.

The chairmen listed in the report were Sens. Howard Cannon, James O. Eastland, Henry M. Jackson, Russell B. Long, Warren G. Magnuson, John L. McClellan, Edmund S. Muskie, William Proxmire, Jennings Randolph, Abraham Ribicoff, John J. Sparkman, John C. Stennis, Herman E. Talmadge and Harrison A. Williams Jr.

The 15 chairmen named in the House report were Reps. Jack Brooks, James J. Delaney, Thomas S. Foley, Robert N. Giaimo, Harold T. Johnson, George Mahon, Carl D. Perkins, Melvin Price, Henry S. Reuss, Peter W. Rodino, Harley O. Staggers, Frank Thompson Jr., Morris K. Udall, Al Ullman and Clement J. Zablocki.

Senate—The chief beneficiary of the lobbyists' contributions in the Senate was Harrison A. Williams Jr. of New Jersey, chairman of the new Human Resources Committee. He was reelected in 1976 with

62% of the vote. Special interest groups donated $257,500, or 47% of Williams' campaign budget.

Another recipient of large contributions from lobbyists was Sen. Warren G. Magnuson of Washington, chairman of the new Commerce, Science and Transportation Committee. In 1974, when Magnuson was reelected with 61% of the vote, special interest groups contributed $126,100, or 27% of his campaign expenses.

Other committee chairmen who received substantial contributions from lobbyists were Howard W. Cannon of Nevada, chairman of the new Rules and Administration Committee, who accepted $89,400 for his 1976 campaign (27% of his budget); Edmund S. Muskie of Maine, chairman of the Budget Committee, $84,800 in 1976 (36%), and John J. Sparkman of Alabama, chairman of the Foreign Relations Committee, $82,300 in 1972 (12%).

All of the 14 committee chairman "occupied nearly invulnerable political positions in their home states," according to the Times. Only one of the group was reelected with less than 60% of the vote—Sen. James Eastland of Mississippi, chairman of the Judiciary Committee. He was returned to office in 1972 with a 58% plurality.

Despite their preeminent positions with voters, the Times noted, all but one of the committee chairmen had spent heavily in their latest campaigns. The exception was Sen. William Proxmire of Wisconsin, chairman of the Banking, Housing and Urban Affairs Committee. Proxmire spent $1,800 in 1976, all of it his own money, to win reelection in 1976 with 73% of the vote. On average, the other 13 committee chairman spent $350,000 in their last races.

Several chairmen reported their contributions had exceeded their expenses. Sen. Herman E. Talmadge of Georgia, chairman of the Agriculture Committee, was reelected in 1974 with 72% of the vote. He received $57,700 from special interest groups, most of them business and professional associations, or 88% of his $65,200 in expenses. Because Talmadge accepted another $197,200 in contributions from other sources, he

ended the campaign with a $189,700 surplus.

Other chairmen who reported substantial surpluses were Williams ($76,200); Sen. Russell B. Long of Louisiana, chairman of the Finance Committee, $57,900; Sen. Henry Jackson of Washington, chairman of the new Energy and Natural Resources Committee, $43,000, and Magnuson, $35,800.

House—Beneficiaries in the House of the largest contributions from special interest groups were Al Ullman of Oregon, chairman of the Ways and Means Committee, with $37,700 in donations; James J. Delaney of New York, chairman of the Rules Committee, $37,300; Thomas S. Foley of Washington, chairman of the Agriculture Committee, $35,100; Robert N. Giaimo of Connecticut, chairman of the Budget Committee, $32,600; Morris K. Udall, chairman of the Interior and Insular Affairs Committee, $31,300, and Henry S. Reuss of Wisconsin, chairman of the Banking, Finance and Urban Affairs Committee, $30,700.

Five chairmen collected more in special interest contributions than they spent on winning reelection. Lobbyists' donations to one of them, Foley, represented 228% of the $15,400 he spent in the 1976 election. Since Foley accepted another $7,000 from other sources, he reported an overall campaign surplus of $25,700. Others whose special interest contributions exceeded their expenses were Harold T. Johnson of California, chairman of the Public Works and Transportation Committee; Harley O. Staggers of West Virginia, chairman of the Interstate and Foreign Commerce Committee; Frank Thompson Jr. of New Jersey, chairman of the House Administration Committee, and Clement J. Zablocki of Wisconsin, chairman of the International Relations Committee.

(Other committee chairmen who reported large campaign surpluses were Jack Brooks of Texas, chairman of the Government Operations Committee, with a $63,700 surplus; Udall, $30,300; Giaimo, $26,000, and Peter W. Rodino of New Jersey, chairman of the Judiciary Committee, $25,400.)

In addition to the five whose entire campaign costs were financed by special interest contributions, another six accepted lobbyists' donations that paid for at least half their campaign expenses. They were Delaney (76%), Brooks (59%), Udall (58%), Giaimo (56%), Ullman (54%) and Melvin Price of Illinois, chairman of the Armed Services Committee (53%).

Committee chairmen who were least dependent on contributions from special interest groups were George Mahon of Texas, chairman of the Appropriations Committee, who accepted $14,400, or 11% of his expenses, and Carl D. Perkins of Kentucky, chairman of the Education and Labor Committee, who accepted $400, or 21% of his expenses. (These chairmen also were the only ones who received no contributions from labor groups.)

Of the 15 chairmen, only three were re-elected with less than 60% of the vote. They were Foley with 58%, Giaimo with 55% and Mahon with 54%. Two of the chairmen, Brooks and Zablocki, ran with no Republican opposition.

"Despite such apparent invulnerability," the Times said, "the 15 chairmen raised over $826,000 for their 1976 campaigns and spent $548,000 of it, for a collective surplus of more than $278,000." The average cost of their 1976 campaigns was $36,500.

Interest groups aided key legislators. Members of two key congressional fiscal panels, the Senate Finance Committee and the House Ways and Means Committee, received more than $2 million in contributions from special-interest groups the last time the legislators sought reelection, the New York Times reported March 7, 1977.

The 49 committee members who sought reelection each received an average of $42,000 from the interest groups. That was about 65% more than the average $25,000 contribution accepted by House and Senate members the last time they ran for Congress.

The two committees were of vital importance to corporate, professional and labor interests because the panels handled all legislation involving taxes, Social Security and welfare, according to the Times.

Three members of the Finance Com-

mittee each were able to pay 30% of their 1976 political expenses with special-interest contributions. They were Sen. Herman E. Talmadge (D, Ga.), who accepted $57,700; Sen. Mike Gravel (D, Alaska), $179,000, and former Sen. Vance Hartke (D, Ind.), $202,600.

Finance Committee members who received the largest contributions from business and professional groups were Sen. Lloyd M. Bentsen (D, Tex.), who accepted $129,600; former Sen. Bill Brock (R, Tenn.), $128,900; Sen. Robert J. Dole (R, Kans.), $80,600, and Hartke, $75,900.

The committee's chief beneficiaries of labor contributions were Gravel, who accepted $145,500; Hartke, $126,700 and Vice President Walter F. Mondale, a former Democratic senator from Minnesota, $58,800.

Eleven of the 32 members of the Ways and Means Committee who sought reelection in 1976 were able to pay more than 40% of their campaign expenses with donations from special-interest groups. Two of the 11, Rep. Omar Burleson (D, Tex.) and Rep. Joe D. Waggonner Jr. (D, La.), reported that their special-interest contributions exceeded the total cost of their campaigns.

Ways and Means Committee members who accepted the largest contributions from business and professional groups were Reps. John J. Duncan (R, Tenn.), who received $53,800; Waggonner, $41,-300, and Donald D. Clancy (R, Ohio), $45,400.

The largest labor contributions went to former Rep. Richard F. Vander Veen (D, Mich.), who accepted $43,900; Rep. Abner J. Mikva (D, Ill.), $35,200, and Rep. Martha Keys (D, Kans.), $34,300.

Maritime union contributions. Rep. Paul N. McCloskey Jr. (R, Calif.) asserted Oct. 6 that two maritime labor unions that had made large contributions to federal election campaign funds in 1976—"Paul Hall's Seafarers' International Union (SIU) and Jesse Calhoon's Marine Engineers' Beneficial Association (MEBA)"—were the "primary" supporters of the cargo preference bill then pending in the House.

McCloskey reported that "in 1976,

MEBA contributed $539,771.25 to federal election campaigns," or $56.81 "for each MEBA member." The SIU contributed $348,720.32, or $29.06 per member, McCloskey said. He inserted in the Congressional Record a Village Voice report in which Phil Tracy asserted that the SIU "pays cash on the barrelhead for every piece of legislation that concerns the shipping industry. It's been that way for 20 years." According to Tracy, the passage in 1976 of the Energy Transportation Security Act, to subsidize U.S. oil tankers, represented a victory in Congress of the Seafarers against the oil lobby (which preferred cheaper, foreign tankers). (The bill was vetoed by then-President Ford.) As Tracy reported:

Congress opted to do the one thing it does well: it lined its pockets. The legislators who had sold out to the Seafarers squared off against the boys who had sold out to the oil companies. The Seafarers won because, obviously, they owned more congressmen. And not just any old congressmen, but the key ones. In the House, for example, Frank Clark, a Democrat from western Pennsylvania, got $18,500 from Hall's maritime lobby last year, which alas wasn't enough to reelect him. Clark was chairman of the maritime subcommittee' that reported out Hall's bill. The chairman of the full committee, Leonor Sullivan, got $5,500 in 1974. Other committee members who voted for Hall included John Murphy (New York), $6238.81; John Dingell (Michigan), $4000; Bob Eckhardt (Texas), $2500; Joel Pritchard (Washington), $2500; and David Bowen (Mississippi), $2000. Tip O'Neill, the House majority leader, got $16,000 ...

On the Senate side, the maritime boys were even more generous. Mike Gravel of Alaska clearly led the pack, with $46,300 in gifts or loans from the Seafarers and the Marine Engineers. He was followed by Russell Long, chairman of the commerce subcommittee that reported out Hall's bill. Long got $22,000. Long was also the floor manager for the bill in the Senate. Warren Magnuson, chairman of the full Commerce Committee, got $12,900. Magnuson sponsored the bill. The other Senate luminaries who voted for the bill and shared in the wealth included Alan Cranston ($18,000); Charles McC. Mathias ($19,000); and Adlai Stevenson III, opposer of oil ripoffs ($12,500) ...

McCloskey had told the House July 13 that "the maritime industry has probably given more money to members of Congress per capita than any other industry" in the U.S. He quoted U.S. Lines as having admitted in a statement filed with the Securities & Exchange Com-

Labor Contributions to House Committee Members

Rep. Guy Vander Jagt (R, Mich.) inserted in the Congressional Record Sept. 22, 1977 the following listing of organized "labor's [political campaign] contributions to individual [House] members" in the 1976 election campaign (based on a report of the Public Policy Research Corp.).

House committee	Contributions to— Democrat members	Republican members	Total
Agriculture	$499,151.06	$6,700.00	$505,851.06
Appropriations	393,572.11	23,622.98	417,195.09
Armed Services	293,728.11	8,550.00	302,278.11
Banking, Finance and Urban Affairs	779,844.29	4,000.00	783,844.29
Budget	365,422.84	1,750.00	367,172.84
District of Columbia	184,081.86	8,008.00	192,089.86
Education and Labor	502,096.40	17,467.20	519,563.60
Government Operations	474,608.72	10,673.97	485,282.69
House Administration	308,683.52	700.00	309,383.52
Interior and Insular Affairs	575,910.72	20,700.00	596,610.72
International Relations	261,431.23	14,749.40	276,180.63
Interstate and Foreign Commerce	680,710.49	24,907.48	705,617.97

House committee	Contributions to— Democrat members	Republican members	Total
Judiciary	229,799.11	6,000.00	235,799.11
Merchant Marine and Fisheries	481,115.30	19,623.97	500,739.27
Post Office and Civil Service	371,898.30	10,841.40	382,739.70
Public Works and Transportation	483,600.89	15,150.00	498,750.89
Science and Technology	203,730.85	3,550.00	207,280.85
Rules	509,749.25	4,425.00	514,174.25
Small Business	413,183.71	24,002.98	437,186.69
Standards of Official Conduct	10,250.00	5,150.00	15,400.00
Veterans Affairs	294,948.52	10,150.00	305,098.52
Ways and Means	345,336.10	2,850.00	348,186.10
Grand total	8,662,853.38	243,572.38	8,906,425.76

mission: "We paid $5,000 to an elected official [not named] of the United States government in an attempt to procure passage of favorable legislation."

Congress Members Accused

Podell pleads guilty to conspiracy. Rep. Bertram L. Podell (D, N.Y.) pleaded guilty in federal district court in New York Oct. 1, 1974 to charges of conspiracy and conflict of interest in a $41,350 payment he received from a small Florida airline seeking government approval of a route to the Bahamas. Podell, whose surprise plea ended his nine-day bribery-conspiracy trial, admitted accepting the money from co-defendant Martin Miller to appear before federal agencies on behalf of Florida Atlantic Airlines. This act, Podell conceded, constituted a conflict of interest for a congressman. The plea by Podell was not an admittance that he had accepted any bribes.

Gurney acquitted. Former Sen. Edward J. Gurney (R, Fla.) was acquitted Aug. 6, 1975 of five felony charges in a bribery-conspiracy trial in Tampa, Fla. On two other charges, including a key conspiracy count, the jurors announced they had been unable to reach a verdict during 10 days of deliberations.

Gurney, a former member of the Senate Watergate Committee, was accused of conspiring to raise secret campaign funds from Florida builders by peddling his influence with the Federal Housing Administration. He was found innocent of a bribery count, accepting unlawful compensation, and three perjury counts relating to his grand jury testimony.

After his indictment was announced in July 1974, Gurney withdrew his bid for re-election. He resigned his Senate seat in December 1974.

Two co-defendants in the case, Ralph M. Koontz and K. Wayne Swiger, were found innocent of conspiracy charges. They had been suspended as Florida officials of the FHA. A fourth defendant, former Gurney aide Joseph Bastien, was acquitted on a charge of receiving unlawful compensation, but a mistrial was declared on a conspiracy charge.

Six other men had pleaded guilty to felony charges stemming from the case against Gurney. Larry E. Williams, former finance director of the Florida Republican Party and Gurney fund-raiser, admitted collecting nearly $400,000 from builders in exchange for favors from FHA officials for subsidized housing contracts.

James L. Groot, Gurney's former chief aide in Washington, and Earl M. Crittendon, former state Republican chairman, entered guilty pleas during the nearly 24-week trial. Both admitted complicity in the shakedown of Florida contractors to raise an illegal $233,000 slush fund for Gurney's 1974 re-election race.

George F. Anderson, a Florida banker and former treasurer of the party, also pleaded guilty to a conspiracy charge. William Pelski, a former FHA administrator in Florida, admitted he had awarded federal contracts to home builders who had made contributions to the Gurney fund and said he had received a kickback for his services. The Miami builder who paid the kickback at Williams' behest, John Priestes, also had pleaded guilty.

Jury selection in the lengthy trial began Feb. 24 at the U.S. District Court in Tampa. The government rested its case June 19 after calling 69 witnesses and presenting 300 items of documentary evidence. The prosecution contended that Gurney had known "all along" of the illegal fund-raising scheme, and that he developed a policy of "deniability" about the shakedown by insulating himself from Williams' pressure tactics and Groot's handling of the cash.

Williams' testimony was the core of the government's case against Gurney. Williams testified, and two other witnesses corroborated, that Gurney had hired him as a fund-raiser in January 1971. Williams said he received his instructions from Groot, who accepted the cash for Gurney to pay office and personal expenses.

Groot claimed Gurney had been aware as early as June 1972 of Williams' efforts to shakedown FHA contractors. Groot also admitted he had accepted $50,000 from Williams in July 1972 and had deposited the money in Gurney's Washington office safe.

(In testimony June 12, Groot also charged that immediately before the 1972 election, he had given $10,000 in cash from the safe to L. A. Bafalis, who was subsequently elected to Congress from Florida's 10th district. Bafalis never reported the secret campaign contribution, Groot testified. Bafalis denied the charge in testimony June 23.)

Gurney testified in his own defense during July, claiming that he had been unaware of the slush fund's existence until the summer of 1973 when the Senate Watergate hearings were underway. He defended his failure to release information on the illegal fund-raising, contending his "effectiveness on the Watergate committee would have been totally destroyed." He added that the information also would have proved an embarrassment to former President Nixon and the Republican Party.

The three other defendants in the bribery-conspiracy case also took the stand to deny participating in the shakedown scheme.

Gurney cleared on last charges—Gurney was acquitted Oct. 27, 1976 of the last of seven felony charges against him.

A jury in U.S. District Court, Orlando, Fla. found Gurney innocent of a perjury charge related to a political shakedown scheme that had involved members of his staff. The trial began Oct. 12. The prosecution claimed that Gurney had lied to a federal grand jury when he said he did not know until the summer of 1973 that $400,000 that had been paid by Florida builders in return for promised favors from the Federal Housing Administration was used to pay expenses of Gurney's Florida field offices. Larry E. Williams, Gurney's fund-raiser, had collected the money.

U.S. District Judge George C. Young, who presided over Gurney's trial in Orlando, Oct. 25 dismissed a portion of the perjury count against him. Young ruled that the government had not introduced sufficient evidence to prove its contention that Gurney had lied to the grand jury when he denied knowing before June 7, 1972 that Williams was raising funds on his behalf.

Williams, 32, served a five-month prison term after pleading guilty to felony charges stemming from the shakedown case. Williams, who was the chief prosecution witness at the Orlando trial, claimed that he had told Gurney about his activities since being hired as a fund raiser in 1971.

Hansen pleads guilty. Rep. George V. Hansen (R, Ida.) pleaded guilty Feb. 19, 1975 to two misdemeanor charges of failing to file a required campaign financing report and lying on another filed during his 1974 primary campaign. Hansen concealed receipts and expenditures totaling $16,150 with these actions, according to a criminal information filed by the Justice Department with U.S. District Court in Washington.

Hansen and his committee later filed amended financial reports that were in "substantial compliance" with the campaign law, the Justice Department noted.

After pleading guilty, Hansen said he viewed the charges as "technical violations" and said he would not resign. "I don't think I've done anything to leave Congress for," he said. Hansen was only the third sitting Congressman to plead guilty in court to a criminal offense and the first sitting member of Congress to be charged under the 1971 campaign law.

Hansen was sentenced April 18 to a year in jail (with 10 months suspended) and a year's probation (but the two-month remaining jail term was revoked April 26 by the same judge).

Before imposing sentence, Chief Judge George L. Hart Jr. of U.S. District Court in Washington, asked, "If the people who make the laws can't obey them, who can be expected to obey them?"

In setting aside the jail term and ordering instead that Hansen pay a $2,000 fine, Judge Hart said, "I had assumed when I sentenced him to jail he was evil. Now, I'm not sure he was. Stupid, surely."

James Jones pleads guilty to campaign financing violation. Rep. James R. Jones (D, Okla.) pleaded guilty Jan. 29, 1976 in federal court in Washington, D.C. to a misdemeanor charge—brought by the office of the Watergate special prosecutor — of failing to report a campaign contribution received in late 1972.

According to evidence summarized by the prosecution, Jones received the contribution—between $1,000 and $2,000 in cash—from Royce H. Savage, a former federal judge and general counsel for Gulf Oil Corp. A man who worked in Jones' campaign had approached Savage for a contribution after the election when it appeared that the campaign would not have money for its debts. Savage obtained the money from Claude C. Wild Jr., at the time the chief lobbyist for Gulf Oil Corp. (Wild and Gulf have already pleaded guilty to violating federal election laws.)

Jones said Jan. 29 that he had "thought the contribution was properly reported by my campaign committee."

Hinshaw convicted. Rep. Andrew J. Hinshaw (R, Calif.) was found guilty Jan. 26, 1976 on two felony counts of taking bribes while he was assessor for Orange County, Calif. The bribes—a payment of $1,000 and stereo equipment—were received from Tandy Corp. in 1972. He was acquitted of a charge of soliciting a bribe from a lawyer of another corporation.

One of his aides said Jan. 29 that Hinshaw was appealing the California superior court conviction and planned to run for reelection. After the verdict, Hinshaw said, "My conscience is clear. I hope the jury's conscience is. I sleep well."

With his conviction, Hinshaw fell under the Congressional rule that prohibited members convicted of felony charges from voting or taking part in the actions of committees to which they belonged.

During the course of the trial, Hinshaw was divorced from his wife.

Hinshaw was sentenced Feb. 24 to serve one to 14 years in prison.

While Hinshaw was free on appeal, the House Oct. 1 tabled and so killed a move to expel him. (Hinshaw had been defeated for renomination in a June 8 primary.)

The ouster bid, which was tabled by voice vote, had been brought before the full House by Rep. Charles E. Wiggins (R, Calif.) after the House Committee on Standards of Official Conduct had rejected it, 10–2, on Sept. 2.

Sikes charged with conflict of interest. Common Cause, the self-described citizens' lobby, lodged a complaint with the House ethics panel April 7, 1976 charging that Rep. Robert L. F. Sikes (D, Fla.) had committed several violations of House conflict-of-interest rules. In a press conference the same day, John Gardner, Common Cause chairman, announced the action and also condemned the Ethics Committee for its inactivity in the matter.

The complaint against Sikes alleged that from 1968 to 1973 he had failed to disclose ownership of 1,000 shares of stock in Fairchild Industries, a major defense contractor, although the holding came under a House rule requiring disclosure in annual financial reports filed by House members. The same charge was made regarding stock in the First Navy Bank in 1974.

Sikes also, according to the complaint, voted in 1974 on an appropriations bill that contained funding for a Fairchild contract. A House rule requires a member to abstain from voting on bills that could financially benefit the congressman.

The complaint further alleged that Sikes, in violation of House and federal service ethics rules, had sponsored legislation that removed restrictions on commercial development of some Florida land in which Sikes had a proprietary interest, and had thereby received financial gain.

Finally, Sikes was charged with using his office to influence government officials to allow the establishment in 1973 of the First Navy Bank at the Pensacola Naval Air Station. Sikes, according to the complaint, was an initial shareholder in the bank.

In the press conference, Gardner dwelt more on the failure of the Ethics Committee to look into Sike's activities than on the activities themselves. He noted that the charges against Sikes had been reported in detail in "reputable newspapers." Gardner said that he had written to every member of the committee, and then to every member of the House, without evoking any response.

Gardner ended by saying that the Ethics Committee "exemplifies the buddy system at its worst.... The committee is the worst kind of sham, giving the appearance of serving as policeman while extending a marvelous protective shield over members of Congress."

Forty-five members of the House agreed to transmit the complaint to the Ethics Committee.

Sikes reprimanded—The House July 29, 1976 voted, 381-3, to reprimand Sikes. He told reporters he had expected the vote "because of the atmosphere regarding public officials at this time."

In a statement issued July 29 Sikes denied practicing any concealment in his business affairs. He said that he had "no intent to violate any rule of this House, and any inadvertent and technical violation did not benefit me in any way."

The House vote followed a July 26 recommendation by the Committee on Standards of Official Conduct (the ethics committee) that Sikes be reprimanded on two of three charges the panel had been studying.

The two charges preferred by the panel involved Sikes' failure to report ownership of stock in Fairchild Industries and in the First Navy Bank. The complaint also said that Sikes had used the influence of his office to persuade government officials to permit First Navy to be established.

The third charge alleged that Sikes had pushed legislation that removed restrictions on development of land in which Sikes had an interest. The committee formally abstained from judging the case, since the alleged incidents involved took place before it was created.

A reprimand was the lightest sanction the ethics panel could recommend. The committee's vote for the action was 10-2.

Sikes ousted as panel head—House Democrats, acting in caucus Jan. 26, 1977, voted, 189-93, to remove Sikes as chairman of the Military Construction Subcommittee of the House Appropriations Committee.

Supporters of the move argued that it was needed to prove that the House was serious about requiring higher ethical standards of its members.

Defenders of Sikes argued that the 1976 reprimand had been sufficient punishment.

The two top Democratic leaders in the House, Speaker Thomas P. O'Neill (Mass.) and Majority Leader Jim Wright (Tex.), had expressed support for Sikes, but both had disclaimed attempts to influence other representatives. Nevertheless, Common Cause chairman John W. Gardner called the vote to strip Sikes of his chairmanship a "major defeat" for the House Democratic leadership.

Metcalfe probe dropped. The Justice Department said April 15, 1976 that it would not seek an indictment against Rep. Ralph H. Metcalfe (D, Ill.). Metcalfe had been under investigation for alleged tax evasion in 1969.

The Justice Department did not give any details concerning the investigation when it made the announcement. However, the Washington Post reported April 16 that department sources had said that the possibility of tax evasion had arisen from the alleged concealment of bribes received from real estate developers while Metcalfe was chairman of the Chicago City Council's Committee on Buildings and Zoning. Metcalfe had been the first black to attain the presidency of the City Council.

Metcalfe, 65, said after release of the Justice Department statement that he was "grateful to God that justice had been done ... I have never broken the public trust."

The Justice Department, which normally did not announce decisions not to indict, explained that the statement was made "to offset any possible adverse effect" reports of the investigation might have caused for Metcalfe.

Helstoski indicted. Rep. Henry Helstoski (D, N.J.) was indicted by a federal grand jury in Newark, N.J. June 2,

1976, several days before he was due to stand for renomination, on charges of having taken $8,735 in bribes to gain permanent residence for illegal South American aliens. Three of Helstoski's top aides were also named as having taken part in the alleged scheme.

The indictment, announced by U.S. Attorney Jonathan L. Goldstein, charged Helstoski with "both conspiring to and with the actual corrupt asking, demanding, accepting and receiving of cash payments from Chilean and Argentinean aliens" in return for the promise to introduce private bills that would allow the South Americans to remain in the country permanently. He was also accused of "obstructing and impeding justice by supplying and producing false and misleading testimony to the grand jury."

Also charged with obstruction of justice were two aides serving as Helstoski's attorneys, Alfred A. Porro and Vincent L. Verdiramo, and D. John Mazella, treasurer of Helstoski's reelection campaign, who was further accused of perjury. Named as an unindicted co-conspirator was Albert DeFalco, a former aide, serving a prison term for accepting bribes from the aliens and promising Helstoski would get them citizenship.

(Helstoski was renominated in a primary runoff Sept. 21 but was defeated in the election Nov. 2.)

The prospect of wrongdoing was first raised in 1973 when a Chilean alien threatened with deportation told officials of the U.S. Immigration and Naturalization Service that he had paid a bribe to get Rep. Helstoski to introduce a private immigration bill. This information was passed along to the Federal Bureau of Investigation, and in April 1974 a Newark grand jury began its investigation.

Rep. Helstoski defended himself against the charges June 2, describing the indictment as "an outrage" and "a lot of nonsense." He said there was "always some garbage that keeps me tied up in the courts during election time," and he accused U.S. Attorney Goldstein of harassment. (A civil suit in which Helstoski had alleged harassment by Goldstein was dismissed May 27 in Newark by U.S. District Court Judge H. Curtis Meanor, who said his decision was not based on merit but on U.S. Supreme Court rulings giving prosecutors immunity from civil litigation designed to restrain them.) Helstoski asked the House Ethics Committee June 3 for a "thorough, fair and impartial investigation" of the indictment.

Federal jury clears Maraziti. Former U.S. Rep. Joseph J. Maraziti (R, N.J.) had been cleared of charges that he had criminally misused funds by putting a woman friend on his congressional payroll even though she was working full time elsewhere, U.S. Attorney Jonathan L. Goldstein announced June 23, 1976. According to Goldstein, a Newark federal grand jury had found insufficient evidence under House rules that a crime had been committed.

Maraziti's woman friend, Ann Leclerc, had earned $20,000 in 1973 and 1974 as a staff aide, while working full time as a legal secretary in Whippany, Morris County, under the name Linda Collinson.

Hastings sentenced. Former Rep. James F. Hastings (R, N.Y., 1969-76) was sentenced Jan. 31, 1977 to a term of 20 months to five years on charges stemming from a payroll kickback scheme involving employes in his congressional district.

U.S. District Judge June L. Green said the sentence was intended to "put on notice those few [public officials] whose actions do violate the law." The sentence was thought to be the most stringent imposed on a current or former congressman in at least a decade, according to the Washington Post Feb. 1. Hastings' lawyer said the former representative had decided not to appeal his conviction.

A federal jury Dec. 17, 1976 had convicted Hastings on 20 counts of mail fraud and eight counts of making false statements to the House Finance Office. The charges stemmed from the kickback scheme. The prosecution said Hastings had received more than $30,000 in kickbacks.

Tonry admits guilt. Former Rep. Richard A. Tonry (D, La.) pleaded guilty in New Orleans July 1, 1977 to four of ten misdemeanor counts charging him with conspiring to accept illegal political contributions, accepting illegal contributions and promising favors to campaign contributors. Felony charges against him were dropped. U.S. District Court Judge Charles Schwartz sentenced him July 28 to a year in prison and fined him $10,000.

Tonry had resigned from the House May 4 after vote-fraud charges had cast a cloud on his victory in the 1976 Democratic primary in Louisiana's first congressional district.

The indictment by a federal grand jury on 10 counts took place eight days later. The charges included receiving illegal campaign contributions and conspiring to block a grand-jury probe into the contributions and into charges of vote fraud.

Tonry pleaded not guilty to all the charges against him during a May 18 hearing. John W. Mumphrey, a partner in Tonry's law firm who had been indicted with Tonry on a number of charges, also pleaded not guilty.

Tonry had been certified the winner of the Oct. 2, 1976 Democratic primary runoff by a 184 vote margin. His opponent, James A. Moreau, had filed suit charging vote fraud. Eventually, a state court judge ruled that there had been fraud and voting irregularities sufficient to affect the outcome of the election, but the judge added that only the House of Representatives had the power to unseat Tonry or order a new election.

Tonry's resignation occurred before a House Administration Committee subcommittee, which was looking into the vote fraud charges, delivered its report. It had been generally expected that the panel would recommend that Tonry resign. After Tonry's resignation, a spokesman for the panel said that no recommendation would be made regarding Tonry, saying "the question is moot."

The indictment specifically charged Tonry with accepting a total of $59,500 in campaign contributions from five individuals (federal law barred contributions of more than $1,000 from an individual), promising jobs and federal benefits to three individuals who contributed a total of $24,000 and obstructing justice by providing false information to federal investigators.

When Tonry resigned, he said he would run and win in the new election that would

be ordered for the district. He acknowledged there had been vote fraud in his favor, but said his opponent had also benefited from vote fraud. Tonry said he believed he still would be the winner if only legitimate votes had been counted.

But when the primary was held June 25, Tonry was defeated by Ron Faucheux by a vote of 52,592 to 45,320.

Charges against Garmatz dropped. Federal bribery charges against former Rep. Edward A. Garmatz (D, Md.) were dropped Jan. 9, 1978 when the government's attorneys revealed they had discovered that their key witness had lied about an alleged payoff.

The witness was Edward J. Heine, president of U.S. Lines Inc. He insisted that his testimony before a grand jury was truthful.

Garmatz, 74, had been accused of having conspired to obtain $25,000 from two shipping lines in exchange for pushing legislation favorable to the lines. Garmatz had been chairman of the House Merchant Marine Committee. He left Congress in 1973.

Garmatz had been indicted by a federal grand jury in Baltimore Aug. 1, 1977.

The dates of the alleged conspiracy, according to the indictment, were from early September 1971 to April 1973, when Garmatz was said to have conspired to obtain a total of $25,000 from the two lines, but $10,000 of the amount apparently was not paid.

The lines involved were Moore McCormack Lines, a subsidiary of Moore McCormack Resources Inc., and U.S. Lines Inc.

The legislation involved, which was passed by Congress, authorized the lines to sell certain ships to the U.S. government or foreign buyers. Such authorization was required for sale of U.S. ships built with federal subsidies.

Diggs indicted on kickbacks. Rep. Charles C. Diggs Jr. (D, Mich.) was indicted March 23, 1978 by a federal grand jury on 35 counts involving an alleged scheme of kickbacks and illegitimate payments. The kickbacks and payments totaled more than $101,000 between 1973 and 1977, according to the indictment.

Diggs's office released a statement in which he said he was "innocent of the charges being leveled against me."

Diggs was on a tour of several African nations when the indictment was handed up. He complained that the timing of the indictment showed "an unfortunate insensitivity" to his "mission to Africa."

According to the indictment, Diggs had increased the salaries of several of his congressional employees and used the increases to pay for "various personal, business and House of Representatives expenses."

Diggs also had put people on the federal payroll who worked for a funeral home business Diggs had owned, not for the government, the indictment alleged.

The senior black member of the House, Diggs was chairman of the Committee on the District of Columbia and had been the first chairman of the Congressional Black Caucus.

Reportedly, with the funeral home failing to prosper (Diggs sold it in 1975) and with alimony and child support payments from two divorces, Diggs had been beset with financial difficulties.

The specific charges against Diggs were 14 counts of mail fraud and 21 counts of making a false statement to the government.

U.S. Attorney Marston Fired During Probe of Flood & Eilberg

The Carter Administration became embroiled in controversy in January 1978 over the dismissal of David W. Marston as U.S. attorney in Philadelphia. Marston had been investigating two Democratic members of Congress from Pennsylvania—Reps. Daniel J. Flood and Joshua Eilberg—before he was ousted.

Bell dismisses Marston. Attorney General Griffin Bell Jan. 20, 1978 dismissed David W. Marston as U.S. attorney in Philadelphia despite the controversial political overtones of the move.

Marston emerged from a meeting with Bell to protest his ouster as "purely political."

"He said we have a system and that he has to accept that system," Marston said of Bell. "I don't agree with that. They had a system in Philadelphia, too, . . . and I didn't accept that system. I threw it out and eliminated politics. . . ."

Marston, a Republican, was credited with several successful prosecutions of leading Democratic politicians for corruption.

President Carter had acknowledged at his news conference Jan. 12 that he had received a request from Rep. Joshua Eilberg (D, Pa.) to "expedite" Marston's removal. Eilberg, according to local press reports, was being investigated by Marston's office.

Bell confirmed Jan. 12 he had received a call from Carter asking "why is it taking so long" to replace Marston. The President and Bell said they did not know at the time about the investigation of Eilberg.

Eilberg's complaint about Marston reportedly was that he felt Marston was using the prosecutor's office as a platform for higher office.

Marston told reporters after his meeting with Bell Jan. 20 that the call from Eilberg "clearly expedited my removal." "I think that raises very grave questions," Marston said.

Marston said Bell had offered to let him stay on until the appointment of a successor but he had declined to "be a lame duck prosecutor."

"He said that my situation had caused quite a controversy," Marston reported, "and I told him that the way to stop controversy would be to let me stay a full four-year term. He told me that had never been an option. I am very disappointed."

Marston's term ran until June 1980. He had held the post since mid-1976.

Bell declined to meet with reporters following his meeting with Marston. He issued a written statement pledging that in the choice of a successor for Marston "it would have to appear to me personally that no investigation or prosecution would be impeded."

Carter had been asked three times at his Jan. 12 press conference to explain the Administration's decision to remove Marston. He replied that Bell was handling the matter.

"I can't say Mr. Marston has or has not done a good job," he said. "The only criticism about him was that he had a very heavy commitment to calling news conferences."

Carter said he had not discussed the case with Bell and inquired specifically what was wrong with Marston. The decision to replace Marston had already been made when he first heard the name, Carter said.

Bell, in an appearance before the National Press Club Jan. 10, conceded the political aspect of the situation. "He's a fine young man and has a good record, indeed," he said of Marston. "But this is a political system in the country."

Marston's ouster had evoked a flood of protest from Philadelphia residents, much of it directed to the White House.

The move to oust Marston was condemned Jan. 13 by Republican National Chairman Bill Brock and Common Cause, a public-affairs lobbying organization.

Brock said the incident had "overtones of political cover-up." Common Cause said it made "a mockery" of Carter's campaign pledge to appoint federal prosecutors on the basis of merit.

The issue brought into question Carter's campaign promise to appoint federal prosecutors on the basis of merit without consideration of political aspects.

According to a Justice Department count, reported by the Washington Post Jan. 13, the Carter Administration had named 65 new U.S. attorneys across the country since assuming office, all but one of them Democrats.

Carter insisted Jan. 30 there was "nothing improper in the handling" of the Marston case. He thought Bell had "handled the case as well as possible."

"I made a campaign commitment that any appointee to a position as U.S. attorney or a judgeship would be appointed on the basis of merit," he said, "and this campaign commitment will be carried out."

The President was questioned in particular about his statement at his news conference Jan. 12 that he had not known, in relation to the Marston affair, of any investigation of members of Congress. (Carter had told Justice Department investigators, in a statement released Jan. 24, that he had first learned of an "investigative interest" in Eilberg just prior to that news conference.)

Was there any "conflict" in his statement that he did not know of any probe when he did know? he was asked.

Carter replied that the question on Jan. 12 "obviously related" to what he had known at the time of his telephone talks with Eilberg and Bell and "the answer was no; no discussion ever had been made" at that time.

"This was a routine matter for me," Carter said, "and I did not consider my taking the telephone call from Congressman Eilberg nor relaying his request to the attorney general to be ill-advised at all."

"If it occurred now, I would do the same," he said.

Internal Probe Clears Carter, Bell—The Justice Department investigation cleared both Carter and Bell of obstruction of justice or improper conduct.

The finding, made known Jan. 24, was that neither man knew Eilberg "might be of investigative interest" to the Justice Department "when the decision was made to expedite the replacement of Mr. Marston after a telephone call to the President from Congressman Eilberg."

The finding was made by Solicitor General Wade McCree and Michael Shaheen Jr., head of the department's office of professional responsibility.

Robert N. deLuca, 37, for eight years an assistant to the U.S. attorney in Philadelphia, was named Jan. 24 as temporary successor to Marston.

DeLuca said he would continue Marston's investigation of the two Democratic Congressmen.

House panel probes Flood & Eilberg. The House Committee on Standards of Official Conduct—the ethics committee—announced Feb. 8 that it was informally investigating allegations that Rep. Daniel J. Flood (D, Pa.) had taken money in exchange for political favors.

News reports before and after the ethics committee announcement described a number of occasions on which Flood had allegedly received money in return for influencing the actions of federal agencies, particularly the awarding of contracts and aid.

Flood, 74, was chairman of the labor and health, education and welfare subcommittee of the House Appropriations Committee. He had become well-known for finding ways to bring federal money to his district.

Ethics committee Chairman John Flynt Jr. (D, Ga.) said Feb. 8 that his panel was also informally investigating Rep. Joshua Eilberg (D, Pa.).

Hahnemann Hospital—Reportedly, Marston had been investigating links between Flood and Eilberg and the Hahnemann Medical College and Hospital of Philadelphia. Flood had been a key figure in congressional approval of a $14.5-million grant to help enlarge the hospital. Eilberg was connected to the hospital through his law firm, which had been hired in April 1975 to represent the hospital. The firm reportedly had received $500,000 in fees from the hospital.

Stephen Elko, a former administrative assistant to Flood, reportedly had urged officials at Hahnemann to hire Eilberg's law firm.

(Elko was convicted in 1977 on bribery charges. It was revealed at his trial that he had reached an agreement with the Justice Department under which he received immunity from prosecution on other matters in exchange for giving testimony about alleged wrongdoing by members of Congress and federal agency officials.)

Elko said that Flood, when he was maneuvering the Hahnemann appropriation through Congress, had expected to receive a $50,000 kickback from Eilberg's law firm, the New York Times reported March 9.

The Times had reported Feb. 19 that the Justice Department was looking into allegations that Flood had supported the Hahnemann addition to benefit two Pennsylvania contractors who had supported him politically. The contractors,

according to the Times' sources, were brothers, Edward F. and John P. Dixon.

The Times story March 9 carried denials by Flood and Eilberg. Flood had claimed that he supported the hospital because it would aid low-income families in Philadelphia's inner city.

Other Charges—Elko was the source of a number of other accusations against Flood. According to an Associated Press report, Jan. 27, Elko had given federal investigators an affidavit in which he charged that:

■ Walter Verblosky (who was not identified) paid Flood $50,000 between 1972 and 1974, perhaps for assistance in getting government contracts.

■ Flood received between $40,000 and $50,000 worth of First Valley Bank of Pennsylvania stock for helping with a merger.

■ Murdock Head, executive director of the nonprofit Airlie Foundation in Warrenton, Va., gave $59,000 to Flood (and $18,000 to Elko) between 1971 and 1973 for assistance in getting federal funding for a conference center. (According to the Times March 9, Elko said the money received by himself and Flood actually totaled $42,000, not $77,000 as in the AP report.) Head also gave $10,00 to former Rep. Otto Passman (D, La. 1947–77) between 1973 and 1974, according to the AP report of Elko's affidavit. Head and Passman, as well as Flood, denied Elko's charges. (Head said March 7 he believed Elko had made the accusation because Head had refused to give an $8,000 contribution Elko sought to help pay his legal expenses.)

■ Flood had received about $10,000 between 1974 and 1976 from Rabbi Lieb Pinter, head of the B'Nai Torah Institute of Brooklyn, N.Y. for help in connection with a training program for Jewish immigrants from the Soviet Union.

Another charge against Flood was made by Deryl E. Fleming, a lobbyist formerly connected with West Coast Schools. (Elko's bribery conviction stemmed from charges that he had used his position as Flood's aide to obtain government favors for West Coast Schools, which was a group of private vocational schools that went out of business in 1973.)

Fleming told federal investigators, according to a Times report Feb. 15, that he had given Flood $1,000 in cash after a letter bearing Flood's signature was sent to former U.S. Education Commissioner Sidney Marland Jr. Flood had pressed Marland to have the West Coast Schools accredited. The schools were never accredited, but pressure from Flood's office helped West Coast Schools become temporarily eligible for student loans from the federal government.

Flood had testified that he did not know of the bribes paid to Elko in the West Coast Schools matter. But Elko said that Flood had known of the payments; Elko further charged that one of Flood's former attorneys had arranged a payment of $28,-000 to Elko so that he would remain silent about the payments.

News reports identified John Ingoldsby, a Washington lawyer and old friend of Flood, as the lawyer who allegedly tried to buy Elko's silence. Ingoldsby acknowledged helping Elko pay the costs of his trial, but he denied trying to obtain the former Flood aide's silence.

House Actions—Thirty-two House Democrats sent a letter to the ethics committee Feb. 17 urging the panel to upgrade its informal inquiry into Flood's and Eilberg's activities to a formal investigation.

The representatives said that such an investigation was necessary to show that Congress "has the will and the desire to properly police the behavior of its members."

The ethics committee March 15 decided to continue its informal probe of Flood and Eilberg. However, committee member Charles Bennett (D, Fla.) said the panel was taking steps to hire an attorney to head the Flood-Eilberg probe, indicating that the panel was moving toward launching a formal investigation.

Rabbi admits bribing Flood. Rabbi Lieb Pinter pleaded guilty in U.S. District Court in New York May 11, 1978 to charges of bribing Rep. Flood. Pinter admitted to giving Flood more than $1,000 on each of five occasions between late 1974 and early 1976.

Pinter had testified before a grand jury that in return for the payments, Flood had:

■ Influenced officials of various federal agencies on matters affecting Pinter's B'Nai Torah Institute. The institute had grown from a small religious school in Brooklyn, N.Y. into a multimillion-dollar organization administering federally financed summer food and job-training programs.

■ Worked to increase federal appropriations for employment programs, so that B'Nai Torah would have a greater chance of obtaining money.

■ Asked former Rep. Otto Passman (D, La.) to exercise his influence with the Agency for International Development to obtain a $1-million grant for a school Pinter wished to build in Israel.

Flood, who was still the subject of a number of bribery allegations, issued a statement "categorically denying" that he had taken bribes from Pinter.

Civiletti confirmation reopens Marston ouster dispute. The Senate May 9, 1978 voted, 72 to 22, to confirm Benjamin R. Civiletti as deputy attorney general, the second-ranking post in the Justice Department. All those voting against confirmation were Republicans.

Republicans had used the Civiletti confirmation hearings as a forum to examine the firing of David Marston as U.S. attorney in Philadelphia. Sen. Malcolm Wallop (R, Wyo.) claimed that Civiletti's credibility was in question because of a conflict between his testimony to the Senate Judiciary Committee and an affidavit filed with the committee by another Justice Department official.

The other official, Russell T. Baker Jr., had said that Civiletti in November 1977 had spoken of the Justice Department's investigation of Rep. Joshua Eilberg (D, Pa.). Civiletti had referred to the Eilberg case as "alive," Baker said in his affidavit. Civiletti had told the committee that he did not recall such a conversation with Baker.

The significance of the conflict concerned the question of whether there had been an ongoing Justice Department investigation of Eilberg in November 1977. That was the time when Eilberg called President Carter to ask that Marston be dismissed. Supporters of Civiletti had claimed that there was no investigation of Eilberg at that time, and so the decision to dismiss Marston had not been an attempt at a cover-up.

The Senate May 4 rejected a report that had cleared Civiletti of any responsibility for Marston's ouster.

Sen. Richard Schweiker (R, Pa.) objected that the report had been sent from the Judiciary Committee to the Senate without being shown to any member of the committee except the chairman. Schweiker called the report a "misleading whitewash."

Schweiker April 25 had charged that the report was "apparently fashioned in the White House and Justice Department."

Sen. William Scott (R, Va.) said he would be "ashamed to sign my name to such a whitewash as this report is."

On a motion by Sen. Strom Thurmond (R, S.C.), the Senate without objection ordered the report returned to committee. The Senate instructed the committee to send back to the Senate only a recommendation on Civiletti's confirmation. The committee earlier had voted to recommend that he be confirmed.

Sex Scandals

Hays admits affair with aide. Rep. Wayne L. Hays (D, Ohio), House Administration Committee chairman, admitted to the House May 25, 1976 that he had had a "personal relationship" with Elizabeth Ray, a member of that committee's staff. Hays denied, however, that he had given Ray the $14,000-a-year job so that she could be his mistress.

The May 23 Washington Post carried the first report of Hays' affair with Ray. In that story, Ray, 33, said that Hays had hired her to be his mistress, and that she spent only a few hours a week at her office. Ray denied having the secretarial skills required for the job, saying, "I can't type, I can't file, I can't even answer the phone." Hays, Ray said, visited her once or twice a week for sexual relations.

When the story first broke, Hays, 65, denied having any intimate relationship with Ray. In his House speech, however, Hays said he had "committed a grievous error in not presenting all the facts" of the matter. The relationship, Hays said, occurred after he had been separated from his first wife, and before he married his second wife. Ray had not been hired, Hays said, on the condition that she sleep with him; the sexual relationship, he said, had been "voluntary on her part and on mine."

Hays admitted that he had helped Ray get a job on the office staff of a representative in the summer of 1975. (She was later transferred to the Administration Committee.) He said she had worked previously for the Administration Committee and that he knew her to be capable of performing "normal office duties."

Hays called Ray a "seriously disturbed young woman." He said that she had threatened both suicide and blackmail when he told her that their relationship must end because he was getting married. (Hays was married six weeks before the speech.) Hays said that Ray's accusations in the Washington Post showed that "Miss Ray had kept her promise to try to destroy my marriage and my career."

On May 25 both Hays and a group of about 25 House members made separate requests that the House Committee on Standards of Official Conduct (the so-called ethics committee) investigate Ray's charge. The Justice Department had said the previous day that it was investigating the case.

Hays said May 26 that Ray had extorted over $1,000 from him during the preceding five weeks by threatening to disclose their relationship. Hays fired Ray May 24.

Hays' attacks on public figures, including other members of the House, and his conduct as chairman of the Administration Committee, had earned him the dislike of many representatives. He noted this in his May 25 speech, saying that he had "been called more names than any member of Congress in my memory. I have been called arrogant, ruthless, cold-blooded, vicious, tempermental and mean ... just to mention a few of the ones that are printable."

Rep. Thomas P. O'Neill (Mass.), House majority leader, asked Hays June 2 to temporarily resign his committee chairmanships—one a Democratic Party post, the others congressional jobs—until the charges made against him by Ray were resolved. Hays headed the Democratic National Congressional Committee (which distributed funds to Democrats seeking election to the House), the House Administration Committee, the Joint Committee on Printing and the subcommittee on operations of the House International Relations Committee.

Hays June 3 agreed to give up the Democratic party post, but refused to let go of the others. House Democratic leaders and members expressed dissatisfaction with Hays' stand. They noted that Hays might be stripped of his chairmanships by the House Democratic Caucus if he did not resign them.

The House Committee on Standards of Official Conduct voted 11-0 June 2 to proceed immediately with an investigation of Hays. On June 9, the House voted 388-0 to comply with a Justice Department subpoena for personnel and payroll records of Ray and three other past or present employes of the Administration Committee.

Hays, who had won renomination in his bid for a 15th House term in the June 8 Ohio primary, was rushed to a Barnesville, Ohio hospital the morning of June 10. He was in a coma that his doctor said was caused by "an overreaction to a commonly prescribed sleeping pill." Hays' doctor June 12 said that Hays was "back to normal, ordering people around, asking about his farm." The doctor said he did not know whether the incident represented a suicide attempt.

The Washington Post June 12 called into question Hays' use of federal payroll funds in relation to another individual, Don R. Gosny. According to the Post story, Gosny lived in Ohio, earning $19,140 a year as a "field" representative for Hays. The Post said that Hays had also given Gosny a $10,000-a-year job as an assistant clerk for the House Administration Committee. The Post quoted Gosny as saying he did not "know the difference between Hays' staff work and his committee responsibilities."

Hays resigns—Hays announced Sept. 1 that he was resigning from the House, "effective immediately." He announced ·his decision just two days after the House Committee on Standards of Official Conduct (known informally as the Ethics Committee) had voted (Aug. 30), 11-0, to hold public hearings on his case in September The New York Times reported Sept. 2 that Hays had tried to win a commitment by the House to drop any action against him if he resigned. The Times reported that the bid was unsuccessful, but the Ethics Committee voted 12-0 Sept. 1—after Hays' resignation had been announced—to abandon its probe of Hays and cancel the hearings. The criminal investigations of Hays would not be affected by his resignation.

Hays had been described by his aides as being in a "severely depressed mental state." Carol Clawson, one of his aides, said Aug. 30 that Hays was under the care of a psychiatrist and that his mental stress since the scandal broke had brought on an impairment in the use of his right hand.

Hays' 28 years in the House, plus a stint in the Army during World War II, entitled him to a pension of about $30,000.

Some Democratic congressmen had feared that Hays' continued presence in the House would hurt them at the polls in November by lending weight to GOP charges of corruption in the Democratic-controlled Congress.

Taxpayer suit dismissed—U.S. District Judge Thomas A. Flannery Oct. 26 dismissed suits brought against Hays by three "taxpayers" seeking restitution of federal funds. They said in the suits that Hays had arranged for Elizabeth Ray to receive a federal salary in return for being Hays's mistress. Flannery dismissed the suits at the request of the Justice Department, which said that it could reinstate the suits later if the action appeared warranted. The Justice Dept. announced Dec. 8 that it had decided not to press charges against Hayes.

Aide accuses Rep. Young. Colleen Gardner, 33, charged in a story in the New York Times June 11, 1976 that Rep. John Young (D, Tex.) had paid her primarily to have sex with him. Gardner was hired by Young in 1970 as a secretary with an $8,500 annual salary. She quit in 1973 and told unemployment officials that she did so because of sexual pressures. A Justice Department investigation at that time resulted in no prosecution of Young. Gardner went back to work for Young in 1974, and was earning close to $26,000 a year by the time she quit again in March 1976. Gardner, the Times reported, was entering her fourth year as an undergraduate, majoring in accounting, at American University in Washington.

The Times story quoted Gardner as saying, "It wouldn't have been so bad going to bed with him if he'd at least have let me work, but he wouldn't . . . He did not want me to have any definite responsibility because he wanted me to be available to him whenever he wanted."

Gardner said she had met with Young in motel rooms, rented by Young under the name of "George Denton." Gardner had tape recordings of a number of phone calls between her and Young. The Washington Post reported June 14 that Gardner's lawyer had said that the recordings would be turned over to federal authorities.

Young refused June 11 to verify the reported affair but he emphatically rejected Gardner's claim that her salary had been paid principally for sexual favors. Young admitted having rented motel rooms under the name of "George Denton," but he said that he had done so to meet confidentially with Defense Department officials.

Young refused to comment on charges made by another former secretary, Melanie Hall, who said that Young had made advances Feb. 14 when they were alone in Young's office. She said that he had offered her a "substantial" raise the next week but that she had refused it and had quit shortly afterwards.

Gravel & Gray accused. The New York Times reported June 12, 1976 that "sources close to the investigation" had indicated that federal authorities were probing charges by Elizabeth Ray that former Rep. Kenneth J. Gray (D, Ill.) had ordered her to have sex with Sen. Mike Gravel (D, Alaska) in order to gain Gravel's backing for legislation favored by

Gray. Ray had worked on Gray's office staff before going to work for Hays' Administration Committee.

The Times story reported that Colleen Gardner had given an independent account of the alleged sexual encounter between Gravel and Ray. Gardner claimed to have accidentally witnessed the supposed incident, which, Gardner said, took place on board Gray's houseboat. Gardner's description matched an episode in Ray's novel in which a meeting aboard a houseboat with a "Senator Boulder" is described. The novel, entitled "The Washington Fringe Benefit," was described by the publisher as a *roman à clef,* based on Ray's experiences in Washington.

Gravel June 11 termed Ray's charges "ridiculous." He said that he did not remember ever having met anyone named Elizabeth Ray. Gray June 12 also emphatically rejected the charges.

Gardner said that Gray had told her in a telephone call made after the Hays-Ray affair became public, that she should forget what she had seen on the houseboat. Gray denied the charge June 11, saying, "I never told her not to talk to anyone about anything."

The alleged sexual favor was supposed to have been given in connection with legislation to authorize construction of a National Visitors' Center at Union Station, near the Capitol. Gray and Gravel were chairmen of the House and Senate subcommittees with jurisdiction over the bill. According to a June 12 AP report, Ray had told federal investigators that the date of Gravel's visit to Gray's houseboat was Aug. 10, 1972. That was shortly before the legislation passed Congress.

Young cleared—The Justice Department Aug. 16 confirmed press reports that an investigation had cleared Young of charges that he had paid Gardner primarily to act as his mistress. A department spokesman said that the probe had turned up no evidence to support charges made by Gardner. A spokesman said Aug. 18 that it had been decided to end the investigation.

Gardner never said she had performed no office duties. She had charged, rather, that her salary was disproportionate to her official duties. She said that the difference had been earned by complying with Young's sexual wishes. Young had not denied having an affair with Gardner, but he had maintained that the relationship played no part in determining Gardner's salary. A Justice Department official said Aug. 18 that Gardner's admission to having performed some legitimate duties made it particularly difficult to assemble a case against Young.

The department spokesman also said that no evidence of financial misdealing by Young had been found to support allegations that he had used checks sent to his office by constituents for personal expenses.

Howe convicted on sex charge. A jury of three women and one man found Rep. Allan Turner Howe (D, Utah) guilty July 23, 1976 of soliciting sex acts for hire. Judge Raymond S. Uno sentenced Howe to 30 days in jail and fined him $150.

Howe immediately appealed, exercising an automatic right to have a new trial in state court with an eight-member jury. The defense had called no witnesses during the trial. The prosecution case relied mainly on testimony by two part-time policewomen who had arrested Howe while they were on duty as prostitute decoys in Salt Lake City's red-light district.

A jury of five men and three women Aug. 24 rejected Howe's bid to reverse his conviction.

The jury deliberated less than half an hour before rejecting Howe's explanation that he had gone to Salt Lake City's red light district to attend a party where he could "shake some hands, meet some good people and win some votes." He maintained that he had fallen into a conversation with the decoys under the misconception that they might be going to the party too.

Howe was sentenced Aug. 25 to 30 days in jail and court costs, the jail term to be suspended on the payment of the costs.

Rep. Richmond's plea on sex charge. Rep. Frederick W. Richmond (D, N.Y.) pleaded not guilty in Superior Court in Washington April 6, 1978 to a misdemeanor count of sexual solicitation.

In a statement released April 5, Richmond admitted that he had offered money for sex to an undercover male police officer in February. Richmond, 54, also said he had "made solicitations with payment of money to a young man beginning almost a year ago."

The charge related only to the incident with the police officer.

After making his plea, Richmond was enrolled in a treatment program for first offenders. The prosecutor's office said that the charge would be dismissed if Richmond complied with the requirements of the treatment program. This was the customary procedure for first offenders, a government spokesman said.

Twenty members of the New York delegation to the House of Representatives issued a statement April 6 in which they expressed "compassion and understanding" for the Brooklyn representative. They called Richmond "one of the most effective and hard-working members of Congress."

Other Developments

Travel expense probe. The Justice Department announced Oct. 27, 1976 that Rep. William L. Clay (D, Mo.) had made "full restitution" of disputed travel funds that he had received from Congress, and that the department accordingly would drop a suit against the congressman. At the same time, the agency named nine other House members whose claims for travel expenses had been under investigation. They were: Ray J. Madden (D, Ind.); Margaret M. Heckler (R, Mass.); Tim Lee Carter (R, Ky.); Walter Flowers (D, Ala.); Otto E. Passman (D, La.); Bill D. Burlison (D, Mo.); George E. Shipley (D, Ill.); Robert E. Jones (D, Ala.), and Gene Taylor (R, Mo.).

The department, without specifying individuals, said that restitution "where appropriate" had been made to the government, and that therefore no suit would be brought against any congressmen.

The sum Clay repaid was $1,754.24. (The suit against Clay originally had been brought by a law student, acting under a federal law that permitted a taxpayer to sue "on behalf of the United States" to recover government money obtained through false claims. The Justice Department later had taken over the suit.)

The Wall Street Journal had reported March 23 that Congress had repaid Clay for trips to his home district of St. Louis that, according to the vouchers he submitted, took place at the same time or overlapped with trips made to other destinations. The dates of some other reimbursed trips, the Journal said, coincided with roll-call votes at which Clay had been present.

Clay March 23 denied that he had billed Congress for any trips not actually made. Vouchers, he noted, were often submitted some time after trips were made, and clerical errors could have caused the inconsistencies in dates.

Another type of Congressional travel expense often criticized was luxury travel aboard military planes at military expense. Rep. Robert J. Lagomarsino (R, Calif.) inserted in the Congressional Record Oct. 4, 1977 a Santa Barbara News-Press article in which Jerry Rankin discussed some of these criticized expenses.

According to Rankin, "the military planes the politicians and their parties travel on are well stocked with food and liquor, but the bill is paid by military congressional liaison money . . . [and the committee] thus doesn't have to report it. . . ."

Rankin reported that when Lagomarsino and six other Congressmen toured the Mideast Jan. 3–16, 1976, "their military VC-137 jet was stocked . . . with $422.30 worth of liquor and mix. . . . Another $372.49 was spent . . . to stock the plane with frozen food, including chocolate eclaires, fruit, different types of cake and pies, vegetables, beef stroganoff, veal parmesan and pigs in blankets. In all, the military laid out $1,690.38 just to stock the plane during the trip. On the return leg, the plane landed in Naples Jan. 14 and supplies were made available by the Navy captain escorting the trip for consumption there and on the return journey. He paid $425.25 for: 12 bottles of Old Forester, 24 of Johnnie Walker Black Scotch, 12 of Tanqueray gin, 12 of Smirnoff vodka, 12 of Jack Daniels Black bourbon, one bottle of Martini & Rossi vermouth, one of Bacardi rum, a six-pack of Old Milwaukee beer, plus mixers and nuts. The previous night, the military spent $51 in Athens for 10 bottles of whisky, a case of beer, a case of Coke and three cartons of cigarettes for the group. In total, the military paid $4,838.46 on that trip . . . for meals and beverages, in addition to money spent for regular meals by the congressmen out of their $75 daily living expense allowance."

Rankin added that Lagomarsino's wife went along on the trip, "but her expenses are paid entirely by Lagomarsino on such trips, including her air fare."

Brooke admits false disclosure. Sen. Edward W. Brooke (R, Mass.) conceded May 26, 1978 that he gave false information about a $49,000 loan in a sworn deposition taken in 1977 for his divorce proceedings.

In the deposition, Brooke said he had accepted a total of $49,000 in interest-free loans from a long-time friend, A. Raymond Tye, a Massachusetts liquor distributor.

The loan did not show up, however, in the public financial disclosure report Brooke filed with the Senate on May 11, although loans of more than $2,500 were required to be listed.

The omission, disclosed by the Boston Globe, led to Brooke's admission that he had made "a misstatement and a mistake" in the deposition.

Only $2,000 of the $49,000 personal loan came from Tye, Brooke said, and $47,000 came from his mother-in-law, since deceased. The funds from Brooke's mother-in-law derived from an insurance settlement of $100,000 on an automobile accident.

The money was turned over to him and he spent it "according to her wishes," Brooke said, including medical and funeral bills.

Some $30,000 of the personal loan was still outstanding, Brooke said, and "I always intended in my head and heart to pay it back."

He had not put it this way in the deposition, he said, because "I didn't want to get into the whole thing of family obligations" during the divorce proceedings.

He denied that he was trying to hide the money from his wife and insisted that he intended to distribute the money to his mother-in-law's heirs after the divorce became final.

The mistake he made in the deposition, he said, "was in the person to whom" the liabilities were owed.

Brooke denied that this constituted perjury since he had revealed the sum of his personal liabilities. He contended the deposition had no legal standing because he did not sign it and it was never used in court.

Brooke's accounting could clarify the omission of the loan from his Senate report, since loans from relatives need not be reported. But the question of possible perjury for a false statement on a sworn deposition remained.

Corporate Funds & Political Favors

Improper Payments Under Attack

Bribery of government officials for business reasons is an ancient practice. In some parts of the world it is so traditional as to be virtually respectable, although illegal. In the United States, bribery and illegal political contributions also have a long tradition although they are not respectable.

Fresh attempts were made in the mid-1970s to root out these illegal activities. These efforts owed much of their impetus to the revelations of the Watergate period and to discoveries not only that American corporations were making questionable political payments to win foreign business but also that many U.S. firms were using illegal "slush" funds for illegal political contributions at home.

$412 million in questionable payments. Between 1970 and 1976, 233 U.S. companies had disclosed making $412 million in questionable payments, according to a private study reported by the Wall Street Journal Jan. 21, 1977.

The analysis, by Charles E. Simon & Co. of Washington, was based on information filed with the Securities and Exchange Commission. Included in the payments total were agents' fees, commissions and over-billing, which, the research firm said, "may not be deemed improper."

According to the study, an additional 55 companies had admitted making questionable payments but had not disclosed the amounts.

Seventy of the 233 firms that specified the dollar amounts accounted for nearly 90% of the payments reported. (Ten companies disbursed 57% of the total.) Boeing Co., which had admitted making $70 million in questionable payments, topped the list. Others making large payments were Exxon Corp., $46 million; Northrop Corp., nearly $32 million; Lockheed Aircraft Corp., $25 million, and Armco Steel Corp., $17.5 million.

An earlier study, undertaken by the Library of Congress and made public Nov. 17, 1975, found that since only January of that year, more than 20 U.S. firms had admitted making about $306 million in questionable payments in the U.S. and abroad.

Among the illegal payments listed in the report were fees and commissions paid to overseas agents, bribes, kickbacks, political contributions and laundered funds. Also included in the total were questionable payments made to agents and political figures. Not included were payments that had been admitted, but had not been quantified. The report was prepared at the request of Rep. Les Aspin (D, Wis.), who released the findings.

Lockheed Aircraft Corp., the nation's largest defense contractor, made the largest amount of questionable payments, according to the report. Lockheed admitted paying $22 million to foreign officials and political groups abroad in connection with its foreign sales, particularly the sale of its F-111 fighter bomber, and $202 million to foreign consultants.

The next-largest payment, $30 million, was made by Northrop Corp., also a defense contractor and Lockheed's competitor in the sale of a fighter bomber to NATO. Ranked third was Gulf Oil Corp., which admitted paying $5 million abroad and in the U.S.

Other corporations cited in the 1975 report included General Motors Corp., McDonnell Douglas Corp., United Brands Corp., Occidental Petroleum Corp., Exxon Corp., Phillips Petroleum Co., Cities Service Co., Ford Motor Co., and Chrysler Corp.

Another study of business payoffs overseas was made by Business International, a private research group in New York that produced its report for its corporate clients. The study, reported in the New York Times Dec. 20, 1976, was based on confidential interviews with executives of 55 multinational corporations in the U.S., Canada and Europe.

The report concluded that the pattern of corporate bribery and payoff of foreign officials and agents was deeply embedded in international business. The practice was not confined to U.S. firms, the report stated. "The most important element by far in setting payments pattern is the attitude of the host country," the study said. The second most important factor was the nature of the industry involved.

In addition to the four industries cited in the council's report—drugs, oil and gas, aerospace and chemicals—Business International added construction, communications, automobiles and shipping as most likely to make questionable payments.

These industries were cited because their sales hinged largely on decisions made by government officials or purchasing agent who were in a position to demand payoffs. These sales also were of such a magnitude that it was relatively easy to hide a kickback in the purchase price.

The inquiries into questionable political payments abroad frequently produced information on illegal payments made to U.S. political groups. The revelations helped spur a growing attack on politico-corporate corruption in the U.S. and the movement to improve ethical standards in American government.

Corporate bribery ban passed. Legislation barring U.S. corporations from bribing foreign officials was passed by Senate voice vote Dec. 6, 1977 and by 349-0 vote of the House Dec. 7.

Under the bill, a corporation could be fined up to $1 million for paying bribes to foreign government or political party officials, or to foreign political candidates. Corporate officers or employes involved in the bribing would also be subject to penalties, with a maximum prison sentence of five years and fine of $10,000.

Prompting the legislation were disclosures that over 350 U.S. firms had made questionable payments to foreign officials to obtain business.

Bribes were defined in the bill as money paid to close business deals. Sponsors of the bill said that the wording meant that a corporation would still be able to make small "grease" payments to minor functionaries for such purposes as expediting customs clearances.

The bill's penalties would not apply to foreign subsidiaries of U.S. companies. However, officials of the parent U.S. firm could be prosecuted if they were aware of the bribes.

The bill also mandated certain reforms in corporate accounting practices. The purpose of this provision was to make it more difficult to disguise or obscure slush funds that were used to finance bribes.

Contractor largess attacked. Sen. William Proxmire (D, Wis.) Oct. 24, 1977 charged that major defense and space contractors commonly provided free entertainment to government officials in an attempt to create an atmosphere of goodwill that would aid the firms in contract negotiations. The corporate gratuities—which included meals, sports tickets and hunting trips—were forbidden by Defense Department regulations.

Proxmire based his charge on a study,

covering the period 1973–75, by the Joint Congressional Committee on Defense Production. The study, Proxmire said, showed that the practice of providing free entertainment to government officials was "much more pervasive . . . than previously suspected."

Proxmire said that although individual gratuities were not large, the total corporate largess "probably exceeds several million dollars annually."

Proxmire said that previous congressional inquiries in 1967 and 1959 had resulted in merely temporary reductions of corporate gift-giving because the Defense Department lacked a firm commitment to preventing conflict-of-interest situations.

Companies Under Fire

Northrop secret fund alleged. A vice president of Northrop Corp., a major defense contractor, admitted that the Los Angeles-based firm maintained a secret $1.2 million fund for political purposes, according to the New York Times Oct. 11, 1974.

The disclosure was made in an unsigned deposition given by James Allen in connection with a shareholders' suit filed after the firm, Allen and Thomas V. Jones, Northrop chairman and chief executive, pleaded guilty in May to violating a federal law barring campaign contributions from federal contractors.

According to the civil suit filed in May, the illegal donations were concealed from shareholders by falsifying corporate documents as part of a complex international scheme to "launder" the donations. The class action suit was brought by the Center for Law in the Public Interest.

An affidavit filed by Northrop shareholders based on the Allen deposition and others given by company officials, contended that "secret campaign contributions were begun in 1961 and have been made in virtually every federal campaign since 1961." The fund reportedly was used to aid Richard Nixon in 1968 and 1972, and Sen. Hubert Humphrey (D,

Minn.) in 1968 when he was the Democratic presidential nominee. At least five other California candidates for federal and state office (of both parties) also received contributions from the Northrop fund, according to court documents.

The affidavit, which was sealed Oct. 10 by federal district court in Los Angeles, stated that Allen had identified William A. Savy as the person responsible for laundering the corporate funds. Savy, Northrop's Paris-based consultant whom Allen had hired in 1961, had also been identified in a report prepared by the Senate Watergate Committee.

The Securities & Exchange Commission accused Northrop April 16, 1975 of maintaining a $30 million slush fund for "unlawful political contributions and other unlawful purposes."

The SEC charges, contained in a complaint filed with U.S. District Court in New York, also named Jones and Allen.

According to the SEC complaint, Northrop's involvement in illegal campaign funding activities was far larger than previously indicated. The SEC charged that beginning in 1961, Northrop, Jones and Allen caused "in excess of $76,-000 in corporate funds to be paid for political contributions and related expenses, a substantial portion of which was unlawful."

The money was laundered through over-payments made in Paris to Savy, who converted the disbursements to cash and returned the money to an agent in New York, the complaint stated. Allen then picked up the cash from this agent, according to the SEC.

The Northrop slush fund was greatly expanded from 1971 through 1973, according to the SEC, until "approximately $30 million in Northrop corporate monies was or would be disbursed."

Northrop settled the SEC suit April 17 without admitting or denying the charges. The defendants accepted a permanent decree barring them from making false entries in corporate books and from maintaining any secret or unrecorded fund of corporate monies or assets.

In a statement issued with the settlement announcement, Northrop said that the $30 million fund "consists of fees and sales commissions that have been or will be paid over a number of years in relation to sales of company products and services abroad totaling $777.4 million."

Northrop, convicted of making an illegal $150,000 donation to the Nixon re-election campaign, also distributed $250,000 in illegal cash contributions to Democratic and Republican political figures from 1962 to 1973, according to documents filed with the SEC.

Disclosure of Northrop's additional political payments was made to the SEC in 1974 in a special audit report prepared by Ernst & Ernst, an accounting firm hired by the company to investigate its secret slush fund transactions. Northrop had agreed early in 1975 to make the disclosures as part settlement of a stockholder's suit, filed in connection with the illegal Nixon gift.

A breakdown of the political payments, based on the Ernst & Ernst report filed with the SEC, appeared May 6, 1975 in the Washington Post and May 6 and 8 in the New York Times. According to the Post, the accounting firm was advised by a Washington law firm that of the $338,000 in donations made through the slush fund and uncovered in the audit, some $250,000 in contributions were believed to violate the 1971 federal campaign law. No determination was made whether Northrop's political contributions may have violated other federal or state laws, the Post reported.

Among the candidates for federal office who received the Northrop payments:

Sen. Alan Cranston (D, Calif.), a total of $26,200 for the years 1966, 1968, 1972, and 1973; former President Richard M. Nixon, $10,000 for his 1968 campaign; former Sen. George Murphy (R, Calif.), $8,000 for 1970; Sen. Hubert H. Humphrey (D, Minn.), $6,175 for 1966 and 1968; Rep. Charles H. Wilson (D, Calif.), a member of the House Armed Services Committee, $2,350 for 1966, 1971, and 1973; Sen. John V. Tunney (D, Calif.), $2,000 in 1970; the late Sen. Richard Russell (D, Ga.), former chairman of the Senate Armed Services Committee, $1,000 in 1966; Sen. Henry M. Jackson (D, Wash.), $1,000 for his presidential bid in 1972; Sen. Mike Mansfield (D, Mont.), $250 in 1964; and former Sen. Thomas H. Kuchel (R, Calif.), $250 in 1964.

Eugene Wyman, a prominent Democratic fund raiser in California, was given $20,000 for the years 1962-1973 and Holmes Tuttle, a Republican fund raiser in the state, received $30,000 over those years.

Candidates for state office in California who received Northrop payments: former Gov. Ronald Reagan (R), $6,000 in 1970; former Gov. Edmund G. Brown (D), $5,000 in 1966; Treasurer Jess Unruh, $1,085 in 1970; Gov. Edmund G. Brown Jr. (D), $800 in 1970 when he ran for secretary of state; and Mayor Thomas Bradley (D, Los Angeles) $100 for his unsuccessful 1969 mayoralty bid.

Pentagon's hospitality users. The Defense Department Nov. 11, 1975 sent letters of reprimand to 22 employes who had visited a Maryland hunting lodge as guests of Northrop. The 22 military personnel were among a group of 170, which included members of Congress, who had used a goose-hunting lodge provided by the defense contractor.

A Pentagon spokesman said the 22 government employes also had been reprimanded privately for their "severe error of judgment in conflict with the existing rules of the department."

The Pentagon notified Sen. William Proxmire (D, Wis.), chairman of a Senate subcommittee investigating alleged improprieties in the relationship between defense contractors and the Defense Department, that it had taken formal action against Pentagon personnel.

Proxmire had sharply criticized an earlier finding by the Pentagon's acting general counsel that more than 40 high-ranking military officers and civilians who had accepted Northrop's hospitality between October 1971 and January 1974 "weren't necessarily in technical violation" of the Pentagon's rules barring officials from accepting any gift, gratuity, entertainment or favor from government contractors.

Most were personal friends of Northrop employes and accepted the invitation "on a social basis," the counsel said in a letter Oct. 3 to three congressional committees.

Proxmire termed the finding an "obvious whitewash" and an "absurdity."

With congressional criticism mounting,

James R. Schlesinger, then defense secretary, Oct. 6 ordered a "broad inquiry" into the gratuity issue.

Newsday reported Nov. 1 that Schlesinger had reversed the counsel's ruling and formally reprimanded a top aide, Erich F. von Marbod, for violating the "spirit" of the department's code-of-conduct rules. Newsday also reported that von Marbod had been reassigned recently to Iran as the Pentagon's representative for arms sales made there by U.S. firms, including Northrop.

The Pentagon announced Nov. 25 that it had tightened its policy against acceptance of gratuities offered by defense contractors, and had expanded the number of military officers required to submit financial statements.

According to Proxmire's investigative subcommittee Oct. 22, Northrop was not the only defense contractor that had entertained Pentagon officials at hunting lodges. Lockheed Aircraft Corp., Rockwell International, Raytheon Co. and Martin Marietta Corp. also were cited. General Dynamics Corp. was added to the list Oct. 24.

Proxmire charged Oct. 18 that Rockwell also had entertained employes of the National Aeronautics and Space Administration. The company held a $6.4 billion NASA contract to develop a space shuttle.

Four months later Defense Secretary Donald Rumsfeld March 16, 1976 issued a reprimand to the Pentagon's chief of research and engineering, Malcolm R. Currie, and admonished Navy Secretary J.. William Middendorf 2nd for visiting fishing and hunting lodges operated by Rockwell International Corp.

Currie, the 4th ranking official at the Pentagon, also was ordered to forfeit about four weeks pay, totaling $3,200, and reimburse Rockwell for all expenses incurred during a two-day stay at a fishing lodge on Bimini Island in the Bahamas.

The Pentagon said Currie, his daughter and an unidentified friend spent the 1975 Labor Day weekend at the lodge with Rockwell chairman Robert B. Anderson, his wife and two daughters. According to the Pentagon, "at no time was any official or corporate business or either the department or Rockwell discussed." Anderson

was said to be a long-time personal and business friend.

Middendorf received a "letter of admonition" from Rumsfeld, a less serious form of reproof than Currie received. Middendorf was admonished for accepting an invitation from Ardeshir Zahedi, the Iranian ambassador to Washington, to spend a day at a hunting lodge in Maryland. According to the Pentagon, Middendorf was unaware until recently that Rockwell leased the lodge.

Rockwell was the principal contractor for the Air Force's new B-1 bomber. Because it was still in the development stage, the project was within Currie's purview as director of research. Currie had been expected to participate in the Pentagon's decision later in 1976 whether to put the plane into production.

The Currie-Middendorf case was embarrassing to the Pentagon because Deputy Defense Secretary William P. Clements Jr. had declared in October 1975 that the department's civilian and military employes "must be above reproach" and "avoid even the appearance of a conflict of interest" by not accepting hospitality, gratuities, or favors from defense contractors. (Middendorf's visit to the Maryland lodge reportedly occurred the same day Clements issued a "standards of conduct" memo to service secretaries.)

At a news conference in February, Rumsfeld reiterated Clements' warning and said he would "land all over individuals" who violated the department's rules. Rumsfeld reportedly considered firing Currie to emphasize the department's displeasure over the incident.

Rockwell March 17 informed Sen. Proxmire that the chairman of the Joint Chiefs of Staff and the director of the Defense Intelligence Agency had been among 41 military and civilian employes of the Department of Defense who had been guests of the company at its Maryland hunting lodge between 1973 and 1975.

Named were Adm. Thomas H. Moorer, who retired as chairman in June 1974, and Vice Adm. Vincent de Poix, former director of the DIA.

A Pentagon spokesman said that Rockwell's list was being studied to see if disciplinary action should be taken against any of the group.

Rockwell's list of 39 Pentagon guests was in addition to another list that Proxmire provided the department Feb. 3 after Clements contended the Pentagon had been unable to determine who had been entertained at the Rockwell lodge. Proxmire's list, culled from hunting licenses and other records, named 55 high-ranking Pentagon employes.

Secret Gulf political fund charged. The Securities and Exchange Commission March 11, 1975 accused Gulf Oil Corp. and its former vice president, Claude D. Wild Jr., of funnelling more than $10 million through a wholly owned Gulf subsidiary, Bahamas Explorations Co. Ltd., from which secret political contributions were made beginning in 1960.

Gulf signed a consent agreement without admitting or denying the charges but Wild chose to contest the charges.

According to the SEC, at least $5.4 million was returned to the U.S. from the now-defunct Bahamiam firm. Most of the money was disbursed as illegal campaign contributions, the SEC charged. The remainder of the fund was distributed abroad by Gulf and unidentified "others."

According to testimony taken by the Senate Watergate Committee, Wild, who had headed Gulf's Washington office, decided which political candidates should receive donations from Gulf. He then ordered William C. Viglia, comptroller of the Bahamas firm, to send him the desired amount of cash for disbursal as contributions.

Company records showed that the board of directors of the Bahamas firm voted Aug. 7, 1973 to cease operations of the company. That date was three days before Gulf voluntarily disclosed to the Watergate special prosecutor's office that an illegal $100,000 contribution had been made to the Nixon re-election campaign and contributions totaling $25,000 had been given to two Democratic candidates for the presidential nomination. Gulf and Wild later pleaded guilty to violating the federal campaign finance law.

The SEC named Viglia as disburser of the $5.4 million and also claimed that

Royce H. Savage, former general counsel and director of the Bahamas company, also had known of the contributions. Neither man was charged in the SEC complaint. Savage currently was serving as court-appointed trustee of the bankrupt Home Stake Production Co.

In accepting the consent judgment, filed with U.S. District Court in Washington, Gulf revealed that a special committee, headed by John J. McCloy, former U.S. high commissioner in Germany and former chairman of Chase Manhattan Bank, had been established to review the company's investigation of its corporate contributions.

McCloy report details political payments —Gulf Oil Corp. made political contributions in the U.S. and abroad totaling $12.3 million, most of it donated illegally and funneled through a slush fund maintained at Gulf's Bahamian subsidiary, from the early 1960s to the early 1970s, according to the special panel headed by John McCloy.

Gulf quickly accepted a consent order settling the complaint and agreed not to violate securities laws in the future. Gulf also accepted the SEC's chief condition for the settlement and agreed to an independent examination of Gulf's books and management to reveal the full extent of the company's unlawful contributions. The special review panel's report was filed with the SEC and with U.S. District Court in Washington Dec. 30, 1975 in compliance with the terms of settlement.

The report also was submitted to Gulf's board of directors and provided the basis for the board's subsequent ouster of Gulf chairman Bob R. Dorsey and three other top officials of the company.

Noting that 11 company executives admitted having some knowledge of the covert transfer of Gulf funds through the Bahamian slush fund, the McCloy report said, "The pattern and nature of this use of corporate funds, in large part not recorded on the books of the company, has raised serious questions as to the policy and management of the company in regard to this matter."

The panel was unable to prove that Dorsey was aware that Gulf's former vice president in Washington, Claude C. Wild Jr., was illegally distributing more than $5 million in laundered corporate cash to politicians; however, the report "concluded that Dorsey was not sufficiently alert and should have known Wild was involved in making political contributions from an unknown source."

"If Dorsey did not know of the nature and extent of Wild's unlawful activities," the report continued, "he perhaps shut his eyes to what was going on. Had he been more alert to the problem, he was in a ready position to inquire about it and put an end to it."

The panel also blamed E. D. Brockett, who had preceded Dorsey as Gulf chairman, for failing to question Wild's "extracurricular" activities.

Of the 11 executives with direct knowledge of the slush fund, only two remained with the company, the report stated, three having died and six retired.

The two men, William L. Henry and Fred Deering, both vice presidents of Gulf and former comptrollers with the company, denied "knowledge that company funds were being used for domestic political contributions," according to the report.

However, the commission concluded that Henry "had an obligation" as comptroller to question the covert transactions, and that Deering, also while comptroller, "did not act in a manner consistent with the responsibilities of his office in connection with the transfer of funds to the Bahamas."

Herbert C. Manning, a lawyer and secretary of the company, also was blamed for failing to make inquiries about the source of funds used to make donations. Henry, Deering and Manning were dismissed by Gulf's board in the shakeup resulting from Dorsey's ouster.

The commission was unable to pinpoint when the Bahamian slush fund was created, but believed it occurred around 1960. One of the former company officials said to have knowledge of the fund told the commission that the late William K. Whiteford, then chairman of Gulf, established the fund in 1960 "to help maintain a political atmosphere conducive to [Gulf's] foreign expansion plans" and "to give the company some 'muscle' in [domestic] politics."

The commission offered several recommendations to prevent a recurrence of the political payments scandal. These included prohibiting the use of "off-the-book [unrecorded] funds, whether legal or not"; strengthening the company's internal audit department; and giving the company's chief legal officer direct access to the chief executive and charging the lawyer with the "responsibility of calling to the attention of management any operations of the company which ... constitute illegal political activities."

The commission acknowledged, however, that these safeguards would not necessarily prevent future abuses. "The illegal use of corporate funds for political purposes was originally instituted by the top management of Gulf and in the last analysis it will be in the tone and attitude of top management that the eradication of the practice will be insured in the future," the report stated.

The commission said it was unable to trace most of the $5.4 million that the SEC said was donated illegally to U.S. politicians. However, the panel concluded that the domestic contributions made by Gulf were "shot through with illegalities."

Although the commission was unable to prove that politicians knowingly accepted corporate cash in violation of federal laws, the report said, "It is hard to escape the conclusion that a sort of 'shut-eyed sentry' attitude prevailed upon the part of both the corporate officials and the recipients as well as on the part of those charged with enforcement responsibility."

Senate Minority Leader Hugh Scott (R, Pa.) was among those whom company officials said had received laundered cash from the slush fund—$5,000 in the spring and $5,000 in the fall of each year for several years. The report noted that Scott had filed a written statement with the commission denying he "knowingly" received illegal contributions.

(The Senate Ethics Committee said Feb. 4 it was working with the Justice Department, the SEC, and the Internal Revenue Service on an "in-depth investigation" of the charges against Scott and several other senators who allegedly received Gulf donations.)

The commission's estimate of Gulf's total political payments differed from the SEC's figure because the report disclosed payments made in Sweden, Canada and Italy that were termed legal.

Wild acquitted—Former Gulf Vice President Claude C. Wild Jr. was acquitted July 27, 1976 of charges of having made an illegal contribution in 1973 to the campaign of Sen. Daniel K. Inouye (D, Hawaii). The court ruled that in Wild's case the three-year statute of limitations governing campaign contributions had expired.

Federal Judge Joseph C. Waddy of U.S. District Court in Washington, who heard the case without a jury at the defense's request, ruled that the Watergate special prosecutor's office had failed to prove that Wild made the contribution in the three years prior to his indictment March 12.

(Waddy June 24 dismissed another count against Wild involving an illegal contribution made to Sen. Sam Nunn's [D, Ga.] 1972 campaign. Waddy ruled that Wild's statute of limitations waiver on the Nunn donation was ineffective.)

During the two-day trial, Wild admitted that he had acted illegally in giving $5,000 in cash on Gulf's behalf to Inouye's 1974 re-election campaign on the condition that the money not be reported, as required by federal law. Wild testified, however, that the money was turned over to Inouye's administrative assistant, Henry Giugni, before Feb. 7, 1973.

The Senate Watergate Committee was established on that date. Inouye was a member of the committee. Speaking of the donation, Wild testified, "I just thought it would be too sensitive a matter to get involved in after Feb. 7."

Giugni, who said he had solicited the money from Wild in December 1972, testified that he had received the cash in March or April 1973, a period that fell within the statute of limitations.

In ending the trial, Waddy said he "found the evidence of the defendant worthy of greater credence than that of Mr. Giugni."

Giugni admitted during the trial that he had committed perjury in September 1975 before a federal grand jury investigating his handling of the Gulf contribution.

Giugni said he had discussed the Wild donation with Inouye for the first time after Giugni's grand jury appearance. (Inouye, who also took the stand during the Wild trial, testified that he had received $1,200 in cash from Giugni for campaign expenses in April, May and June 1973, but never asked the source of the cash.)

Giugni said that after his talk with Inouye and with the prosecutor's office, he had returned to the grand jury with immunity and testified truthfully about the Wild donation.

After months of negotiations, with the prosecutor's office, Wild appeared before the grand jury in January 1976 and testified with immunity on all 1973 contributions he had made on Gulf's behalf, except the Inouye donation.

During his trial, Wild said he had told the prosecutor's office of eight senators and representatives who had received up to $5,000 from him in 1973. Only one member of Congress had been indicted as a result of Wild's alleged testimony—Rep. James R. Jones (D, Okla.), who pleaded guilty in January.

While the special prosecutor's office was investigating illegal corporate contributions to legislators, Congress had passed a new campaign fund law that reduced the statute of limitations on illegal donations from five years to three years.

Viglia sentenced—A federal court in Tulsa Aug. 4, 1976 sentenced William C. Viglia, 71, a former Gulf official, to a year in jail for his part in making illegal corporate contributions.

Viglia, who the SEC said had acted as Wild's courier in handling the cash contributions, was the only Gulf official to receive a jail sentence in connection with the payments.

Charge vs. Dole withdrawn—Sen. Robert J. Dole (Kan.), then Republican candidate for vice president, was accused Sept. 6, 1976 of campaign-fund irregularity, but the accuser quickly withdrew the charge.

The charge was made by Claude C. Wild Jr., who said he had given Dole $2,000 in cash in 1970 to distribute to Republican candidates. The contribution had surfaced several days earlier in a report on Gulf's secret fund for political contributions.

Dole denied receiving any money from Gulf Oil or Wild. The contribution itself, as described, was legal, but if received, it would have entailed an illegality by Dole for failing to register as a campaign committee.

Dole also denied reports, emanating from a federal grand jury investigation in January of Gulf Oil's political contributions, of a secret Gulf Oil contribution of some $5,000–$6,000 allegedly given by Wild to Dole's aide William A. Kats in 1973. Kats said he could not recall receiving the funds from Wild. Such a contribution was required to have been reported under the Federal Elections Law.

Wild announced Sept. 8 that he was in error about the 1970 contribution of $2,000 to Dole. He issued a public apology to the senator.

Gulf fined for laundering money—The Treasury Department Nov. 13, 1977 imposed a $229,000 civil penalty on Gulf Oil in connection with Gulf's illegal campaign contributions made in 1972.

Gulf was fined for violating the 1972 Bank Secrecy Act, which required the reporting of any transactions between the U.S. and a foreign country that involved $5,000 or more. Gulf had admitted concealing its illegal payments by secretly channeling them through a subsidiary in the Bahamas.

According to the Treasury, the penalty represented 90% of the money brought into the U.S. after the law took effect in July 1972. The fine was the largest ever imposed under the law, which had been designed to catch drug smugglers.

Gulf indicted for IRS gratuities—Gulf Oil and two of its tax executives were indicted June 15, 1977, by a federal grand jury in Pittsburgh on charges of "providing illegal gratuities" to an Internal Revenue Service supervisor.

The supervisor, Cyril J. Niederberger, since retired, had been convicted earlier of allowing Gulf to pay for family vacations taken while he was auditing the oil company's books.

SEC charges Phillips Petroleum. The Securities and Exchange Commission March 6, 1975 accused the Phillips Petroleum Co. and four of its current and former officers of illegally diverting more than $2.8 million in corporate money since 1963 to a secret political fund

from which it made illegal political donations.

Named as defendants, accused of falsifying company financial records to conceal the slush fund, were Phillips chairman William F. Martin, vice president Carstens Slack, and two former chairman, William W. Keeler and John M. Houchin. (Houchin currently also served as a director.)

Phillips and the four men consented to a court order enjoining them from further securities law violations, but the defendants neither admitted nor denied the SEC charges. However, in consenting to the court order, Phillips agreed to investigate the illegal activity and report its findings to the SEC.

According to the SEC complaint, filed in U.S. District Court in Washington, Phillips channeled more than $2.8 million in corporate funds to two Swiss corporations which returned $1.3 million in cash to the U.S. The remainder "was distributed overseas in cash," according to the SEC. (Disposition of the money abroad was not revealed.) Of the $1.3 million returned to the U.S., "$600,000 was expended for political contributions and related expenses, a substantial portion of which was unlawful," the SEC charged.

Phillips and Keeler were convicted in December 1973 of illegally donating $100,000 in corporate funds to the Nixon re-election campaign.

In a disclosure that was made later, Phillips admitted that secret contributions totaling $585,000 also had been made to other political candidates from a secret fund. In making the disclosure, the firm also said that more than $700,000 remaining in the slush fund had been discovered in a company safe and had been returned to the corporate treasury.

The SEC asked the court to order the four defendants to repay the $2.8 million diverted out of the company.

Ex-officers settle—Phillips Petroleum said it had been paid $150,000 by William F. Martin as well as four of its former officers to release claims the company might have against it in connection with $395,000 maintained in a cash fund used to make apparently illegal political contributions, the Wall Street Journal reported March 31.

Others party to the agreement were K. S. Adams, Stanley Learned and William W. Keeler, all former chief executives, and John M. Houchin, a director and former deputy chief executive. Disclosure of the arrangement was made in a report on the firm's political contributions that was distributed to stockholders with a proxy statement for the annual meeting.

According to the special report, about $585,000 in corporate funds was contributed from 1964 through 1973. (That was about $100,000 less than Phillips originally reported in an earlier statement that had been sent to shareholders. Out of the total, about $90,000 was contributed to candidates in states that permitted corporate donations, the report stated.

Of the $495,000 in apparently illegal contributions, a $100,000 contribution to the Nixon re-election campaign was recovered, leaving a $395,000 balance. (Nixon fund raisers returned the money after the Watergate Special prosecutor brought charges against Phillips regarding the illegal donation.)

According to the Phillips report, the only disbursements from the cash fund, which was generated from foreign operations, were for political contributions. The report also revealed the existence of several other unrecorded funds of corporate money or assets totaling about $200,000. The funds were obtained in foreign transactions and used abroad in connection with the operation of foreign subsidiaries, according to the report. The funds currently were recorded on the books of appropriate subsidiaries, Phillips said.

The special investigating committee that prepared the report recommended that no further action be taken against chairman Martin because his actions related to the cash fund "amounted for the most part to acquiescence in a program which had been earlier instituted by his superiors." The investigating committee also recommended that no action be taken against Carstens Slack, Phillips'

Washington-based vice president, because, although he distributed some of the political contributions, he "had no knowledge that the funds belonged to the company."

Recipients listed—In a report filed Sept. 26 with the SEC, Phillips Petroleum listed the recipients of $585,000 in largely illegal campaign contributions that it made during 1964–72.

Among the candidates that Phillips supported were President Gerald Ford and former Presidents Richard Nixon and Lyndon Johnson. Johnson received $25,000 for his 1964 presidential campaign. Nixon got $50,000 for his 1968 race and another $100,000 in 1972. Phillips admitted giving a total of $125,000 to Congressional candidates, including President Ford, who received $2,000 in both 1970 and 1972 when he ran for reelection to the House from Michigan.

It was Phillips' admission in 1973 of making the illegal $100,000 donation that led to further disclosures about its secret cash fund and prosecution by the Watergate special prosecutor's office for violating federal campaign finance laws.

The SEC also accused Phillips and four of its officers of falsifying company records to conceal the illegal contributions. Without admitting or denying the charges, the defendants accepted a consent decree barring further violations of securities laws and agreed to file a full report on its activities with the SEC and the court. The list of recipients was prepared to comply with that settlement.

In its report, Phillips also said it spent about $70,000 on tickets for political dinners and contributed $215,000 to candidates for state office, chiefly in Texas, Oklahoma and Alaska where the oil company had business interests. Phillips was based in Bartlesville, Okla.

All but $90,000 of the $585,000 in campaign contributions were made illegally. (Candidates for federal and most state offices were barred from accepting corporate contributions.) Most of the legal contributions were made to Oklahoma candidates for state office.

Phillips said there was no evidence that candidates who accepted the donations knew the money was contributed illegally.

The funds, which were donated in the name of "friends at Phillips," were handled in such a manner as to avoid disclosure under reporting requirements of campaign finance laws.

Phillips said that since no written records were kept on the contributions, they had been unable to reconstruct a complete list. In preparing the report for the SEC, Phillips relied on the memories of such company officials as former president William W. Keeler, convicted of making the illegal $100,000 donation to the Nixon campaign, and Carstens Slack, vice president in charge of Phillips' Washington office, who was named with Keeler in the SEC complaint:

Details of the Phillips list:

Receiving $1,900 each in 1972 were Sen. Howard H. Baker Jr. (R, Tenn.); Sen. Robert P. Griffin (R, Mich.); Sen. James A. McClure (R, Idaho); Sen. Sam Nunn (D, Ga.); and Wesley Powell, who ran unsuccessfully for the Senate seat from New Hampshire.

Ten successful senatorial candidates received $1,000 each in 1972; former Sen. Gordon Allott (R, Colo.); Sen. Carl Curtis (R, Neb.); Sen. Clifford P. Hansen (R, Wyo.); Sen. Mark O. Hatfield (R, Ore.); former Sen. B. Everett Jordan (D, N.C.); former Sen. Jack Miller (R, Iowa); Sen. James B. Pearson (R, Kan.); Sen. Jennings Randolph (D, W. Va.); Sen. Strom Thurmond (R, S.C.); and Sen. John G. Tower (R, Tex.). Another $1,000 contribution went to a congressional committee, earmarked for Sen. Ted Stevens (R, Alaska).

Receiving smaller amounts in 1970, generally $200-500 were Sen. Hiram Fong (R, Hawaii); Sen. Henry M. Jackson (D, Wash.); former Rep. William C. Cramer (R, Fla.); Rep. Clark MacGregor (R, Minn.); Sen. Frank E. Moss (D, Utah); former Sen. George Murphy (R, Calif.); and Sen. Hugh Scott (R, Pa.).

Politicians receiving the largest contributions were generally candidates for federal office from Oklahoma: Ed Edmondson, who ran unsuccessfully for the Senate, got $11,000 in 1972; former Republican Rep. Page Belcher got $3,000 in 1970; House Speaker Carl Albert received $2,500 in 1970 and $500 in 1972; Rep. John Jarman, a Democrat who recently turned Republican, got $3,000 in both 1970 and 1972; Democratic Rep. Tom Steed received $2,000 in both 1970 and 1972.

Other Congressional candidates who received illegal contributions from Phillips included former Rep. Leslie C. Arends (Ill.), who was Republican whip; and Democratic majority leader Thomas P. O'Neill Jr. (Mass.).

In its report to the SEC, Phillips stated that it did not pay "any bribe, commission, contributions or another political payment to any government official, politicians or political party" abroad.

The money paid to U.S. politicians was funneled through two Swiss corporations. Phillips said that a total of $2.9 million was diverted to these firms, and said at least half was spent legally abroad.

Tax fraud indictment—Phillips Petroleum, its chairman and two former chief executive officers were indicted Sept. 2, 1976 on tax-fraud charges related to its corporate fund used to make secret and illegal political contributions.

A federal grand jury in Tulsa, Okla. returned the seven-count indictment Phillips, William F. Martin, Stanley Learned and William F. Keeler. They were accused of conspiring to conceal from the Internal Revenue Service nearly $3 million that was deposited in Swiss bank accounts or held as cash at the firm's headquarters in Bartlesville, Okla.

According to the indictment, the money was generated through "confidential transactions" involving agreements made by Phillips and its Panamanian subsidiary with an Illinois construction firm and its French subsidiary, a New York ship broker and a refinery in India.

The indictment said that Phillips used "international couriers, code names, misleading [bookkeeping] entries, and false invoices and billings" to conceal the company's true expenses and incomes from the IRS. The income from the secret transactions was not reported on corporate tax returns for 1963–71, according to the indictment. The company also was accused of filing false returns for 1969–71. Martin was accused of assisting in their preparation.

Ashland Oil payments. A special panel investigating possibly illegal political payments made by Ashland Oil, Inc. disclosed June 29, 1975 that $801,165 in corporate funds might have been used for such payments in the U.S. and abroad in 1967–74.

In earlier disclosures at the firm's annual meeting, Ashland had told stockholders that $533,000, excluding an illegal $100,000 donation to the Nixon reelection campaign, had been contributed to politicians.

The investigation, by a committee of Ashland's board of directors, was initiated under court order as part of a settlement with the Securities and Exchange Commission, which had charged the Kentucky-based firm with filing false reports on its secret donations, in violation of U.S. securities laws.

The panel said Chairman Orin E. Atkins, who had pleaded no contest to authorizing the Nixon donation, agreed to repay Ashland $175,000 over five years. In other five-year installments, Vice Chairman William R. Seaton agreed to repay $105,000 and President Clyde M. Webb agreed to reimburse $45,000. Ashland already had been reimbursed $135,310 by some recipients and two officers, the report stated.

Report details domestic donations— Ashland made a total of $780,465 available for domestic political contributions, the special panel's report stated in disclosures published July 8. From 1967 through 1972, actual contributions made directly by the oil company totaled $612,-000 and another $105,000 was funneled through an intermediary to "selected candidates for Congress."

Among the recipients of Ashland's contributions was Gov. Hugh Carey (D, N.Y.), whose 1974 gubernatorial campaign was given $5,000.

The report also said that a "political figure" in Hudson County, N.J. extorted $15,000 from an Ashland unit; he was subsequently convicted on federal extortion charges, the report noted.

The report was ambiguous on whether Ashland's regular accountants, Ernst & Ernst, were aware of the political payments. "There is conflicting evidence which suggests, but does not establish, that Ernst & Ernst obtained knowledge during the course of its 1969 audit engagement that the corporation was making political contributions," the report stated.

Cash recipients—Bowing to SEC pressure, Ashland Oil Aug. 9 disclosed the names of recipients of its foreign and domestic political contributions totaling more than $1.1 million. The payments were made from September 1967 to January 1973, officials of the company said.

Among those who accepted money from Ashland were President Omar Bongo of Gabon, former President Richard Nixon, the Democratic National Committee, and numerous candidates for federal, state, and local elections.

Ashland had refused to make the list public, saying Aug. 7 "no useful purpose would be served by public disclosures of the names." The SEC responded by threatening legal action against the firm, which earlier had accepted a settlement of the SEC's charges alleging violations of financial reporting laws in connection with illegal political contributions in the U.S.

As part of the consent judgment, Ashland had agreed to reveal the recipients of its cash payments "to the full satisfaction of the commission."

Ashland listed more than $342,000 paid in corporate cash to government officials abroad.

Ashland admitted distributing a total of more than $730,000 to politicians at federal, state and local levels.

Among Ashland's reported contributions to U.S. politicians:

■ $30,000 in 1968 to Robert Short, former treasurer of the Democratic National Committee; a total of $50,000 in 1970 and 1972 to Robert S. Strauss, former treasurer and current chairman of the Democratic National Committee.

■ A total of $60,000 to the late Rep. Michael J. Kirwan (D, Ohio), for distribution to Democratic congressional candidates; $50,000 to Rep. Wilbur Mills (D, Ark.) "to help elect a Democratic congress in 1972"; a total of $40,800 to several campaigns of Louis Nunn, former Republican governor of Kentucky; $35,000 to several campaigns of John C. Watts, a former Democratic congressman from Kentucky; $30,000 to Gov. James A. Rhodes' (R, Ohio) 1968 race for the Senate; a total of $23,000 to Gov. Arch A. Moore (R, W. Va.); a total of $20,000 to the late Sen. Allen J. Ellender (D, La.), $5,000 of which was for distribution to other candidates; $14,000 to Katherine Peden, a Kentucky Democrat, for an unsuccessful Senate race in 1968 and $6,000 to her successful Republican opponent, former Sen. Marlow Cook; $13,000 to Sen. Wendell H. Ford's (D, Ky.) successful gubernatorial race in 1971; nearly $12,000 to Sen. Hubert H. Humphrey's (D, Minn.) various campaigns.

Others who received money from Ashland included: Sen. James O. Eastland (D, Miss.) $5,000; Sen. Carl T. Curtis (R, Neb.) $5,000; Sen. J. Bennett Johnston Jr. (D, La.) $5,000; former Sen. Jack Miller (R, Iowa) $5,000; former Sen. B. Everett Jordan (D, N.C.) $5,000; former Sen. Gordon Allot (R, Colo.) $5,000; Sen. Vance Hartke (D, Ind.) $3,500; Sen. Milton R. Young (R, N.D.) $3,500; Sen. Birch Bayh (D, Ind.) $3,000.

Airlines probed. The enforcement bureau of the Civil Aeronautics Board (CAB) in March 1975 ended a year of inquiry into political funding actions of American Airlines and Braniff Airways. Dispute over the scope of the CAB's investigation had surfaced after the death of the bureau's chief, William M. Gingery, who committed suicide Feb. 17.

Gingery left a note charging that his predecessor as head of the enforcement bureau, acting CAB chairman Richard J. O'Melia, had terminated several investigations into illegal political contributions and ordered the files "impounded," according to the New York Times March 4. Gingery said that he had discovered the locked files Feb. 14.

Before his death, Gingery had been scheduled to give testimony to the Senate Judiciary Committee's subcommittee on administrative practice and procedure, which had been investigating the CAB's regulatory policies. Gingery asked that his suicide note be sent to the subcommittee. It was also forwarded to the Watergate special prosecutor's office.

O'Melia told the subcommittee March 21 that in November 1973 when he had headed the bureau, then-CAB chairman Robert D. Timm ordered an abrupt end to the investigations of political gift-giving by airlines. O'Melia testified that he had received the order in a memo from Timm, but said he refused to accept a copy of it.

Timm, who remained a member of the CAB after President Ford refused to reappoint him chairman because of alleged improper ties to the airline industry, denied the existence of the memo. In his testimony before the subcommittee March 21, Timm admitted, however, that he had strictly limited the scope of questioning the enforcement board could pursue when investigations were initiated in July 1973.

O'Melia admitted he had ordered all "politically sensitive" material related to the investigations placed in a safe, but denied he had blocked the bureau's probe of unlawful campaign contributions.

Braniff accused—The CAB enforcement bureau March 13 filed a complaint alleging that Braniff Airways maintained a political slush fund that was financed by the sale of "at least 3,262 unaccounted-for" flight tickets to the public. "Off-the-book" income from these sales totaling at least $641,285 and as much as $926,955, was diverted to a secret fund "for the use of Braniff management ... at least in part for unlawful purposes," the enforcement bureau charged. Some of the money allegedly was laundered through Panama.

With the exception of an illegal $40,000 contribution to the Nixon campaign, none of the revenue from the slush fund was reflected in Braniff's books, the bureau charged. Braniff and Harding L. Lawrence, the airline's chairman, had pleaded guilty in 1973 to making the unlawful donations and were fined.

The enforcement bureau charged that Lawrence and C. Edward Acker, Braniff's president, had access to the secret fund. Five other airline officials also were accused of participating in or having knowledge of the ticket scheme.

In the complaint, which was still pending before the five-member CAB board, the enforcement bureau asked that the board consider modifying or suspending Braniff's operating authority. Federal law did not allow the CAB to set criminal penalties, but the Justice Department had jurisdiction to follow up CAB actions.

American Airlines fined—American Airlines agreed May 19, 1975 to pay a $150,000 fine in settlement of the CAB enforcement bureau's March 13 complaint about the airline using a slush fund to make illegal campaign payments. The CAB accepted the settlement May 27.

The March 13 complaint was a charge

against the airline and eight of its current and former officers. According to the complaint, between 1964 and 1973, American maintained a secret fund totaling "at least $275,000" that was used in part to make illegal corporate donations to political candidates. Some of the money was funneled through Mexico; other funds were paid as a commission to a Lebanese agent.

American had pleaded guilty in 1973 to unlawfully donating $55,000 to the Nixon re-election campaign and was fined for the violation.

The CAB claimed that $119,546 in donations paid out of the slush fund later was returned to the airline, $117,479 could not be traced, and $57,975 in contributions was not returned. In addition to the Nixon contribution, which was returned in 1973, American donated money to at least 132 other candidates for federal and state office or their campaign committees received money from the airline, the CAB stated. Among the recipients were the Senate Democratic Campaign Committee and the Democrats for Nixon Committee, according to the complaint.

By concealing the slush fund, the CAB charged, American violated federal campaign laws and the agency's regulations dealing with airline accounting and financial reporting requirements. Agency officials said that the civil penalty, the largest fine ever collected by the CAB, would have been larger if American had not voluntarily disclosed the Nixon contribution and cooperated with the agency. Several airline officials also reimbursed American for $125,000, a CAB spokesman added.

George Spater, former American Airlines chairman, had agreed in 1974 to pay the firm $75,000 in settlement of a shareholders' suit arising out of illegal payments.

American had been the first firm to plead guilty to campaign finance law violations after investigations were conducted by the Watergate special prosecutor's office. Spater, who had served as chief executive during the time the illegal donations were made, had not been charged in the case.

American Airlines details payments— American Airlines Feb. 9, 1977 made public details of $275,000 in corporate funds that it admitted paying between 1964 and 1972 "by means of false and fictitious entries" in company books. Most of the money had been diverted to a "secret cash fund" used in part for "unlawful political contributions," the airline said.

The disclosures were made in a report submitted to the Securities and Exchange Commission as settlement of the SEC's charges that American had violated securities laws by failing to report the payments.

The SEC's charges were made in an administrative proceeding against American. The airline, in turn, agreed to settle the case by promising the SEC not to violate its order against future securities law violations.

Under the SEC's enforcement authority, the commission could take administrative action against publicly held companies under its jurisdiction, or it could take the charges to federal court and seek civil injunctive relief against the alleged violations.

In either instance, when a company settled a case, it neither admitted nor denied the SEC's charges but agreed not to commit future violations of securities laws. In an administrative proceeding, the pledge was made to the SEC. In a court proceeding, the company consented to a court injunction barring future violations.

In most other cases involving questionable payments, the SEC had gone to court to settle the charges. Analysts said the more lenient enforcement action had been taken against American because the airline had come forward voluntarily in 1973 to report illegal secret payments of $55,000 to the Nixon presidential reelection campaign.

In its report to the SEC, American listed about 70 politicians from both major parties who had received corporate contributions totaling an estimated $40,000 in 1971 and 1972. Federal law barred corporate contributions to candidates for federal office. It also was illegal for those candidates to knowingly accept corporate contributions.

American's list of politicians who had

accepted corporate contributions included former President Gerald R. Ford, who had received $100 when he was a Michigan congressman; House Speaker Thomas P. O'Neill Jr. (D, Mass), $100, and Senate Minority Leader Howard H. Baker Jr. (R, Tenn.), $500. The political payments ranged from $50 to $2,500, but most contributions were for $100 and $200.

Flying Tiger accused—The CAB Dec. 29, 1976 charged Flying Tiger Line, an air cargo subsidiary of Tiger International Inc., with not accounting properly for 1969–76 contributions to U.S. politicians and foreign officials. The CAB said that the payments, which were recorded as operating expenses, actually were non-operating expenses.

The payments included nearly $12,000 in free air travel in 1970 and 1971 for Sen. John V. Tunney (D, Calif.), $5,000 for a 1971 dinner for then-President Richard M. Nixon, gifts to South Korean officials and their wives, and $25,500 in charitable contributions.

The CAB complaint against the firm and six of its executives, including Anna C. Chennault, the airline's former vice president, alleged only technical violations of reporting requirements, not illegal business practices.

The CAB action was the fifth against airlines for reporting violations that involved political contributions. In the previous cases, the CAB had accepted civil-penalty payments of $300,000 from Braniff International, $150,000 from American Airlines, $75,000 from Aloha Airlines and $50,000 from Continental Airlines.

General Tire accused. In a suit filed May 10, 1976, the Securities & Exchange Commission accused General Tire and Rubber Co. of making a wide array of foreign and domestic payoffs. The charges were the broadest yet in the SEC's post-Watergate investigation of management fraud.

The SEC's wide-ranging probe centered on the payment of illegal corporate contributions to U.S. politicians and on bribes paid to officials of foreign governments.

The suit was settled when a consent agreement and the SEC complaint were filed simultaneously in U.S. District Court in Washington, D.C. The company neither admitted nor denied the charges but accepted a court injunction barring further violations of federal securities laws.

General Tire also agreed to appoint a special review committee to investigate and make a public report of any improper activities by the company or its employes.

The SEC complaint involved alleged contributions to U.S. politicians, payments of "gratuities" to military and civilian employes of U.S. agencies with which the firm did business, overseas bribes, a hidden slush fund, violations of foreign-currency laws, participation in the Arab League's boycott of Israel and the filing of false and misleading financial reports.

The company and its president, Michael G. O'Neil, also were accused of devising and directing various schemes to circumvent U.S. and foreign laws against corporate payoffs. (O'Neil also signed a consent agreement settling the SEC's charges against him.)

According to the SEC, political payments totaling at least $65,000 were made between 1968 and 1972 to candidates for federal and state office. A "substantial portion" of that sum was donated illegally, the SEC said. Recipients of the contributions were not identified.

The SEC complaint gave few details about payments to U.S. government employes; however, the consent agreement directed General Tire's special review committee to investigate the matter further

General Tire's domestic and foreign payoffs were made from an elaborately maintained slush fund, the SEC charged. The money used for domestic purposes was called the General Tire Good Citizenship Fund. It was kept in a wall safe in O'Neil's office at the firm's Akron, Ohio headquarters.

At O'Neil's direction, the SEC charged, a percentage of executive bonuses and salaries, beginning in 1968, were paid into the domestic slush fund.

R. J. Reynolds admits paying $25 million. R. J. Reynolds Industries Inc. of Winston-

Salem, N.C. admitted Sept. 10, 1976 that it gave more than $25 million in questionable corporate payments in the U.S. and abroad since 1968 to promote its business and political interests.

The voluntary disclosure was made in a report filed with the Securities and Exchange Commission. The amount made Reynolds' payment total one of the largest disclosed by the more than 200 companies that had filed such reports with the SEC.

Reynolds said that between 1971 and 1975 its wholly-owned shipping subsidiary, Sea-Land Services Inc., had paid $19 million in "possibly illegal rebates" to "shippers, consignees and forwarding agents."

Reynolds' tobacco subsidiaries made $5.4 million in questionable payments to officials of foreign governments or to employes of companies owned or controlled by foreign governments, the report stated. Most of the overseas payments from the tobacco operations were recorded on company books as commissions, Reynolds said, adding that 75% of the questionable commissions already had been stopped. The remaining payments would be ended shortly, Reynolds said.

Reynolds also admitted paying $190,000 in corporate funds to presidential and congressional candidates between 1968 and 1973. The cash was generated "by diverting a royalty payment due from a foreign license and paying inaccurate invoices, purportedly from other foreign countries," the report said. The money was disbursed through Reynold's Washington office.

In a preliminary report filed with the SEC May 28, Reynolds had said its political contributions totaled $65,000 to $90,000. Three directors responsible for making the contributions on Reynolds' behalf had resigned and agreed to reimburse the company for the illegally disbursed funds, Reynolds said.

At the same time, Reynolds said its preliminary investigation had uncovered "questionable payments" made by Sea-Land. Reynolds also admitted making other payments, totaling $100,000, to foreign officials.

Of the $19 million paid by Sea-Land, Reynolds said, $11.5 million involved the Atlantic market, $7 million went to Pacific

businesses and $500,000 was paid in the Caribbean. Reynolds said that rebates were "traditional and pervasive in the international ocean-shipping industry." Sea-Land "reluctantly joined in the practice after trying to compete without doing so," Reynolds said.

(According to the Sept. 13 Wall Street Journal, rebates paid by returning part of the posted tariff to the shipper or consignee were legal and customary in most foreign countries.)

Sea-Land unilaterally stopped paying rebates in the Pacific in 1973 and in the Atlantic in 1975, but "believes that it has lost business as a result," Reynolds said.

Although the payment of rebates had halted, Reynolds said, Sea-Land continued to pay small bribes, known as "tea money," to shipping clerks in the Pacific until 1976. In one year, the small payments totaled $730,000 according to the report. Reynolds, which had acquired Sea-Land in 1969, said it had first learned of the rebating practices in early 1975.

"Mislabeling of accounts" was involved in paying the rebates, made in part from "off-book funds," Reynolds said.

Reynolds said that Sea-Land and the Federal Maritime Commission were negotiating a settlement involving penalties for payment of the rebates. The Shipping Act of 1916 made payment of rebates and related practices illegal. Reynolds also said that a federal grand jury in New Jersey was investigating rebating practices in the entire shipping industry.

Continental Oil fires 2 aides. Continental Oil Co. Dec. 15, 1976 fired two of its operating officials because, the company said, they had known of, or participated in the making of, questionable domestic and foreign political payments since 1971. The company also accused the officials—Wayne E. Glenn and Willard H. Burnap, both vice chairmen—of withholding information about the payments from a directors' committee that was investigating them.

Burnap Dec. 16 denied the company's charges.

In a filing with the Securities and Exchange Commission Dec. 16, Continental Oil said C. Howard Hardesty Jr., also a vice chairman, had not taken "adequate steps to investigate the possible misuse" of domestic political contributions channeled through a slush fund operated by a subsidiary between 1970 and 1972. Other senior management personnel "were aware or and/or authorized" improper transfers of more than $80,000 from 1970–73 "outside normal accounting channels" to pay unnamed foreign tax officials, Continental Oil said.

The company said that its internal investigation, which was "substantially completed," had uncovered a total of $85,-000 in corporate contributions to U.S. politicians and $148,000 in payments to foreign political parties or officials.

Southern Bell officials indicted. Southern Bell Telephone Co., its president, three vice presidents and a former vice president were indicted Aug. 2, 1977 on charges of conspiring to falsify records in connection with a political slush fund.

The indictment, returned by a Mecklenburg County, N.C. grand jury, named Southern Bell president L. E. Rast, vice presidents Nathaniel R. Johnson, James W. Travis and Robert J. Clontz and retired vice president John J. Ryan.

The defendants were accused of coercing 24 employes at the Atlanta-based phone company's North Carolina facilities to submit false expense vouchers. The proceeds allegedly were turned over to the company's secret political fund. Contributions were made from the slush fund between October 1971 and July 1973, according to the indictment.

Ryan also was charged in a separate indictment with embezzling $17,000. Ryan, who had first disclosed the existence of the slush fund after he was forced to retire, had filed an $85-million libel suit against his former employer.

The company pleaded guilty Feb. 13, 1978 to one count in the 25-count indictment, and the other charges were dropped under a plea-bargaining agreement. The company was then fined $310,712 for conspiring to use corporate funds for political contributions by falsifying vouchers.

SEC sues Occidental. The Securities and Exchange Commission May 3 accused Occidental Petroleum Corp. of spending more than $600,000 on illegal or questionable political contributions, gifts and entertainment in the U.S. and abroad between 1968 and 1975.

Some of this money, the SEC said, was generated by two foreign companies secretly created by Occidental and whose profits were not recorded. At least $165,-000 of the profits were diverted to a slush fund used to make secret political contributions abroad.

When the complaint was filed, Occidental immediately settled the suit, without admitting or denying the charges, by agreeing not to commit future violations of federal securities law. Occidental earlier had admitted making $7,800 in illegal political contributions and $168,000 in questionable payments abroad.

SEC accuses Goodyear. The Securities & Exchange Commission (SEC) Dec. 21, 1977 accused Goodyear Tire & Rubber Co. of maintaining a $1.5-million slush fund to make illegal political contributions in the U.S. and improper payments abroad. Goodyear's foreign payments in 20 countries, made since 1970, totaled more than $500,000, the SEC charged. The money went to political parties, government employes and officials of labor unions.

Goodyear settled the charges as soon as they were filed in U.S. District Court in Washington. Although Goodyear agreed not to violate securities law in the future, it neither admitted nor denied the SEC's charges.

Beasley of Firestone pleads guilty. Robert P. Beasley, former vice chairman and chief financial officer of Firestone Tire & Rubber Co., pleaded guilty Feb. 28, 1978 to five counts of embezzling $1 million from a secret corporate fund established to make illegal political contributions. Indicted Oct. 25, 1977, the executive had pleaded not guilty in November to the 40-count indictment. He later changed his plea to guilty when the government agreed to drop the remaining 35 counts.

Beasley admitted using subterfuge to remove $1 million from the Firestone treasury and conceal it in about 20 bank accounts. Instead of making illegal contributions to politicians from the fund he controlled, Beasley used the money for personal expenses.

Firestone had admitted to the Securities and Exchange Commission in June 1976 that about $300,000 in corporate funds were used for political payments between 1970 and 1973. Beasley had been given control of the illegal program, set up sometime before 1960, after being named executive vice president for finance in November 1968.

The indictment charged that "it was an important part of the Firestone illegal political contributions program that the monies be obtained from the corporate treasury through subterfuge to avoid detection by Firestone's auditors."

Beasley "devised these methods of sub-terfuge" and "utilized them to defraud Firestone by obtaining additional corporate monies without detection for his own personal use," according to the indictment.

In December 1976, after a court-ordered audit of its political payments program, Firestone said Beasley had collected $1.16 million for political contributions. The company said about $300,000 was disbursed, $200,000 was returned by Beasley from outside bank accounts that were under his control and the remainder was unaccounted for.

Firestone had filed suit against Beasley in May, seeking recovery of the more than $600,000 that was missing. Beasley had taken an early retirement from Firestone in June 1976, just after he had been promoted to vice chairman.

Carter Administration

Stress on Ethics

Jimmy Carter was elected President of the United States Nov. 2, 1976 and was inaugurated Jan. 20, 1977. During his campaign and afterwards Carter frequently stressed his religious convictions and his intention to require high ethical standards in his administration.

Carter's conflict-of-interest code. President-elect Jimmy Carter Jan. 4, 1977 issued guidelines intended to guard against conflicts of interest in his administration. He announced at the same time plans to put most of his own business holdings in trust.

Carter's press spokesman Jody Powell, citing Carter's campaign pledge to "restore the confidence of the American people in their own government," said the guidelines were intended to insure that Carter "and the people who serve under him are indeed worthy of trust."

The conflict-of-interest code would apply not only to Cabinet officers but also to nearly 2,000 political appointees and to career federal employes in policy-making posts.

Full public disclosure of financial net worth would be required under the code.

This would be updated regularly and be submitted for two years after an individual had left government service. An official would be required to divest himself of any holdings that would be affected by an official act or that would be "broadly affected by governmental, monetary and budgetary policies." In addition, an official would have to disqualify himself from handling matters that would affect holdings he chose to retain. If this occurred more than "rarely," however, divestiture would be required

The code exempted assets in real estate, savings certificates and accounts and other government securities.

The code would permit divestiture by the trust if the trustee were genuinely independent and given authority to buy or sell without consulting the official.

The code would impose new regulations to close what Carter had called the "revolving door" between federal agencies and businesses and industries affected by the agencies' decisions. An official would not be permitted to handle for two years after leaving the government any paid private business with his former federal agency if it concerned matters he had dealt with during his last year in government. And he would be prohibited for one year after leaving government service from doing business for pay before his former agency on any matter, regardless of whether he had actually worked on the issue as a government official.

Carter said he planned to ask Congress for legislation curbing the "revolving door" practice and to issue an executive order embodying the conflict-of-interest guidelines.

The proposed code went beyond existing requirements on financial disclosure, on the "revolving door" situation and on officials covered.

Currently, public financial disclosure was required of Cabinet officers during confirmation hearings, but reports on other top officials in Cabinet departments, while required, were kept confidential and contained only the name of companies in which a financial interest was held, not the value of the interest.

Under the current U.S. Code, officials were prohibited for one year after leaving the government, from representing private clients before their former agencies on matters they had handled at the agencies.

Carter's statement indicated a problem in the divestiture area, in that "to decree that no person can have any financial interests other than a salary from the government would seriously limit the ability to recruit the most qualified persons." "It is hoped," the statement continued, "that except in rare circumstances divestiture causing severe tax burdens will be unnecessary."

Carter sets up trust—For his own part, Carter was putting his peanut warehouse into a trust, leasing his farmland for a fixed amount—to be set in 1977—for the next four years and selling much of his stock.

The trustee could either lease or sell the warehouse, which Carter owned in partnership with his mother, Mrs. Lillian Carter, and his brother, Billy Carter. Carter's 3,240 shares of American Can Co., valued at about $126,000, also would be put into the trust.

Carter was to sell his other common stock, which included 85 shares of Federated Department Stores Inc., valued at about $4,100, and 956 shares of Advance Investors, a mutual fund, valued at about $10,500.

Carter's net worth, listed in a December 1975 financial statement, totaled $811,982. His land holdings—he owned outright or shared an interest in more than 2,000 acres in southwest Georgia, some of it land that had been in the family for six generations—accounted for $348,444 of his net worth. His warehouse holdings were valued at $330,002.

Common Cause lauds 'breakthrough'— Common Cause, the citizens lobby, hailed Carter's initiatives as "a major breakthrough in the fight to eliminate conflicts of interest in the executive branch." The statement was issued Jan. 4 by John W. Gardner, Common Cause chairman.

Ethics law proposed. President Carter proposed May 3, 1977 an Ethics In Government Act that would require public financial disclosure reports from all policy-making officials in the executive branch. The President previously had required such statements from members of his Cabinet, Cabinet-level appointees and members of his White House staff.

The proposed legislation would apply to 13,000 officials, including presidential appointees and top-level civil servants and military officers. Many of them were currently required to file statements of financial information, but the statements' were not made public.

In his message to Congress accompanying the proposal, Carter said it would "establish far-reaching safeguards against conflicts of interest and abuse of the public trust by government officials."

As part of the proposal, the President called for creation of an office of government ethics in the Civil Service. Its director would be appointed by the president and confirmed by the Senate. The office would issue conflict-of-interest guidelines, including suggestions on how to resolve problems and monitor compliance by agencies and individuals.

The measure would tighten restrictions against "revolving door" practices whereby officials left government service "to accept a job in private industry, where one of their primary responsibilities is to handle contracts with the former employer," as the President put it in his message.

Currently, an official leaving federal service was prohibited for a year from lobbying before his old agency on matters that he had handled. Carter proposed to extend the ban to two years and to prohibit any contact with the old agency for one year. The prohibition in both cases would include informal as well as formal contacts.

Bill for special prosecutor endorsed— In his message, the President endorsed legislation pending before Congress for appointment of a special prosecutor when necessary "to handle cases of misconduct by high-ranking executive branch officials." This would include the president, vice president, members of the Cabinet and White House staff.

Carter said the pending legislation, "with relatively small revisions, will conform to my own principles for sound special prosecutor legislation."

As explained by Robert J. Lipshutz, counsel to the President, at a White House briefing May 3, Carter was not seeking a permanent special prosecutor but a legislative mandate for appointment of a special prosecutor when circumstances warranted. The President also advocated appointment of such a person by a special court panel and removal of that person from office only for extraordinary impropriety or incapacity.

*Text of message—*Carter said in his message on ethics:

During my campaign I promised the American people that as President I would assure that their government is devoted exclusively to the public interest. I began fulfilling that promise by making information on my own financial interests publicly available. I have also required that all Presidential appointees disclose their business and financial interests, to remove any possibility of hidden conflict of interest. In addition, I have obtained a commitment from these officials to adhere to tighter restrictions after leaving government, in order to curb the "revolving door" practice that has too often permitted former officials to exploit their government contacts for private gain.

To expand upon the actions I have taken so far, I am submitting to Congress the Ethics in Government Act of 1977. This bill would establish far-reaching safeguards against conflicts of interest and abuse of the public trust by government officials. The

bill incorporates the standards I have required of my own appointees, and extends their coverage to other high-ranking officials. It builds upon the Comptroller General's two-year investigation of conflict of interest enforcement in the Executive Branch. It also parallels the unprecedented efforts the Congress has made to strengthen ethical standards for its members.

In addition to strengthening conflict of interest controls through the Ethics in Government Act, I am today announcing support for legislation to authorize appointment of a temporary Special Prosecutor to handle cases of misconduct by high-ranking Executive Branch officials.

Both Houses have recently adopted new Codes of Conduct which are milestones in the history of government action to prevent actual or potential conflicts of interest. The leadership of both Houses has also pledged personal support for enactment of these new Codes into law. The Senate is currently considering S. 555, the Public Officials Integrity Act of 1977, and the House, in addition to creating a Select Committee on Ethics to enact its new Code into law, has also been working on legislation to establish government-wide ethical standards. I am confident that through our joint efforts, legislation prescribing government-wide standards of conduct will be considered and passed this year.

The Ethics in Government Act calls for a three-part program of financial disclosure, creation of a new Office of Ethics in the Civil Service Commission, and strengthened restrictions on post-employment activities of government officials.

First, the Ethics in Government Act would require policy-making officials, whether political appointees or top-level career civil servants, to disclose publicly their financial interests. Currently, policy-making employees must file statements of financial interest, but these statements are not available to the public. In addition to requiring public disclosure, the Act would require collection of more extensive information about employees' financial interests than the current Executive Order. Each official's report will include information on:

—income, whether earned or from investments;
—gifts, including travel, lodging, food and entertainment;
—assets, liabilities and financial transactions;
—positions held in business and professional organizations;
—agreements for future employment.

The vast majority of government officials, of course, have always followed strict ethical standards. I respect their efforts and integrity, and I have carefully considered the new obligations that this legislation will place on them. The provisions of the Act would strike a careful balance between the rights of these individuals to their privacy and the right of the American people to know that their public officials are free from conflicts of interest.

Second, the Ethics in Government Act would strengthen existing restrictions on the revolving door between government and private industry. All too often officials have come into government for a short time and then left to accept a job in private industry, where one of their primary responsibilities is to handle contacts with the former employer. To restrict this kind of arrangement I propose:

1. An extension of the current prohibition on appearances before an agency of former employment on matters that were under the official's responsibility:

—by extending the period of the prohibition from one year to two; and
—by including informal as well as formal contacts.

2. A new and broader ban on formal or informal contact on other matters with agencies of former employment, for a period of one year after the end of government service.

These rules also reflect a balance. They do not place unfair restrictions on the jobs former government officials may choose, but they will prevent the misuse of influence acquired through public service.

Third, this Act would establish a new Office of Government Ethics in the Civil Service Commission. Under the existing Executive Order, guidelines have often been unclear, and enforcement has been ineffective in some agencies. An effective oversight office is essential if strict ethical requirements are to be enforced throughout the government.

Because I believe these responsibilities are so important, I am asking that the Office be headed by a Director who is a Presidential appointee, confirmed by the Senate. I want to designate an individual who is clearly accountable to me, to the Chairman of the Civil Service Commission and to the Congress for the supervision of ethical standards in the Executive Branch. The Director and his new Office would:

—issue general guidelines to agencies

on what constitutes a conflict of interest, and how those conflicts can be resolved;

—make recommendations to me on any change needed in laws and regulations governing conflicts of interest;

—monitor compliance by agencies and individuals with established requirements; and

—increase understanding throughout the government and on the part of the American people of the ethical standards of conduct required of Executive Branch employees.

This new Office will ensure vigilant enforcement of the standards that are established to protect the honesty and integrity of our government.

To complement the Ethics in Government Act, I am also announcing my support for legislation which would require appointment of a Special Prosecutor to investigate and prosecute alleged offenses by high government officials. I am not submitting my own bill, for legislation has already been introduced in the Congress which, with relatively small revisions, will conform to my own principles for sound Special Prosecutor legislation. Under those principles the Special Prosecutor would be appointed by a specially empaneled court. He or she could be removed from office only upon a finding of extraordinary impropriety or incapacity. The Special Prosecutor's jurisdiction would extend to alleged misconduct by the President, the Vice President, members of the Cabinet, and White House staff members.

This approach will eliminate all appearance of high-level interference in sensitive investigations and prosecutions. The American people must be assured that no one, regardless of position, is above the law.

I look forward to working with the Congress to enact both the Ethics in Government Act and Special Prosecutor legislation, so that we can help restore the faith of the American people in their government.

The Bert Lance Affair

In a controversy involving ethics in the Carter Administration, Bert Lance, a close friend and adviser of President Carter's, resigned as director of the Office of Manage-

ment & Budget Sept. 21, 1977. In the dispute over Lance, however, his actions as a member of the Carter Administration were never at issue. The controversy was concerned entirely with his alleged manipulations as a Georgia banker.

Senate panel clears Lance on finances.

The Senate Governmental Affairs Committee July 25, 1977 decided against a full investigation of the personal finances of Budget Director Bert Lance.

Lance's problem centered around the more than 200,000 shares of stock he held in National Bank of Georgia, of which he was president prior to joining the Carter Administration. The stock, acquired over a period of time, cost $3.4 million, or an average $16.62 a share.

When Lance entered government service, the holding was put in a blind trust under a conflict-of-interest requirement by President Carter that the bank shares be sold by Dec. 31.

Partly because of the impending required sale of the large block of stock, the price of the stock had plummeted. The drop deepened with a recent report from the bank that it was writing off $2.3 million in problem real estate loans and it expected to report a net loss for the first half.

The stock, which had sold over the counter for more than $15 a share at the beginning of the year, stood at $8.50 a share on July 6–7. Sale of his holdings at that level would represent a loss of more than $1.5 million to Lance.

Lance also was facing a potential loss of $153,000 in annual dividends from the Atlanta bank, if the dividends were dropped because of the loss.

Lance had brought the matter to the attention of the President. The problem at the time seemed to be the deadline for selling his bank stock, which was having a depressing effect on the value of the stock. Carter asked the Senate Governmental Affairs Committee, in a letter to Chairman Abraham A. Ribicoff (D, Conn.) disclosed July 12, to remove the deadline and permit Lance an indefinite period in which to sell the bank stock. Carter said the deadline imposed "an undue financial burden" on Lance and the bank. The President proposed as well that

the stock be transferred to a corporate trustee for the transaction. The stock, as other Lance assets, were in a blind trust under control of trustee Thomas Mitchell of Dalton, Ga., a Lance friend.

The Ribicoff committee met with Lance July 15 and indicated the deadline problem could be removed if Lance could work out with the Senate Banking Committee a way to insulate himself from banking policy issues. Banking Committee Chairman William Proxmire (D, Wis.) had accused Lance of having violated his pledge not to get involved in banking policy matters. Lance had sent a letter to Congress urging rejection of legislation to force banks to make more loans in local communities.

Lance told the Ribicoff committee July 15 he had considered the legislation, which was designed to end "redlining," or avoidance of loans in high-risk neighborhoods, a housing rather than a banking measure.

"If I violated that pledge," Lance said, "and there is some weight of opinion that I did—then I apologize to this committee and to Sen. Proxmire." He promised to work out some guidelines on the issue with the Proxmire panel.

"What bothers me," Sen. William V. Roth (R, Del.) remarked at the hearing, "is to make the overpromises and then, when the going gets rough, to ask for an exception."

The committee scheduled a vote on extending the deadline for Lance to sell his bank stock, but before the meeting took place there were press reports that National Bank of Georgia had opened a correspondent account with First National Bank of Chicago a month before Lance obtained a $3.4-million loan from the Chicago bank. Lance had used the loan to acquire the Atlanta bank stock.*

The possibility of impropriety existed if the Georgia bank's assets had been used for Lance's personal benefit, that is, if the loan had been obtained in exchange for the correspondence account.

At the July 25 hearing before the Ribicoff panel, Lance said there was no

---

*In a correspondence relationship, a smaller bank paid a larger urban bank, through the deposits into a noninterest-bearing account, to perform certain services that usually involved check clearing, foreign-exchange transactions and securities handling.

"quid pro quo" relationship between the loan and the correspondent account and both were proper. He had borrowed the $3.4 million, he explained, to refinance a $2.7-million loan from a New York bank. The New York loan had been obtained to purchase shares in the Atlanta bank, he said, and he had promised to pay it off if he left the Atlanta bank, which he had in order to join the Carter Administration. He said the interest rate on the Chicago loan was three-quarters of a percentage point above the prime lending rate, which was not considered an unusually favorable rate for a private loan.

The correspondent account, he said, had fluctuated from $37,000 to $357,000 and the Georgia bank had received the check-clearing services, as well as cash management and training services.

Asked about reports that Teamsters union pension-fund money had been placed with the Georgia bank, Lance described it as "desirable business" and probably part of an effort by the Teamsters to "clean up" their pension-fund affairs by putting money in the Georgia bank and four other institutions during the same period.

Lance also confirmed recent reports that his trustee had found a prospective buyer of his Atlanta bank holdings, making the need for waiver of the deadline no longer urgent.

The testimony more than satisfied the committee. "You've been smeared from one end of the country to the other, in my opinion, unjustly," Ribicoff said. Sen. Charles Percy (Ill.), ranking Republican on the panel, said he was "satisfied completely" with the explanations.

No objection was raised when Ribicoff asserted that there was no need for the committee to undertake a full investigation. The committee indicated as well that there would be no problem about removing the deadline if the prospective sale did not go through.

Ribicoff disclosed that John Heimann, comptroller of the currency, would investigate the circumstances of the loan Lance received from the Chicago bank and the correspondent account opened there by Lance's Atlanta bank.

The identity of the prospective buyer of Lance's bank stock was disclosed July 26

by the Atlanta Journal and the Atlanta Constitution. He was David N. Smith, 39, of Atlanta, who reportedly had met Lance twice but doubted that Lance would remember him. Smith was head of International Horizons Inc., which sold books and cassettes abroad, primarily in Japan and Brazil, giving instructions for learning English. The sale reportedly was shaping up near or above the price per share paid by Lance originally.

Currency comptroller clears Lance of illegalities. A federal investigation cleared Bert Lance Aug. 18, 1977 of any criminal wrongdoing in his financial affairs while president of the National Bank of Georgia. However, the report did raise questions about the propriety of some of Lance's earlier activities as president of another, smaller Georgia bank.

President Carter, who had had little comment on the matter during the 30-day investigation by John G. Heimann, comptroller of the currency, delivered a personal endorsement of his long-time friend when the report was made public.

Carter interrupted a vacation at Camp David, Md. to return to Washington and appear with Lance at a nationally televised news conference at the White House. "My faith in the character and competence of Bert Lance has been reconfirmed," Carter said, adding, "Bert, I'm proud of you."

Carter's remarks were made shortly after the Heimann report was made public following its presentation to Chairman Ribicoff of the Senate Governmental Affairs Committee.

Questions had been raised about the circumstances under which Lance had obtained several large personal loans and about his stewardship of the two Georgia banks, one in Atlanta and the other in Calhoun.

Much of the controversy focused on a $2.6-million loan Lance had obtained from Manufacturers Hanover Trust Co. of New York in June 1975 when he was president of the Atlanta-based National Bank of Georgia (NBG). During the same period, NBG's large noninterest-bearing correspondence account in New York was transferred to Manufacturers from Citibank

In his report, Heimann said, "There is some documentary and circumstantial evidence suggesting the possibility that" Lance had obtained the loan in return for maintaining the bank's correspondence account with Manufacturers. But, the report added, "All the principals involved denied under oath that such an arrangement existed and that such an arrangement was ever discussed. . . . In light of the uncontroverted testimony, there appears to be no violation of any applicable laws or regulations." Heimann said the Georgia bank's account with Citibank had been unprofitable for the New York institution, and that officials of both banks had expressed "dissatisfaction" with the relationship.

"We do not believe the information developed to date in the inquiry warrants the prosecution of any individual," the report said.

Lance had used the loan from Manufacturers to purchase 148,118 shares of stock, or a 21% ownership, in the National Bank of Georgia.

The report also found no evidence of wrongdoing in Lance's conduct regarding a $3.4-million loan obtained Jan. 7 from First National Bank of Chicago. Lance received the loan one month after the Atlanta bank opened a correspondence account with First National.

Lance, who had just been named to head the Carter budget office, needed the money because he had promised Manufacturers he would repay that loan if he left the National Bank of Georgia. Lance used $2.8 million obtained from the Chicago bank to pay off his Manufacturers loan, and another $600,000 went toward repaying other debts.

The comptroller's office also investigated the relationship between Lance's National Bank of Georgia and a third institution, Chemical Bank of New York. Heimann concluded, "Although it appears that Chemical became a correspondent bank of NBG in part because Chemical lent money to Mr. Lance and Mr. Dan [B.] Patillo [another major shareholder in the Georgia bank], no evidence was discovered indicating that loans to Mr. Lance or Gwinnet Industries Inc. [Patillo's company] were preferential in treatment because of a correspondence relationship."

Lance also obtained loans from the Calhoun First National Bank (the Georgia bank he had headed before moving to the Atlanta bank), the Citizens and Southern National Bank of Atlanta and two separate banks in Knoxville and Nashville, Tenn. that were both named United American Bank. The report uncovered no connection between Lance's personal borrowing at those banks and correspondence accounts maintained there by the Atlanta bank.

Although the report said it had discovered no illegalities in Lance's transactions, Heimann said in a covering letter to Ribicoff that Lance's "recurring pattern of shifting banking relationships and personal borrowing needs raises unresolved questions as to what constitutes acceptable banking practices."

The report said that while Lance was president of the Calhoun bank, "the management from 1972 to 1975 permitted officers, directors and some employes and their families to overdraw checking accounts in substantial amounts for considerable periods of time."

According to the report, Lance's wife, LaBelle, was overdrawn "generally in the $25,000 to $110,000 range between September and December 1974." Nine Lance relatives also were overdrawn a total of $220,000 to $450,000 between September 1974 and April 1975.

The report criticized these actions as "unsafe and unsound banking practices." The report said that after the comptroller's office had complained in 1975 the practices stopped. At the White House news conference, Lance said, "I regret very much that it [the overdrafts] happened," but he denied they constituted improprieties.

The investigation also examined Lance's borrowings from the Calhoun bank during his unsuccessful 1974 race for the Georgia governorship. The report said Lance's Calhoun bank account was overdrawn at times by up to $76,000. After a 1975 investigation, the comptroller's office had turned the matter over to the Justice Department. No charges were filed and the case was closed two days after Lance was nominated as OMB director.

The report also criticized Lance for failing to "file with the banks of which he was an officer certain reports of outside business interests and personal borrowing and of borrowings by his affiliates as required by statute or regulation."

Heimann said Lance did not make the mandatory disclosures on 50 loans obtained between 1970 and 1977.

Regarding the reporting of his outside business activities, Heimann said the law in this area was "new and complex" and therefore he could not conclude that Lance "knowingly" had filed incomplete and inaccurate reports.

Lance comments—Lance said at the news conference that his "ability to carry out my job has not been damaged" by the controversy surrounding his financial affairs. He termed the Heimann study a "very favorable report on my activities," an interpretation that was challenged by reporters in a lengthy and detailed period of questioning that followed.

Jody Powell, White House press secretary, said the report exonerated Lance both "as a matter of law and of ethics." Hamilton Jordan, who, like Lance, was one of Carter's closest political advisers and friend of many years, discounted suggestions that Lance would be forced to resign because of new disclosures that might surface in upcoming congressional investigations.

Jordan had been in close touch with Lance in recent weeks while the President made efforts to keep some distance from his budget director. The White House adopted a "no comment" policy on the matter Aug. 11 and spokesmen said Aug. 12 that Carter would not hold an expected press conference during the next week.

In his ringing endorsement of Lance at the press conference, Carter committed his own credibility and prestige to Lance's defense.

The only question that Lance refused to answer during the press conference involved whether Carter, as a presidential candidate, had ever used the airplane owned by National Bank of Georgia, which Lance then headed. Since the matter was under investigation, Lance said, it would be inappropriate to respond.

Powell later said Carter had made five trips in 1975 and 1976 on the corporate aircraft. Two trips were personal and three might have involved campaign activity, Powell said, adding that the circumstances were being investigated.

Carter backs Lance. The continuing controversy over Bert Lance's financial affairs dominated a presidential press conference Aug. 23, 1977.

Carter reaffirmed his faith in Lance but conceded that the government investigation into Lance's conduct as president of two Georgia banks revealed the need for a reform of banking regulations.

Commenting on the probe by John G. Heimann, comptroller of the currency, Carter said, "I don't know of anything illegal or even unethical that Bert Lance has ever done."

"I have spent a great deal of time trying to become acquainted with the charges or allegations against Bert Lance," Carter said. "It means a lot to him. It means a lot to me personally as a friend of his. It means a lot to me as President, responsible for the integrity and reputation not only of my Cabinet officers but myself."

Carter was asked whether the size and extent of Lance's personal debts, held in a public trust, created the appearance of a conflict of interest for the budget director. The President said he knew of no alternative to the way problems of personal financial matters were handled by the Administration.

"I have holdings in Carter's Warehouse and in my farms," he said. "You can't expect a public official to dispose of all their net worth because they come to government," he added.

Carter was asked whether "the American taxpayer has reason to question the competence of a man in charge of the federal budget, who, after he has taken that job, wrote seven overdrafts in his own account?"

Carter, who appeared surprised, responded, "I didn't know. . . . It's obviously better had he not had them [the overdrafts] but it's no reflection on his basic judgment or competence." Carter added, "Bert Lance is one of the more competent and intelligent people I have ever known in my life."

The President added that he and his wife occasionally had overdrawn their own bank accounts.

Later Aug. 23, in an interview with the Public Broadcasting Service's MacNeil-Lehrer Report, White House Press Secretary Jody Powell said Carter had known about Lance's overdrafts and personal borrowing practices before nominating him as budget director.

Powell also defended what he called the bank's "liberal overdraft policy" that permitted Lance and his family to be overdrawn by large amounts. Powell said this was a common practice among country banks.

Resignation pressure increases—Senate Democratic Leader Robert C. Byrd (W. Va.) told reporters Sept. 10 that Lance's "effectiveness has been destroyed" and his resignation was "inevitable."

Margaret Costanza, assistant to the President for public liaison, said in a television interview in Rochester, N.Y. Sept. 10 that the Lance controversy had "preoccupied" both him and President Carter. Lance "should relieve the President of this burden," Costanza said.

Lance said Sept. 13, "I'm not going to quit and that means I'm not going to quit." He made the remark after a regularly scheduled meeting with the President.

Via a telephone hookup, Carter told a group of broadcast news directors meeting in San Francisco Sept. 15 that he was "keeping an open mind" about Lance's future until the Senate hearings were over. He had no reason to believe that Lance was "dishonest, incompetent or that he has acted unethically," he said. If he believed all the allegations involving Lance, Carter said, "I would have discharged him immediately."

Lance confronts senators. Bert Lance confronted the Senate Governmental Affairs Committee Sept. 15, 1977 and presented a point-by-point defense of his financial affairs. He accused critics on the committee of unfairness and rejected allegations against him as "erroneous."

After he finished his 49-page opening statement, presented at a televised hear-

ing, Lance received a statement of regret from committee chairman Abraham A. Ribicoff (D, Conn.) and an apology from vice chairman Charles H. Percy (R, Ill.).

Lance had complained about having been linked in press comments to a former fellow bank official currently in jail for embezzling. Ribicoff expressed regret that certain press reports had contained "lies" about this. The stories had originated from a meeting Ribicoff and Percy held with reporters following a meeting with President Carter.

Percy agreed with Ribicoff. He also apologized for a suggestion he had made at a committee hearing Sept. 9 that Lance might have backdated some checks early in the year to take some improper tax deductions for the previous year.

Lance had covered the matter in his statement. He said, among other things, that no such tax deduction had been taken.

Percy said, "It was wrong of me to even raise the possibility" of an illegality. He had done it, he said, only to bring all possible allegations out so Lance could deal with them in his defense statement.

In his statement, Lance maintained that he had done his part to inform the committee about his financial affairs during the confirmation process. "I apprised this committee in some detail of my past financial and personal background and answered fully and accurately all questions that any senator or staff member asked," he said.

On the allegation that his bank maintained correspondent accounts to help him secure personal loans, Lance cited reports by the comptroller of the currency absolving him of any illegality.

As for his practice of overdrafts in checking accounts, Lance said there was nothing illegal about overdrafts. An overdraft policy of a bank "simply involves the decision to extend credit to depositors," he explained.

The Calhoun First National Bank, which he formerly headed, had "a liberal" overdraft policy, he said, because the bank's management believed that such a policy was "a valuable tool for the bank to use in attracting and retaining customers."

The practice was available to all depositors, Lance said, and it was a common practice of small rural banks, where the bank personnel knew the customers and could readily determine whether a check ultimately would be covered. Besides, he said, citing statistics, losses charged off on overdrafts at the Calhoun bank were minimal compared to service charge income on deposit accounts.

Lance said that all overdrafts attributed to him or his family had been paid in full and that he had kept on deposit in other accounts funds exceeding the overdrafts.

The questioning begins—Lance handled the opening interrogation by the individual committee members with an easy confidence. There were long stretches of reprieve for him as the committee broke down into frequent partisan bickering.

Denies improper influence—Lance denied allegations that he had used his relationship with President Carter to exert improper influences on federal decisions that could have been harmful to his appointment as budget director.

One decision concerned an agreement between the Calhoun bank and the comptroller of the currency to remedy some banking practices criticized by the comptroller, such as the overdrafts. The agreement, which could be followed by a "cease and desist" order from the federal office, was lifted the same day, Nov. 22, 1976 that Lance paid a visit to Donald Tarleton, Atlanta administrator of the comptroller's office.

Lance said he had not asked nor told Tarleton to remove the agreement, nor had he suggested that it should be rescinded. The bank had complied with the terms of the agreement, Lance said, and the only thing of concern to him at the time was the paperwork involved in filing monthly progress reports with the federal office. Tarleton not did lift the reporting requirement when he rescinded the agreement, Lance pointed out.

Another federal decision was made by the U.S. attorney's office in Atlanta to terminate an investigation into possible violations of law arising from the financing of Lance's 1974 gubernatorial campaign.

Lance said the investigation originated with the comptroller's office and focused on two accounts maintained by Lance's campaign committee at the Calhoun bank. He gave a deposition on the matter, Lance said, then heard nothing about it until more than a year later when his attorney, in December 1976, called the comptroller's office concerning release of confidential information contained in the Calhoun bank agreement. In the course of the conversation, Lance said, his attorney learned that the investigation of the campaign accounts had been turned over to the Justice Department, which had jurisdiction in such cases.

The lawyer further learned that the Justice Department "had closed the case because they had determined that no violation had occurred." Lance said the file was returned to the Atlanta office for further determination of possible prosecution. His lawyer advised him of this in December 1976, he said, and talked with the U.S. attorney in Atlanta, John Stokes, who reported back that he had concluded that no prosecution was appropriate and the investigation had been terminated.

Lance said he had not talked to Stokes, did not ask that the investigation be terminated, nor was such a request made on his behalf by his counsel.

The Ribicoff committee had heard conflicting, and at times contradictory, testimony on these matters Sept. 12–14.

The investigation itself concerned whether the bank's activity constituted illegal contributions to a political campaign. It was dropped, Lance said, because the bank suffered no loss and "all amounts were repaid."

At the outset, Lance said, he had sent the bank $5,000 as a credit to the campaign account, and he had told the bank to notify him for payment of any amounts due because of insufficient funds in the campaign accounts. To back this up, he had a savings certificate pledged at the bank in the amount of $110,000, he said.

Airplane use—Another matter currently under investigation by the Justice Department was whether Lance improperly used business airplanes for personal purposes.

During his campaigning, he said, he had leased an airplane from the Calhoun bank and later, in partnership with his wife, bought a plane. He paid all the expenses incurred, Lance said.

When he joined the National Bank of Georgia as president in 1975, he said there was an agreement with the bank's officials that a plane would be purchased for his use. The bank purchased the Lances' plane.

"It was generally understood that I was to be creating a new image for the bank," he said, "and would be seeking new business whenever . . . I traveled . . .

"To assume that one can readily distinguish personal use of the plane from business use simply ignores the realities involved in developing new business. Such ready pigeonholing of the plane's use is impossible."

'Sloppy' banking practices—To refute the allegation that he had engaged in "sloppy" banking practices, Lance reported that during his tenure as bank president the Calhoun bank showed a growth in total assets from $11.9 million in 1964 to $54.1 million by the end of 1976. National Bank of Georgia showed a 60% increase in total assets to $404 million from $254 million in the two years since January 1975.

Fighting for the system—"I did not ask for this fight, but now that I am in it I am fighting not only for myself but also for our system," Lance told the committee.

He had been a successful businessman, he said, and he had worked hard in Washington the past eight months and was proud of the job he had done. "But is it part of our American system that a man can be drummed out of government by a series of false charges, half-truths, misrepresentations, innuendos and the like?" he asked.

"I have long felt that businessmen should be willing to take positions in our government. They can bring new ideas, new attitudes, new philosophies and, as a result, our government can be more responsive to the views of all our people.

"I speak, more in sorrow than in anger, when I suggest that it won't be any easier to get these men and women to volunteer for public service after my experience of these past weeks."

Powell apologizes to Percy—White House Press Secretary Jody Powell apologized to Sen. Percy Sept. 14 for trying to plant damaging allegations against Percy in several newspapers. One was that Percy had improperly used corporate aircraft while head of Bell & Howell and that he had not fully reimbursed a Chicago bank for facilities used in his 1972 campaign.

One of the papers Powell contacted, the Chicago Sun-Times, reported that Bell & Howell had never owned an airplane and that Percy had offered a canceled check as proof of the bank's reimbursement. The paper also named Powell as the source of the charges.

Powell confessed to reporters that his action was "inappropriate, regrettable and dumb." He said the President agreed with the description. Powell telephoned his apology to Percy.

Powell had offered an earlier confession Sept. 12. He said he and two other Carter aides saw a critical FBI background report on Lance prior to his confirmation but had not informed President Carter. The comptroller's office had informed them that bank overdrafts were common practice in small, rural banks, Powell said. The other two aides were Robert Lipshutz, currently a White House counsel, and Hamilton Jordan, currently special assistant to the president.

Senate ends probe. The Carter standard of ethics as it applied to Lance's background was the key target of the Senate inquiry Sept. 17, 1977 when Lance underwent his third and final day of questioning by the Governmental Affairs Committee.

Republican members zeroed in on certain circumstances in Lance's background as a banker. They were that:

—An enforcement agreement between the Calhoun bank and the U.S. comptroller of the currency had been rescinded a day before Lance's nomination became known.

—A criminal case involving Lance had been dropped by the U.S. attorney in Atlanta the day before Lance's appointment was announced.

—Lance had paid off two New York bank loans, possibly backed by the same collateral, two or three days before he presented his net worth statement to the committee.

—His campaign committee had operated on an overdraft basis from Lance's bank.

—Overdrafts had continued to be drawn by Lance and his family in 1974 and 1975 despite Lance's pledge to the contrary in a letter to the regional administrator of the comptroller's office in 1973.

"Would you say you were a man of your word?" Sen. William V. Roth Jr. (R, Del.) asked about this point.

Lance replied the situation should be viewed in light of "the circumstances at the time." He was referring, as he frequently did, to his preoccupation during this period with his post as state highway administrator and later as candidate for governor of Georgia.

Another recurrent defense theme by Lance was that the practice, such as overdrafts, was common among country banks. "Was it your understanding of President Carter's standard of ethics that it would be the average . . . what everybody does?" Sen. Jacob K. Javits (R, N.Y.) asked.

It was generally assumed that Lance had aided his cause in his nearly 20 hours of testimony, particularly during the first day of the hearings when he presented a lengthy and vigorous defense. Public response reportedly shifted with his appearances from condemnatory to sympathetic.

The committee, on the other hand, showed itself as bickering, partisan and unsure of itself. The hearings themselves were a reminder of the committee's initial failure to meet its responsibility to thoroughly investigate the nominee.

Many of these weaknesses were highlighted when the committee reverted, on the final day of hearings Sept. 19, to investigating itself. The panel called its own staff members to testify that Lance had misled them before confirmation.

Lance 'misled' the staff—Lance had told them in January that news reports of overdrafts by his wife were "false and misleading," the staffers said, when, in fact, evidence to the contrary was developed later.

The staff reported that Lance had blamed overdrafts by his wife's family on the November 1974 suicide of Mrs. Lance's brother. Because of his death, the family's assets had been frozen in estate proceedings. Lance was reported to have said it would be "painful" to the family if

the subject came up in Senate hearings on his nomination. Later reports showed that overdrafts by the family had been practiced for years prior to 1974.

Other problems—Another problem for Lance concerned his use or misuse of his bank's funds to obtain personal loans from other banks.

Still another was a pending Justice Department probe of possible illegal use of corporate aircraft for personal or political trips.

Sen. Charles Percy (R, Ill.) brought out at the Sept. 17 hearing that 1,343 flights, apparently with Lance aboard, had been made by planes owned by the National Bank of Georgia in the two years he was head of the bank. Furthermore, he had sold the bank one of the planes at a $40,000 profit to himself.

Lance admitted he had not reimbursed the bank for most of the flights, including ones to a college football game, to New Orleans for the Mardi Gras, to Warm Springs, Ga. to attend the opening of Carter's presidential campaign. Lance contended there had been some business purposes for all the trips.

More new developments—One of the most serious aspects of the Lance controversy was that new developments kept cropping up.

At the Senate committee hearing Sept. 16, chairman Abraham A. Ribicoff (D, Conn.) questioned Lance's statement that bank examiners had "never" accused him of violating banking laws limiting loans to bank officers. Ribicoff produced a 1971 bank examiner's report on the Calhoun bank stating that Lance had "direct liability in excess of $5,000" in violation of the limit.

"Senator, when I said 'never,' I was referring to the years 1972 to 1977," Lance told Ribicoff.

On Sept. 20, the day after the hearings ended, the Ribicoff committee released an affidavit by a government lawyer that said Lance had sought to have the critical federal agreement removed from the Calhoun bank. While this was not illegal, it was another ethical issue and, in any event, the affidavit contradicted Lance's testimony to the committee.

On Sept. 19, the Justice Department announced that a special three-member panel had been established to handle the various files and materials it had collected and received on the Lance case.

Lance resigns. Bert Lance's resignation as director of the Office of Management & Budget was announced by President Carter at a televised news conference Sept. 21, 1977. The President, who appeared near tears, said, "Bert Lance is my friend. I know him personally as well as if he was my own brother. I know him without any doubt in my mind or heart to be a good and an honorable man."

The resignation, which Carter accepted "with the greatest sense of regret and sorrow," came in the wake of a continuing controversy over Lance's personal financial dealings.

Carter emphasized that Lance's performance in office had never been questioned. He conceded that part of the problem stemmed from "the extraordinary standards that we have tried to set in government and the expectations of the American people that were engendered during my own campaign and my inauguration statement."

As for the allegations against Lance, Carter said, "Nothing that I have heard or read has shaken my belief in Bert's ability or his integrity." Referring to the Senate hearings on the matter, Carter said, "He told the truth.... He was able to clear his name."

In his letter of resignation, which Carter read to open the news conference, Lance said, "My conscience is clear." He was resigning, he wrote, "because of the amount of controversy, and the continuing nature of it."

"I think he's made the right decision," Carter told the reporters, "because it would be difficult for him to devote full time to his responsibilities in the future."

In the question session that followed, Carter denied that he had been "remiss" in checking Lance's qualifications for office and he insisted that the allegations against Lance "in my opinion, have been proven false and without foundation."

"I don't think any mistake was made," he said of Lance's appointment. "I think he was qualified then; I think he is qualified now."

At the time of the appointment, Carter said the only thing he had heard of a controversial nature about Lance's background involved questions about the Calhoun First National Bank, which Lance had headed, and overdrafts. The overdrafts related to Lance's 1974 race for governor of Georgia, Carter said, and he was informed on Dec. 1, 1976 that an investigation into the overdrafts had been closed.

That was the first time that he or Lance knew, the President said, that the Justice Department had been involved at all in investigating the campaign funds.

Carter said a later Federal Bureau of Investigation check on Lance was favorable.

(Carter's recollection was corrected Sept. 22 by White House Press Secretary Jody Powell. He said the President "misspoke himself." The campaign overdrafts and "problems in the comptroller's office" were the only things Carter knew prior to Lance's appointment, Powell said. In the "misspoken" version, Carter would have known that his prospective nominee was under criminal investigation and he would have known the investigation was being dropped the day before it was terminated.)

The President countered suggestions raised at the news conference that Lance's background might be contrary to the standards of propriety and "the appearance of propriety" set forth by Carter in the campaign. "The standards were high at the beginning; the standards are still high," Carter insisted.

As budget director, Lance was considered the Carter Administration's best and most influential spokesman for business and conservative fiscal policy. The continuing controversy, however, was said to have threatened Carter's broad legislative program and to have blemished his reputation as a different politician with ethical standards sterner than most.

Personal debt huge—Lance's immediate personal financial problem, which helped launch the entire controversy, remained in front of him. It involved the sale of 200,767 shares of National Bank of Georgia stock. Dividends from the shares had been his largest source of income while in Washington, but the stock had undergone a considerable decline and the dividend had been discontinued.

Meantime, Lance faced huge interest payments on million-dollar debts. Sen. Charles Mathias (R, Md.), one of Lance's critics on the Ribicoff committee, had estimated Lance to have $5 million in debts and $400,000 in annual interest payments.

(Lance also had a campaign debt estimated in excess of $250,000 left over from his 1974 race for governor.)

Lance returned to his hometown of Calhoun Sept. 22. About a third of the residents turned out to welcome him back.

It was reported in 1978 that Lance had repaid the bank loans with the proceeds from the sale of $2.4 million worth of stock in the National Bank of Georgia to Ghaith R. Pharaon, a Saudi Arabian businessman.

The middleman in arranging that deal was Agha Hasan Abedi, according to the New York Times Feb. 13.

It was disclosed March 22 that Abedi had paid off Lance's bank loans without asking Lance to sign a note or otherwise arrange the terms of repayments.

Lance had surrendered his diplomatic passport to the White House March 20 but held onto his special White House pass that gave him special access to President Carter.

A White House spokesman said the close friendship between Carter and Lance had not changed because of the SEC complaint, the Washington Post reported March 23.

A diplomatic passport, which was given to high-ranking government officials, entitled the bearer to special treatment in international travel, such as freedom from customs searches.

When Lance had resigned as budget director in September 1977, the State Department had routinely asked him to surrender the passport. At Lance's request, however, the White House intervened and he was permitted to retain the passport.

Lance's critics claimed that the passport, a symbol of his continuing close ties to the President, had helped Lance establish contacts with Middle East businessmen.

Further charges against Lance. A civil complaint filed by the SEC March 18, 1978

was settled March 19 by Bert Lance and nine other investors in a Washington bank-holding company.

The SEC accused Lance and the other defendants, among them four wealthy Arabs, of failing to report their attempted takeover of the Washington firm, Financial General Bankshares Inc.

Financial General was Washington's second-largest bank-holding company, with assets of $2.2 billion. It controlled 15 banks in Washington, Maryland, Virginia, Tennessee and New York.

Other defendants, beside Lance, named in the SEC complaint were:

Bank of Credit & Commerce International S.A., a London bank that managed Arab funds, and Agha Hasan Abedi, the bank's president;

Sheik Sultan bin Zaid al Nahyan, crown prince of Abu Dhabi, a member of the United Arab Emirates;

Abdullah Darwaish, financial adviser to the Abu Dhabi royal family, who acted as agent for the crown prince's brother, a minor;

Sheik Kamal Adham, former head of Saudi Arabia's foreign intelligence agency;

Faisal Saud al-Fulaij, a Kuwaiti businessman;

Eugene J. Metzger, a Washington lawyer; and

Stephens Inc., a Little Rock, Ark. brokerage firm, and its president, Jackson T. Stephens, who was also a member of the executive committee of the Democratic National Committee.

The SEC alleged that Lance and his associates violated federal disclosure laws, including the Williams Act, when they secretly purchased 28% of the outstanding stock in Financial General.

The SEC also accused J. William Middendorf II, secretary of the Navy in the Ford Administration and currently president of Financial General, of failing to disclose that he acted on behalf of a group when he took control of Financial General in 1977.

The SEC charged that Lance, while still director of the Office of Management and Budget, had helped Middendorf assemble the group, which included Metzger and Stephens.

Metzger and Stephens later became

dissatisfied with Middendorf's management, the SEC said. With the aid of Lance and Abedi, Metzger and Stephens found the four Arab partners willing to join with them in purchasing a block of Financial General stock in order to take control of the firm.

The Arab investors each bought 4.9% of the outstanding shares, for a total of more than 1 million shares. With purchases by Metzger, Stephens and Lance, who bought 13,000 shares for his wife's account, the group obtained control of 28% of Financial General's stock.

(The Williams Act required that the SEC be notified when an individual or group purchased at least 5% of a publicly held company.)

In settling the complaint, the defendants promised not to violate federal securities law in the future, but they neither admitted nor denied the SEC's charges.

As part of the settlement, the members of the Lance group (all of the defendants except Middendorf) agreed that within one year they would buy all the remaining shares in the firm at an above-market price, or sell their interest in Financial General.

(The group agreed to pay $15 a share, which had been the highest price paid so far in acquiring the block of stock. In trading March 17 on the American Stock Exchange, Financial General stock closed at $11.38 a share.)

The Lance group also agreed to set up a $1-million fund, out of which it would make restitution to Financial General stockholders who had sold their shares to the group for less than the $15 court-approved minimum price.

In a speech April 12 to the American Society of Newspaper Editors, Lance accused the news media of slipshod reporting about the controversy leading to his resignation and with regard to subsequent business dealings.

As an example of alleged journalistic inaccuracy, Lance claimed that one of the charges in the SEC's complaint was false—that while budget director, he had become involved in the early stages of the bank takeover dispute.

Lance claimed the SEC charge was false. "Everyone involved says it is false."

None of the reporters who wrote the story ever checked the accuracy of the SEC's charge, he said. (Like the later complaint, Lance had settled the SEC case without admitting or denying the charges.)

Lance had resigned as budget director following investigations into his personal finances by both houses of Congress and six federal regulatory agencies. All of the charges contained in the SEC's and comptroller's complaint were aired during congressional hearings. At that time, Lance denied under oath that he was guilty of any wrongdoing.

Bank practices assailed—Lance was charged April 26, 1978 with civil fraud and "unsafe and unsound banking practices and financial irregularities."

The charges were filed jointly by the Securities and Exchange Commission and the Comptroller of the Currency.

Also named as defendants were the two Georgia banks that Lance had headed before joining the Carter Administration in January 1977. Lance was president and later chairman of Calhoun First National Bank from 1963 until 1977, and president of National Bank of Georgia (in Atlanta) from 1975 to 1977.

The banks were accused of engaging in or acquiescing in Lance's questionable dealings.

Lance and the banks settled the government's complaint as soon as it was filed in U.S. District Court in Atlanta. They promised not to violate in the future the banking and securities laws cited in the complaint, but they neither admitted nor denied the charges. Lance also agreed not to become involved in the management or control of any bank for "at least the next six months."

These were some of the specific charges against Lance in the complaint:

■ He used "devices, schemes and artifices to defraud" past, present and prospective shareholders of both banks.

■ At both banks, loans were made on favorable terms to Lance, his relatives, friends and business associates.

■ "Substantial and prolonged overdrafting" privileges also were extended by the Calhoun bank to the Lance group that were not extended to other Calhoun customers. At one point, their overdrafts to-

taled $800,000—more than 70% of all
overdrafts at the bank.

■ These credit extensions jeopardized
the Calhoun bank's financial stability in
1975, when the bank had a "severe
liquidity problem."

■ "In order to create the appearance
that these problems had been eliminated,
Calhoun engaged in a series of undisclosed
or misrepresented transactions . . . [that
included] the making of misleading entries
on Calhoun's books."

■ Lance submitted loan applications
that were false and misleading statements
of his net worth. One of these statements
also was submitted to the Senate committee considering his nomination as budget
director. Lance and his wife overstated
their net worth by $1.2 million.

■ He used the Calhoun bank's general
funds to pay $80,000 of his initial expenses
in the 1974 Georgia gubernatorial race.
Three checking accounts maintained at
the Calhoun bank to pay campaign
expenses also "were overdrawn during
their existence" by amounts that, at
times, totaled more than $240,000.

The White House had no comment on
the charges and Lance's settlement of the
complaint.

Other Developments

Byington resigns. S. John Byington
resigned Feb. 8, 1978 as chairman of the
Consumer Product Safety Commission,
claiming that he was a victim of "political
harassment" by the Carter Administration. Byington, a Republican, had been
nominated for a seven-year term by
President Ford in 1976. The Senate had
approved his appointment for a term of
two and a half years until October 1978.
Byington resigned effective June 30.

The Civil Service Commission had
issued a report Jan. 12 charging Byington
and the CPSC with favoritism in hiring,
misuse of consultants and promoting unqualified persons. Byington was also the
target of Justice Department investigations of those allegations. One such probe
centered on an assertion that a Los
Angeles consulting firm, Terzian
Associates, had done unpaid public relations work for Byington after he had
awarded the company two contracts for
government work.

In his letter of resignation, Byington
claimed that the investigations were begun
shortly after he refused requests from the
White House to hire some of Carter's
campaign workers to work at the CPSC.
He would not name those who asked him
to do the hiring.

Miller confirmed to Fed. G. William
Miller, President Carter's choice as
chairman of the Federal Reserve Board,
won Senate confirmation March 3, 1978
by voice vote.

The only dissenting vote was cast by
Sen. William Proxmire (D, Wis.),
chairman of the Senate Banking Committee. Proxmire also had cast the only nay
vote when the banking panel recommended Miller's confirmation March 2.

Proxmire said after the Senate vote that
Miller would take office "under a cloud of
investigation and suspicion."

The Banking Committee had spent
more than five weeks investigating
Miller's possible involvement, as
chairman of Textron Inc., with a $2.9-
million foreign payment by a Textron subsidiary in connection with a large arms
sale to Iran.

The questionable payment was made to
Air Taxi Co., an Iranian firm that acted as
sales agent for Textron's Bell Helicopter
division in connection with the awarding of
an Iranian government contract in 1973
valued at $650 million.

The sales agency allegedly was controlled in part by the late Gen. Moham-
med Khatemi, Iran's air chief and the
Shah's brother-in-law. Khatemi died in a
glider accident in 1975.

The Securities and Exchange Commission currently was conducting its own
investigation of the payment. The SEC
went to court March 2 seeking a subpoena
to force Textron to release certain documents related to the probe. Textron had
refused to turn over the material, saying
the SEC could not guarantee that the
documents' confidentiality would be
protected.

During committee hearings Feb. 28, Proxmire had asked Miller to withdraw voluntarily as a nominee because of the continuing SEC investigation. Miller heatedly refused. He said he had tried to run a "super-clean" company and repeated his earlier testimony that he had no knowledge of Khatemi's alleged link with Air Taxi. Had he known, Miller said, he "wouldn't have approved" paying the money to a government official.

Miller termed the $2.9-million payment a legitimate sales commission, not a bribe. "A bribe must be a payment with intent to influence a decision, and since Textron officials knew of no secret ownership [of Air Taxi by Khatemi], there could be no bribe," Miller said.

Under questioning, however, he admitted that $300,000 paid in 1971 to Nigerian sales agents in connection with Bell Helicopter sales in Ghana was a "strange transaction."

Questions about the previously undisclosed payment to Air Taxi were first raised by Proxmire during hearings Jan. 24. He said he had the "strongest kind of assurances" that Khatemi was a secret partner in the Iranian firm.

Proxmire did not disclose his source, but the Wall Street Journal reported Jan. 25 that the information came from the Central Intelligence Agency.

CIA, Pentagon Knew of Khatemi Link—The Journal reported Feb. 17 that both the CIA and the Pentagon, which administered the Iranian contract for Bell Helicopter, were aware of Khatemi's link to Air Taxi. The Journal report was based on CIA and Defense Department documents.

The Journal said this "proof of the U.S. government's knowledge that a major U.S. corporation was paying a ranking Iranian military officer . . . strengthens a theory that has been gaining currency in recent months. At times, it's asserted, the CIA in particular viewed such payments as a way of buying intelligence information, cementing valuable friendships for the U.S. and, especially in Italy and Japan, financing pro-American, anti-Communist parties."

Despite several weeks of investigation by the committee staff, no evidence was uncovered to contradict Miller's claim that he knew of no connection between Khatemi and Air Taxi.

Proxmire remained unconvinced, however. "The facts ring loud and clear," he said Feb. 28. "Textron bribed Khatemi."

"Senator," Miller replied, "everything you've said I disagree with."

Many Democrats on the Banking Committee, angered by Proxmire's hostile questioning of Miller, were near open revolt against the chairman by Feb. 28. Several members tried to end the hearings without consulting Proxmire.

That effort failed, but with Proxmire's concurrence, the committee ended its probe March 2 with a 14–1 vote in favor of Miller's nomination.

"No member of the committee wants the investigation to become an inquisition," Sen. Adlai Stevenson (D, Ill.) said Feb. 28. (He had been a backer of Proxmire's lengthy examination.)

During Senate debate preceding the confirmation vote, Stevenson said Miller's "reputation is without blemish."

Proxmire, however, termed Miller a "glib, articulate amateur" unqualified by training, background or experience to direct the nation's monetary policy.

Miller was sworn in as chairman of the Federal Reserve Board at a White House ceremony March 8.

Gartner appointment attacked. Sen. Orrin G. Hatch (R, Utah) in the Senate June 7, 1978 resumed an attack on President Carter's appointment of David Gartner to a $50,000-a-year job on the Commodities Futures Trading Commission.

Hatch noted that Gartner was nominated "after he had received, as the parent of four children, about $18,000 of stock in Archer-Daniel-Midland for each of those children, for a total of $72,000, while he was administrative assistant to Sen. Hubert Humphrey [D] of Minnesota and while Sen. Humphrey sat on the Agriculture Committee, which I understand supervises the Commodities Future Trading Commission." Hatch continued:

"I indicated that I cannot believe that any Republican could get away with having his administrative assistant accept, for his children, $72,000 of Archer-Daniel-Midlands stock, a company which does $3 billion annually in the commodities markets of the United States. "I do not believe that, under the present hiring policies of the Commodities Futures Trading Commission, Mr. Gartner even would be qualified or even would be able to get a job with them, had it not been for this appointment, which was rushed through on the floor of the Senate about 5:40 p.m. one day, I think basically unexpectedly.

"Hardly anybody raised a voice against this appointment. Yet, Mr. Gartner is now in the enviable position of being a very close friend of Dwayne Andreas, who owns Archer-Daniel-Midlands, among other things, which gave the $72,000 worth of stock in trust for his children while he was employed by a Senator who sat on the Agriculture Committee.

"Mr. Gartner was appointed to this commission as a board member. The commission supervises the commodities of the United States, supervises more billions of dollars in commodities than all the business combined that is done by the stock markets of the United States, including the New York Stock Exchange, the American Stock Exchange, and the other stock exchanges of this country.

"I had the temerity to criticize this appointment because I think it is wrong, when a man would not qualify if he applied for a job with the commission, to be appointed to the commission, when he has such a blatant conflict of interest. I cannot imagine anybody, whether he is a Democrat or a Republican, who is a Member of the Senate and has an administrative assistant who had taken gifts for some big oil company, being able to sit on any power commission or any other commission in Government which

has to do with oil companies, without having all problems break loose on the floor of the Senate. ...

"I might also add that the gifts he took were from people who had a direct interest in the commission which he will be sitting upon, and a notorious group of people at that, who he characterized as his friends, and I believe that the record of the proceedings before the Agricultural Committee will show that he said that he would not participate in any matters directly involving Archer-Daniel-Midlands, but almost everything directly or indirectly involves Archer-Daniel-Midlands with regard to its business in the commodities field which is its principal business. ... "

Sen. Howard M. Metzenbaum (D, Ohio) asked Hatch whether he found "any difficulty, using the same line of reasoning, as to the appointment of Lynn Coleman, for whom I believe the senator [Hatch] voted, coming directly from the oil and gas industry, as an attorney for the past 12 years, and then being appointed as general counsel of the Department of Energy?" Hatch replied: "Not at all, because he was not an administrative assistant for a sitting senator who supervised the Federal Power Commission...."

Metzenbaum continued: "... I have the feeling that there is this kind of conflict of interest that becomes so apparent where people are so identified with an industry, whether it be by reason of acceptance of $72,000 in trust for your children or whether it be by reason of coming directly from that industry and then going onto one of our regulatory commissions or, as the case may be, becoming general counsel for an agency of government that is going to regulate the very industry from which you came."

Other Political Issues

Financial Abuses Charged

The Watergate investigations continued to produce evidence of political-financial misdeeds not specifically involved in the actual Watergate break-in and cover-up.

Operation Townhouse. Former White House aide Harry S. Dent pleaded guilty Dec. 11, 1974 to taking part in Operation Townhouse, an illegal fund raising effort mounted by the Nixon Administration to secretly funnel more than $3 million to Republican Congressional candidates in 1970.

In pleading guilty to the misdemeanor charge filed by the Watergate special prosecutor's office, Dent claimed the operation had been "under the direction of the President . . . and I believed, and in fact was told, that the program was legal." Judge George L. Hart Jr. of U.S. District Court in Washington said Dent was "more an innocent victim than a perpetrator" and sentenced him to one month of unsupervised probation. He had faced maximum penalties of one year in jail and a $1,000 fine.

Dent, a South Carolina lawyer and protege of Sen. Strom Thurmond (R), had been President Nixon's chief political strategist. He was known as the architect of Nixon's "Southern strategy," an effort to win Republican support in an area that had traditionally voted Democratic.

Dent had quit the White House in 1972 and later served as general counsel to the Republican National Committee, a post he resigned Dec. 6.

Jack A. Gleason, another former employe of the Nixon White House, who had pleaded guilty to organizing the illegal $3 million Operation Townhouse project, was also placed on unsupervised probation by Judge Hart Jan. 17, 1975. Gleason's lawyer told the judge that his client had been assured by his White House superiors that the secret project was legal.

Babcock & Hammer plead guilty. During more than a year of legal maneuvering, former Gov. Tim M. Babcock of Montana and Chairman Armand Hammer of the Occidental Petroleum Corp. pleaded guilty to making illegal contributions to the Nixon reelection campaign.

Babcock pleaded guilty Dec. 10, 1974 to charges of aiding and abetting Hammer in illegally donating $54,000. The misdemeanor charges filed by the Watergate special prosecutor's office accused Babcock of violating a federal law that prohibited campaign donations given in the name of another person.

According to the prosecutor's office,

137

Babcock delivered the cash to the Committee to Re-elect the President between September 1972 and January 1973 while serving as executive vice president of a Washington-based Occidental subsidiary. In May 1973 Babcock had told the committee that the money had been given in his name.

Babcock was sentenced by Chief Judge George L. Hart Jr. of U.S. District Court in Washington to serve four months in jail (the term was set aside by Hart June 4, 1976). Babcock was also fined $1,000. (Hart actually gave Babcock the maximum one-year sentence but initially told him he would have to serve only four months and then go on probation for two years.)

Hammer pleaded guilty Oct. 1, 1975 to three misdemeanor charges in the case.

According to court documents, Hammer pledged $100,000 to the Nixon finance committee with the stipulation that the contribution be made anonymously. However, Hammer provided only $46,000 to the committee before April 7, 1972, when a new federal campaign law took effect requiring the disclosure of donors' identities.

Judge William E. Jones of U.S. District Court in Washington almost refused to accept Hammer's guilty plea. The court session opened with Jones asking Hammer routine questions indicating he understood the consequences of a guilty plea, including the possibility that he could be sentenced to three years in jail and fined $3,000. Hammer replied that the prison sentencing provision was in dispute and being tested in the appeals court.

After Jones threatened to reject the guilty plea, which could have made Hammer subject to a jury trial, Hammer acknowledged that he could be sentenced to jail for his misdemeanor offenses.

Jones finally did throw out Hammer's guilty plea Dec. 12 and ordered him tried.

Jones said he believed the guilty plea had no factual basis, a legal condition that was required before a plea could be accepted. Jones based his opinion on a letter, dated Oct. 27, Hammer sent to a probation officer.

In the letter, Hammer claimed he was pressured by the Nixon re-election committee to increase his contributions, and he said he was duped by Babcock, who,

he charged, was largely to blame for the illegal contribution.

Hammer, 78, also told his probation officer that he had a serious heart condition and could not survive the tensions of a trial or a prison sentence.

The U.S. Court of Appeals in Washington ruled Jan. 20, 1976 that Hammer could withdraw his controversial letter and enter a new guilty plea to the misdemeanor charges. The case was transferred to Los Angeles Feb. 5 after court-appointed physicians said Hammer, hospitalized in Los Angeles with a heart condition, was too ill to travel.

Hammer's fresh guilty plea to the three counts was entered in U.S. District Court in Los Angeles March 4, 1976.

Hammer sought to enter his guilty plea with the Los Angeles court from his hospital bed. The request was denied but Hammer was permitted to sit in a wheelchair during the 20-minute hearing.

Judge Lawrence T. Lydick sentenced Hammer March 23 to a year's probation and fined him $3,000. Lydick, who could have sentenced Hammer to up to three years in prison, said the sentence was reduced because of Hammer's age and ill health.

Former Postmaster General W. Marvin Watson pleaded guilty in U.S. District Court in Washington Sept. 23, 1976 to helping Hammer cover up the illegal campaign contributions. Judge George Hart fined Watson $500, the maximum amount. He also could have been sentenced to six months in jail. The charges against Watson had been brought by Charles H. Ruff, Watergate special prosecutor.

Watson became an Occidental official after leaving the Johnson Administration, where he had served first as a top White House aide and then as postmaster general. He admitted arranging in 1973 and 1974 for the delivery of false documents to conceal Hammer's illegal contribution.

Stans pleads guilty. Former Commerce Secretary Maurice Stans, who had been President Nixon's chief campaign fund raiser, pleaded guilty March 19, 1975 to five misdemeanor violations of the federal campaign finance law.

Stans admitted he had "nonwillfully" accepted two illegal contributions totaling

$70,000 and had failed to report three other cash transactions totaling $150,000.

In a statement to reporters after the guilty plea was entered in U.S. District Court in Washington, Stans claimed that disposition of the misdemeanor charges "established once and for all that I had no guilty involvement in the Watergate burglary, the Watergate cover-up, the Segretti sabotage, the ITT case, the White House plumbers affair, or the 1971 dairy industry dealings."

The five counts to which Stans pleaded guilty:

■ Secretly accepting a $30,000 contribution from Minnesota Mining & Manufacturing Co. in March 1972.

■ Secretly accepting an illegal $40,000 contribution from Goodyear Tire & Rubber Co. in March 1972.

■ Accepting a $30,000 contribution from former Philippines Ambassador Ernesto Lagdameo on June 29, 1972 and failing to report the donation to the Finance Committee to Re-elect the President. The finance committee, which Stans headed, did not report the donation to the General Accounting Office (GAO) as required.

■ Giving $81,000 between June 26 and July 4, 1972 to Nixon campaign aide Frederick C. LaRue. The transaction was never reported to the finance committee or to the GAO.

■ Failing to report a $39,000 contribution given by former Montana Gov. Tim Babcock on behalf of Armand Hammer, chairman of Occidental Petroleum Corp.

Although the charges did not say so, money involved in the illegal transactions to which Stans pleaded guilty figured in the Watergate scandal. According to a cash flow chart introduced by the prosecutor's office at the trial of the five cover-up defendants, the $81,000 Stans gave LaRue was used to buy the silence of two Watergate break-in defendants. A portion of the Babcock-Hammer donation also went to LaRue for use as hush money. Stans turned the $30,000 contribution from Lagdameo over to Herbert·Kalmbach, Nixon's personal attorney and also a major campaign fund raiser. At one point, Kalmbach controlled disbursement of the hush money.

Stans was fined $5,000 May 14. The maximum penalty was a year in prison and a $1,000 fine on each of the five counts. Judge John Lewis Smith Jr. of·U.S. District Court in Washington imposed sentence after hearing a brief plea from Stans for the court's "understanding and leniency." He did not "intentionally violate any law," Stans told the court.

No prison term was set, Judge Smith explained, because "it is not alleged that Mr. Stans profited personally, that money went into his own pocket." Another factor in his sentencing decison, the judge added, was Stans' "long public and private career." "The court finds that the ends of justice and the public interest are best served by a monetary penalty," Judge Smith declared.

Former AMPI officials get jail term. Two former officials of the nation's largest dairy cooperative, Associated Milk Producers Inc. (AMPI), were sentenced Nov. 1, 1974 to four-month terms and fined $10,000 each for violating federal campaign contributions laws.

AMPI's former general manager, Harold S. Nelson, and David L. Parr, the firm's former special counsel, were the first individuals charged by the Watergate special prosecutor's office with making illegal corporate payments to politicians to receive prison sentences.

Chief Judge George L. Hart Jr. of federal district court in Washington said he imposed the jail terms to deter other violators. "You pleaded guilty to crimes that hundreds of persons have been guilty of in past years. Nothing was ever done about it," the judge said.

Hart also criticized the Watergate special prosecutor's failure to bring charges against recipients of the illegal contributions. "Is there no violation by the donee?" Hart asked. A spokesman for the prosecutor's office responded, "Some of these events are under active investigation."

The sentences were imposed after Nelson and Parr pleaded guilty in July to conspiring to make illegal corporate donations to Republican and Democratic candidates. Nelson's sentence also covered another charge of conspiring to bribe John B. Connally Jr., then Treasury secretary, for his help in arranging an increase in federal milk price supports.

Nelson and Parr had faced maximum five-year prison sentences. Hart sentenced them to three years in jail, but suspended all but four months of the sentence.

Nelson had also pleaded guilty July 31 to a charge that he conspired to bribe Connally in connection with AMPI's effort to secure the milk price support increase.

Nelson admitted a $1,000,000 AMPI payment made in August 1969 to President Nixon's chief fund raiser, Herbert Kalmbach. The money was paid, Nelson stated, "for the purpose of securing access to White House officials."

Nelson admitted that AMPI funds were used to reimburse the co-op's political affiliate, TAPE, for the Kalmbach payment "to obviate the need for TAPE to report said payment."

Nelson's guilty plea came in a wide ranging, one-count conspiracy charge incorporating the bribery and illegal corporate contributions aspects. Among the other "overt acts" cited in the criminal information filed by the special prosecutor's office were authorizations made by Nelson for a $63,500 payment to the Democratic National Committee for tickets to a fund raising dinner in 1968 to benefit then Vice President Hubert H. Humphrey's presidential campaign; a $23,950 donation to Humphrey's 1970 senatorial race in Minnesota; a $5,000 gift to the unsuccessful senatorial campaign conducted by then Vermont Gov. Philip Hoff (D); a $10,000 donation to Rep. Page Belcher's (R, Okla.) campaign for re-election; an $8,400 payment to committees organized for Sen. Edmund S. Muskie's (D, Me.) re-election campaign in 1970; and payments totaling $82,000 made to a computer mail service firm that performed work for "various Democratic Party candidates for federal elective office in Iowa" ($50,000), Humphrey's 1972 presidential primary race ($25,000) and Sen. James Abourezk's (D, S.D.) 1972 campaign ($7,000).

Many of the payments authorized by Nelson were carried out by TAPE official Robert Lilly, who was also said to have

been on the AMPI payroll while working on the 1968 Humphrey campaign. Lilly, who had been cooperating with the special prosecutor's office under a grant of immunity, had told investigators that former AMPI counsel Jake Jacobsen had sought the Connally payment and that Nelson had authorized it.

According to the special prosecutor's office, Nelson's agreement to plead guilty to the felony violation came after plea bargaining negotiations in which he promised to make a "full and truthful disclosure" of all he knew about AMPI's other political dealings; however, Nelson was not granted immunity on possible violations relating to the President's March 25, 1971 decision to raise milk support prices, the special prosecutor's office added.

Nelson's former deputy at AMPI and the co-op's special counsel, David L. Parr, was the first official charged as a result of the special prosecutor's milk fund investigation. Parr pleaded guilty July 23 to a charge that he had authorized payment of more than $200,000 in illegal campaign contributions to Humphrey and other candidates of both parties.

Others named as unindicted co-conspirators were Nelson, Lilly, Robert O. Isham, also a TAPE official, and Stuart H. Russell, an Oklahoma lawyer cited for his role as a conduit of the illegal payments.

According to the special prosecutor's charge, a total of $150,450 was donated to Humphrey's 1968 presidential race, his 1970 senatorial campaign and his unsuccessful bid for the Democratic presidential nomination in 1972.

Other illegal payments which Parr admitted authorizing were a $50,000 payment to Democrat Richard Clark's 1972 election to the Senate from Iowa; a $10,000 payment to Rep. Belcher in 1972; $7,000 contribution to Abourezk in 1972; and $5,000 to Rep. Wilbur D. Mill's (D, Ark.) unsuccessful campaign for the Democratic presidential nomination in 1972.

It was also alleged that Lilly was paid by AMPI while he worked for the campaign of Patrick J. Hillings, a Republican who lost a California race for Congress in 1972.

The criminal conspiracy to which Parr pleaded guilty did not involve President Nixon's re-election campaign or his controversial 1971 decision to raise federal milk price supports, but like Nelson, Parr's plea bargaining agreement did not extend to protection from possible bribery and conspiracy charges involving the President's price increase action. In a letter attached to the charges, the special prosecutor's office told the court, "It is expressly understood that Mr. Parr isn't receiving immunity from prosecution for possible violations in connection with the March 25, 1971 milk price support decision."

In a separate action, Norman Sherman and Jack Valentine were each fined $500 for "aiding and abetting" the illegal use of $82,000 in corporate funds donated by Associated Milk Producers Inc. to several Democratic candidates for federal office in 1972. Sentence was imposed Oct. 10.

Sherman, a former press secretary to Sen. Hubert H. Humphrey (D, Minn.), and Valentine were partners in a Minneapolis computerized mail service firm which had been hired to prepare voter surveys. They had pleaded guilty in August to a one-count misdemeanor charge brought by the special prosecutor's office.

No limit set on AMPI contributions— Former AMPI general manager Harold Nelson had testified to the Senate Watergate Committee that the co-op had set no ceiling on its proposed contributions to the Nixon re-election campaign, but that the President's fund raisers "bungled" plans for collecting the money and thereby limited the dairy lobby's potential for donations.

The testimony was reported by the Washington Post July 17. According to Nelson, AMPI's total donations would have far surpassed the actual amount given (more than $500,000) if Nixon aides had not been so slow in setting up dummy committees to receive (and conceal) the subdivided contributions. "Even when they gave us the committees, they bungled it," he said. "For instance, one of the committee's address was a ballroom. . . . Another one, the chairman was a Washington lawyer whose name I cannot tell you. He had not even been consulted. . . ,

and it made him so mad that he blew his stack and called the clerk of the House."

Although he urged the White House to set up the conduits for donation early in 1971, Nelson said, the Administration was slow to act until many weeks after the decision was made to increase federal milk price supports. This tardiness worried him, Nelson added. "It was a constant thing in the back of my mind that if we didn't get the names of these committees, we might be read off just because of some inept—for want of a better term, I will say 'bureaucrat'—within the party hierarchy not coming forth and giving us the names of the committees."

"We told them [Nixon fund raisers] from the word go that we would make large contributions," he said. "At various times, $1 million, $2 million or even more money was discussed. And had they given us the names of the committees, they could have gotten much more money from us," he testified.

Co-op fined for campaign violations— Associated Milk Producers Inc. (AMPI) was fined $35,000 Aug. 1 after pleading guilty to a six-count criminal information charging conspiracy and illegal campaign giving.

Rejecting pleas for leniency, U.S. District Court Chief Judge George L. Hart Jr. imposed the maximum fine. "The law against corporations giving political contributions has been on the books for a long, long time." Hart said. "It's been completely disregarded by Republicans, Democrats, independents and whatnot for a long, long time. This type of cavalier violation of the law has got to be put to a stop."

AMPI's lawyer had asked Hart to assess a penalty of $15,000 for the felony charges, contending that the co-op "represents a membership of 40,000 hard-working, sincere, honest dairy farmers" whose board of directors was not "sophisticated in this matter" and thereby had delegated operating authority to the co-op's general manager.

The co-op's membership had "learned a bitter lesson about giving too much power to a few," the group's lawyer told the court, adding that because of publicity linking the co-op to the "overhanging shadow" of Watergate, AMPI now was finding it awkward to deal with government officials.

Hart replied, "I can't believe the directors of the corporations, even though they are farmers, didn't know what was going on." Hart was also critical of the recipients of these illegal contributions, saying "I find it difficult to believe that these [campaign] organizations are so loose that they know so little about what is going on."

Politicians who had received the illegal money had denied any knowledge of its corporate source. AMPI President John E. Butterbrodt issued a statement Aug. 1 saying that the co-op was "aware of no evidence whatever" indicating that candidates who had accepted the dairy co-op's funds "had any knowledge whatsoever of the actions taken in their apparent behalf."

Jacobsen pleads guilty. Jake Jacobsen, a former counsel for Associated Milk Producers Inc., pleaded guilty Aug. 7, 1974 to a federal charge that he had bribed former Treasury Secretary John B. Connally Jr. in an effort to secure Administration support for an increase in federal milk price supports. Connally, who had been indicted on five counts of accepting a bribe, conspiring to obstruct justice and commit perjury, and making false declarations, pleaded not guilty to the charges Aug. 9.

Jacobsen's plea was entered in Washington before U.S. District Court Chief judge George L. Hart Jr.

At the arraignment, Jacobsen told the court he had paid Connally, a long-time political associate in Texas, a total of $10,000 in dairy co-op funds in return for recommending the price increase in March 1971. Jacobsen had been plea bargaining with the Watergate special prosecutor's office in an effort to reduce the charges against him.

A letter to Jacobsen's lawyers detailing the special prosecutor's negotiating conditions, dated May 21, was released Aug. 7. In it, the special prosecutor's office agreed to dispose of federal charges pending against Jacobsen in Texas in connection with the alleged misapplication of funds

from a savings and loan institution. "This understanding," the letter continued, "is expressly conditioned on full and truthful disclosure by Mr. Jacobsen and won't bar prosecution for any false testimony given hereafter or for any serious offenses committed by Mr. Jacobsen of which this office is presently unaware."

(Jacobsen was sentenced Aug. 20, 1976 to two years' probation. He had also been given a seven-year probation term on his plea of guilty to a state charge of swindling the savings and loan association of $825,000.)

Connally acquitted. Former Treasury Secretary John B. Connally Jr. was acquitted April 17, 1975 of charges of accepting $10,000 in illegal gratuities from an Associated Milk Producers Inc. emissary as a "thank you" for his 1971 recommendation that the Nixon Administration raise federal milk price supports.

At the request of the Watergate special prosecutor's office, Chief Judge George L. Hart Jr. April 18 also dismissed the two-count perjury charge and one-count charge of conspiracy to obstruct justice that remained pending against Connally in connection with the bribery case. (In November 1974, Hart had ordered that the charges be considered separately.)

The bribery charge brought against Connally by the Watergate special prosecutor's office was based on the testimony of Jake Jacobsen, AMPI's former lawyer and one-time Connally friend, who claimed he had delivered two $5,000 cash payments to Connally in appreciation for his role in winning the price-support increase.

Jacobsen also claimed that when the prosecutor's office began examining the dairymen's large contributions to the Nixon re-election campaign, he and Connally attempted to cover up the alleged payoff by agreeing to tell investigators that Jacobsen offered him $10,000 in cash for use by political candidates of his choosing, but that Connally twice refused the offer and that Jacobsen then stored the untouched money in a Texas safe deposit box.

The prosecution contended that the first $10,000 Connally had provided as replacement money was not placed in circulation until after 1971, and that when Connally realized this, he substituted another $10,000 in its place. The cover-up went awry, according to prosecution, when it was discovered that this second cache also had not been in circulation at the time of the alleged payoff.

At this point, Jacobsen agreed to cooperate with the prosecution.

The defense charged that Jacobsen was a liar and embezzler who framed Connally to save himself. According to Connally's lawyer, Edward Bennett Williams, Jacobsen told investigators six times—four under oath—that Connally had never accepted an illegal gratuity, and only changed his story when he faced up to 40 years in jail on perjury and bank fraud charges. In pleading guilty to the single bribe-giving count involving Connally, Williams noted, Jacobsen faced only up to two years in jail. Williams also charged that Jacobsen converted the AMPI money intended for Connally to his own use.

Jacobsen testified April 13 that Connally had solicited the alleged payoff and that $10,000 was obtained from AMPI official Bob A. Lilly for that purpose. The first installment was delivered to Connally May 14, 1971 and the second was turned over Sept. 24, 1971, Jacobsen said. Both payoffs occurred at Connally's Treasury Department office in Washington, according to Jacobsen.

The prosecution alleged that the coverup was concocted when Jacobsen told Connally in October 1973 that Lilly was believed to be cooperating with federal investigators probing AMPI's massive illegal political contributions.

After agreeing on the cover-up story, the prosecution alleged that Connally delivered the replacement money to Jacobsen in a cigar box Oct. 29, 1973 at a meeting in Connally's Houston law firm. Jacobsen subsequently deposited the money as arranged in an Austin bank box.

Several days later, the prosecution contended, Connally asked Jacobsen to substitute another $10,000 for the money in the safe deposit box when it was discovered that the first replacement cash bore Treasury Secretary George P. Shultz's signature, and hence, could not

have been circulation in May 1971. (Shultz succeeded Connally in May 1972.) According to Jacobsen, the exchange took place at the Austin home of a mutual friend, George Christian, former President Lyndon B. Johnson's press secretary.

The prosecution claimed that despite the exchange, 16 bills in the second batch "just were too new to have been put" in circulation in May 1971 as Connally and Jacobsen had said.

The prosecution rested April 11 after Jacobsen and 35 other witnesses, including officials of all 12 Federal Reserve regional banks, testified in support of the charges. Although considerable circumstantial evidence was introduced corroborating Jacobsen's accounts of meetings with Connally and bank dealings, the prosecution was unable to produce a witness to the alleged payoff and the case hinged entirely on Jacobsen's testimony.

Unlike other Watergate-related trials, the prosecution produced no incriminating tapes or documents that tied the defendant to illegal activities.

The prosecution also introduced no evidence that Connally banked or spent the alleged payoff and failed to document Connally's source of the $20,000 in replacement cash he allegedly gave Jacobsen.

Lilly testified under a grant of immunity April 8 that he had given Jacobsen $10,000 in May and September 1971 and another $5,000 in December of that year after Jacobsen claimed AMPI was "obligated" to Connally for his help in the price-support increase. Under questioning by Williams, Jacobsen said he could not recall having given the additional $5,000 to Connally, but said he "must have" if Lilly turned the cash over to him.

The defense emphasized Jacobsen's financial difficulties—he had filed for bankruptcy in 1972. During the summer of 1971 when it was alleged he made the payoff to Connally, Williams said Jacobsen had paid off $10,000 in bank debt. On the same day that Lilly gave Jacobsen the third $5,000 installment, Williams said Jacobsen paid another $5,000 debt.

Connally took the stand in his own defense April 14 to deny that he had ever sought or accepted a payoff from Jacobsen on behalf of dairy interests. Seven character witnesses, including Mrs. Lyndon B. Johnson, evangelist Billy Graham, and Rep. Barbara Jordan (D, Tex.), also testified that day on Connally's behalf.

In other testimony April 14, George Christian refuted Jacobsen's story that Connally had passed the second replacement cash to him in a car outside Christian's house.

In cross examination April 15, Connally admitted that he had made several mistakes or omitted information in his testimony under oath before the Senate Watergate Committee and the grand jury examining the bribery allegations. However, he attributed the errors to a faulty memory, misunderstood questions and his lack of preparation for the investigation, which he thought would not amount to a "hill of beans."

Connally was the fourth Nixon Cabinet member to be charged with a crime and he was only the second Cabinet official ever charged with a bribery offense. (Albert Fall, interior secretary under Presidents Warren G. Harding and Calvin Coolidge, had been convicted in 1929 of bribe taking in connection with the Teapot Dome scandal.)

Democrats' funds probed. Records from the Senate Watergate Committee's investigation of campaign finances continued to surface. It was revealed Aug. 1, 1974 that Rep. Wilbur D. Mills (Ark.), a candidate for the Democratic presidential nomination in 1972, received a $100,000 contribution that was secretly funneled into dummy campaign committees by two top executives of Electronic Data Systems, a computer firm owned by Texas millionaire H. Ross Perot.

The money was given by company president Milledge A. Hart 3rd, and a regional vice president, Mervin L. Stauffer, both of Dallas.

Stauffer denied that the money came from corporate funds. The donation was divided into installments and funneled through 17 committees March 30, 1972,

just prior to the period when a new campaign financing law took effect and made such secret donations illegal. Mills did not make a voluntary disclosure of his receipts and expenditures during this period.

Stauffer said he gave the money "because I believe in Mills." The Dallas computer firm was a major processor of health insurance claims. Mills had been a chief sponsor of a national health insurance bill.

Committee records published Aug. 7 showed that oil millionaire Leon Hess made a secret $225,000 contribution to Sen. Henry Jackson's (D, Wash.) campaign for the Democratic presidential nomination in 1972. The contribution was disguised under the names of other persons, records showed.

Hess, who was chairman of the Amerada Hess Corp., used the same methods to conceal a $250,000 contribution to the Nixon re-election campaign in 1972 at the time of an Interior Department investigation of a Virgin Island oil refinery owned by Amerada. Jackson was chairman of the Senate Interior Committee.

Jackson also received $166,000 in secret cash contributions, of which more than half came from oil interests. A Texas oil millionaire, Walter R. Davis, donated $50,000; E. Edmund Miller, president of Time Oil, gave $5,000; Claude Wild Jr. of Gulf Oil Corp. contributed $10,000. (Gulf Oil had pleaded guilty to making an illegal corporate contribution to Jackson's campaign.)

According to the committee's records, Jackson raised $1.1 million during the campaign, nearly half of which was given by donors, including those mentioned above, who also made large contributions to Nixon's campaign. Dwayne O. Andreas, who had backed Nixon and Humphrey, had made a $25,000 cash contribution to Jackson's campaign, records showed.

Chestnut convicted in milk fund gift. Jack L. Chestnut, 42, Sen. Hubert H. Humphrey's campaign manager during his 1970 senatorial race, was convicted May 8, 1975 of wilfully soliciting and accepting an illegal $12,000 campaign contribution from Associated Milk Producers Inc. (AMPI).

Chestnut was the first aide to a prominent Democratic politician to be convicted after a trial stemming from an investigation by the Watergate special prosecutor's office, which had obtained his indictment. The jury verdict was returned in U.S. District Court in New York, where the case had been transferred in December 1974.

Chestnut was sentenced June 26 to four months in prison and was fined $5,000.

The prosecution charged that Chestnut had attempted to conceal the illegal AMPI donation by making the co-op's checks payable to a New York advertising firm, Lennen & Newell, now bankrupt, that had handled the Humphrey campaign's publicity in 1968 and 1970.

The government's case was based on the testimony of two men involved in the campaign transaction, Bob A. Lilly, an aide to Harold S. Nelson, then the dairy co-op's general manager, and Barry Nova, a former executive with Lennen & Newell.

Lilly, who admitted he knew the contribution to be illegal, testified that he had personally delivered two AMPI checks for $6,000 each to Chestnut for forwarding to the advertising firm. The arrangements were made on Chestnut's instructions, Lilly testified.

Nova said that he had sent Lennen & Newell's bill to AMPI on Chestnut's instruction. Eventually, Nova said, he had received payment from the co-op.

Lilly also testified that he had made three other contributions totaling nearly $24,000, two as personal checks and one as cash, to the Minnesota Democratic Campaign Committee through Chestnut in 1970. (Nelson and AMPI's then second-ranking official, David L. Parr, had pleaded guilty to making these illegal contributions. Lilly had won immunity in return for testifying as a government witness in various milk fund cases.)

Lilly described the means by which these illegal contributions were concealed: he took out a personal loan, made the donation with a personal check, the co-op was billed by a law firm for double the amount of the contribution; the bill for the

fictitious legal services was paid; and Lilly received funds to retire the loan.

The prosecution contended that Chestnut must have realized that Lilly's personal checks, which were referred to as "AMPI funds," did not represent a legitimate contribution from C-TAPE, the dairy co-op's political committee, and that this knowledge must have carried over to the donations received on Humphrey's behalf in 1970 that were funneled through the advertising firm.

Chestnut testified that he could not recall having made the arrangements with Lilly, nor could he recall having signed and sent letters to AMPI regarding Lennen & Newell's bill.

Humphrey appeared as the prosecution's first witness on May 5 when the trial opened. He said he had personally solicited a contribution from AMPI but had no "personal knowledge" of the actual financial transaction, which was left to the "campaign committee and Mr. Chestnut."

Ex-Congressman Wyatt fined. Former Rep. Wendell Wyatt (R, Ore.) was fined $750 July 18, 1975 for failing to report expenditures from a secret $5,000 cash fund he controlled while heading the Oregon campaign for former President Nixon in 1972.

Wyatt, a five-term congressman, pleaded guilty to the misdemeanor charge June 11 in U.S. District Court in Washington. He could have been sentenced to one year in jail and a $1,000 fine. According to the Watergate special prosecutor's office, money from the secret fund was given by Time Oil Co. of Seattle.

AMPI lawyer sentenced to jail. Stuart Russell, a lawyer for Associated Milk Producers Inc., was sentenced Aug. 14, 1975 to serve three concurrent two-year prison terms for helping the dairy cooperative illegally funnel corporate money to two candidates for federal office. However, because of a provision added to the sentence by the judge in U.S. District Court in San Antonio, Russell would be eligible for parole immediately.

Russell had been convicted July 11 on

one count of conspiracy involving a $100,-000 contribution given to Nixon fundraiser Herbert Kalmbach, and two counts of aiding and abetting the donation of $8,400 to Sen. Edmund S. Muskie (D, Me.) in 1970–1971.

Prosecutor clears Ford on funds use. Charles F. Ruff, Watergate special prosecutor, said Oct. 14, 1976 that after a three-month investigation his office had found no evidence to substantiate an informent's allegation that Gerald R. Ford, who then was President, had misused political contributions for his own benefit.

In his brief written statement, Ruff also said that on Sept. 30, he had asked for "certain information relating to the President's personal finances." Philip W. Buchen, White House counsel, had complied with the request and had authorized the Internal Revenue Service to provide Ruff with a report on its 1973 audit of Ford's income-tax returns for the years 1968–72.

In refuting the specific charges about Ford's alleged mishandling of campaign funds, Ruff also said that he had found no "reason to believe that any other violations of law had occurred" and therefore had closed the case.

Ruff said that on July 13 Clarence M. Kelley, director of the Federal Bureau of Investigation, had referred an allegation about Ford's campaign funds to Attorney General Edward H. Levi. On July 16, Levi formally referred the matter to Ruff for investigation, Ruff said.

"The information furnished to the attorney general by the FBI concerned a previously unreported allegation that political contributions from certain named unions had been transmitted to political committees in Kent County, Mich. [in Ford's home district], with the understanding that they would be passed on to Mr. Ford for his personal use," Ruff said.

The informant was not named, but the prosecutor said that the investigation had "revealed no apparent motive on the part of this individual to fabricate."

Ruff confirmed earlier press reports that he had issued subpoenas Aug. 19 for finance records kept by Kent County Republican committees and by two New York-based maritime unions, the Marine

Engineers Beneficial Association and the Seafarers International Union, which had been heavy contributors to Ford's congressional campaigns.

Although Ruff's statements did not say so, it also was known that some officials of the two maritime unions had testified recently before a grand jury under grants of immunity.

Ford held a nationally televised news conference only hours after Ruff had announced that he had been cleared of the allegations against him.

In a prepared statement, Ford said that he was "very pleased" that the prosecutor "finally" had put the campaign-funds issue "to rest once and for all."

"I hope today's announcement will also accomplish one other major task," Ford said, "that it will elevate the presidential campaign to a level befitting the American people." Ford charged that the race had been "mired in questions that have little bearing on the future of this nation."

Most of the reporters' questions focused on the propriety of Ford's past actions. He was asked twice to comment on allegations by John W. Dean 3rd, the former White House counsel who had been a prominent figure in the Watergate scandal, that in 1972, when Ford was House minority leader, Ford had intervened at the request of the Nixon White House to block an investigation into the Watergate burglary by the House Banking Committee.

Ford refused to discuss the charge, saying the "matter was fully investigated" by House and Senate committees considering his nomination as vice president. "There was no substance to those allegations then," Ford said, adding that, in his opinion, they were still untrue.

Ford also was asked about reports, based on an Internal Revenue Service audit of his taxes, that he had managed to live on $5 a week spending money in 1972. Ford replied that he wrote checks.

Ford defended his past use of political funds for personal benefit, also uncovered in the IRS audit, saying his campaign account had been reimbursed from personal funds. Ford acknowledged that one of the repayment checks had caused his bank book to show an overdraft, but he said that his bank account had not been overdrawn.

"I think a few people in this country have written checks and then waited until the end of the month and then mailed the checks," Ford said.

When asked about his golfing trips that were paid for by corporate lobbyists, Ford said he could not remember how many times he had accepted such hospitality, but that the only trips he could recall were on the public record.

Columnist Jack Anderson had reported Sept. 21, 1976 that the U.S. Steel Corp. had entertained Ford during a number of golfing weekends in the 1960s and early 1970s. Ford played golf, Anderson said, with company vice-president William G. Whyte, who was a close friend of Ford and also was U.S. Steel's chief lobbyist in Washington. The golf outings were at the company's Pine Valley Country Club near Clementon, N.J.. Anderson said.

Ron Nessen, White House press secretary, confirmed that Ford had been a guest of U.S. Steel at the New Jersey club once in 1964 and once in 1971. Nessen said that Ford and Whyte had been friends for more than 20 years. "Obviously, if the President thought there was something wrong with it he wouldn't have done it," Nessen said.

Whyte issued a statement Sept. 23 saying that U.S. Steel had fully financed five of his golfing outings with Ford between 1964 and 1973. Three trips—in 1964, 1969 and 1973—were at the Pine Valley club, and two—in 1972 and 1973—were at the Bay Hill Country Club, near Orlando, Fla.

The Securities and Exchange Commission said Sept. 23 that it was investigating U.S. Steel's entertaining of Ford and other politicians. The Washington Post reported Sept. 24 that the Justice Department also was looking into U.S. Steel's entertainment of 22 senators and congressmen.

The White House had further comment Sept. 28 on the golfing trips. Nessen said that Ford had played golf as the guest of a number of major corporations while he was a Congressman. Nessen named The Firestone Tire & Rubber Co., Bethlehem Steel Corp. and Aluminum Co. of America. He said that those were the only companies he could recall after discussing the matter with Ford.

After Ford became vice president in 1973, he stopped accepting such invitations, Nessen said. When asked why the trips had stopped if Ford saw nothing wrong with them, Nessen said "circumstances" had changed.

Nessen said that Ford felt he had lived up to the "spirit" of a code of ethics, adopted in 1968 by the House of Representatives, which forbade members from accepting gifts of any monetary value from any person or corporation having an interest in legislation before Congress.

Ford told reporters Sept. 30 that he had never diverted "any campaign funds for personal use."

Ford conceded that he "might" have discussed government business with corporate officials while he was their guest on the golf outings, but he defended the propriety of the practice. Ford said that he had been friends for many years with his golfing partners on those trips. They had not sought or received "special privilege or anything that was improper," Ford said.

At first, Ford had said that he had never discussed legislative business with William Whyte. But when he was reminded by a reporter that Rodney W. Markley Jr., vice president of Ford Motor Co., had stated publicly that he had discussed the Clean Air Act with Ford during a golf outing, Ford said he would "modify" his earlier statement.

"In a casual way, of course," Ford said, "we might informally talk about certain matters, but I happen to feel that they were not asking me and I was not asking them."

Jimmy Carter had kept his cautious silence on the Watergate special prosecutor's investigation until Sept. 29 when he said it was time for Ford "to have a frank discussion with the American public through the news media, which so far he has failed to do."

Speaking at a news conference in Plains, Ga., Carter made no charge that Ford had acted illegally in the handling of campaign funds while a member of Congress or in accepting hospitality from major corporations, but he called for a candid discussion of the matter.

"I think the main thing is complete openness about any sort of relationship where a conflict of interest might be involved," Carter said. He added later, "I think the Watergate tragedy also showed [that] concealment of a mistake or an impropriety can be even more serious in some instances than the impropriety itself."

Carter acknowledged that as governor of Georgia he had accepted transportation on private aircraft owned by major corporations for trips within Georgia and abroad. Carter noted that this practice had been reported in the press.

Carter also said that when he had traveled to 10 or 11 foreign countries as governor, some of his expenses had been paid by the governments of Great Britain and Israel.

Carter said that there was a "great difference" between his trips and Ford's golf outings. "All of the trips I took were strictly business," Carter said. His mission, he said, had been to promote the sale of Georgia-made products abroad and involved no personal recreation.

Carter was asked Oct. 1 about his having been a guest of corporations three times while he was governor of Georgia. It was "not a good practice," he told reporters, although his governmental decisions had never been influenced.

Asked what the difference was between his acceptance of lodging and hunting privileges and President Ford's acceptance of golfing trips paid for by lobbyists when he was in Congress, Carter said that he could not answer "because Mr. Ford has not revealed his relationships with the lobbyists and the golf courses."

Justice Department initiated probe—Attorney General Edward H. Levi and other senior Justice Department officials had initiated the investigation into Ford's congressional campaign finances, the Washington Post reported Oct. 1. The Post report was based on an interview with Harold R. Tyler, assistant attorney general.

Tyler said that the inquiry had begun in July when the Justice Department, acting on information given to the FBI by an informant, referred the allegations to the Watergate special prosecutor.

Tyler's disclosure undercut charges made by Sen. Robert Dole (R, Kan.), Ford's running mate, that the prosecutor's investigation was politically motivated. Dole had said Sept. 27 that the probe smacked of "nothing but election-year politics."

Tyler said that the decision to refer the matter to the prosecutor's office came after discussions involving himself, Levi, FBI Director Clarence M. Kelley and James B. Adams, FBI associate director.

Agnew friend sentenced for campaign gift. J. Walter Jones Jr., 56, a Maryland banker and close friend of former Vice President Spiro Agnew, was sentenced April 4, 1977 to three months and fined a maximum $5,000 for soliciting an illegal $10,000 contribution to the Nixon-Agnew reelection campaign in 1972. The donation from the Singer Co., which was seeking government computer contracts, violated federal law prohibiting campaign contributions from corporations.

Jones had pleaded guilty to the charge March 10 after plea bargaining in which prosecutors agreed to drop other charges including extortion and conspiracy. Jones had been described as Agnew's "bagman" or intermediary, who covered up the contribution as a consultant's fee. The kickback scandal was among the events that led to Agnew's resignation in 1973.

Singer also was charged with conspiring to defraud the government and five counts of violating election laws, including a prohibition against donations by government contractors. Raymond A. Long, president of a Singer division, was charged with two counts of approving the contribution, one count of conspiracy and two counts relating to election law violations. (Unlike charges against other firms brought by the Watergate special prosecutor's office, the indictment did not accuse top officers of Singer of being aware that the illegal donation was made.)

Two other men were indicted on misdemeanor charges: John W. Steffey was accused of allegedly accepting the Singer donation and James F. Fanseen, a former Nixon appointee to the Federal Maritime Commission, was accused of acting as Jones' emissary in the scheme. Fanseen pleaded no contest to the two counts March 6.

Two others were named unindicted co-conspirators—Martin A. Leader, a Singer employe, and Lester Matz, a Maryland engineer. Matz had testified against Agnew in the case that led to his resignation as vice president.

The indictments against Jones, Singer and the other three men arose out of the continuing investigation conducted by U.S. Attorney George Beall into charges of widespread corruption involving payments made by Maryland architects and engineers to Agnew and other Maryland associates.

The indictment of Jones had been delivered by a federal grand jury in Baltimore March 6,1975.

Case against N.J. leader dismissed. U.S. District Court Judge Vincent P. Biunno Jan. 7, 1976 dismissed a four-count obstruction-of-justice indictment against ex-Bergen County (N.J.) GOP Chairman Anthony J. Statile because of insufficient evidence.

Statile, 60, had been indicted nearly two years earlier on charges that he had counseled Republican campaign contributors to deduct illegally their donations in Bergen County campaigns as legitimate business expenses and that he had then hindered a federal grand jury probe of the alleged wrongdoing.

Biunno's ruling was made on the request of the U.S. attorney. The government's key witness, Henry Stumpf, the former party treasurer, died in September 1975. Statile said after the ruling he "considered this a complete vindication of me and the Republican Party in Bergen County."

Laws, Rules & Legal Decisions

Supreme Court rules on election law. The Supreme Court, in a landmark ruling Jan. 30, 1976, upheld some parts of the 1974 Federal Election Campaign Act and struck down others. The decision (different parts of which were supported by different numbers of justices) upheld government financing of presidential campaigns and campaign contribution disclosure requirements, but struck down limits on political expenditures (except for presidential candidates who accepted federal subsidies). The decision also upheld ceilings on political contributions, and ruled that the Federal Election Commission (the agency created to enforce and administer the law) was unconstitutional as then set up.

The 1974 law was challenged by a number of groups, as well as by the former Democratic senator from Minnesota, Eugene McCarthy, and by the Conservative Party senator from New York, James L. Buckley. They argued that the law violated the First Amendment guarantee of freedom of speech, and discriminated against minority parties and non-incumbents.

The challengers greeted the voiding of limits on political expenditures as an essential triumph. Brice Clagget, the main lawyer for the challengers, was reported in the Feb. 1 New York Times to have said in reference to a part of that ruling, "If that had gone the other way, the First Amendment would have been dead." In ruling as it did, the Supreme Court held that political spending was "speech," and so protected from limitation by the constitution.

But supporters of the election law also found reason to approve of the ruling, in its upholding of major portions of the 1974 law.

The rulings on specific parts of the law were as follows:

Public financing of presidential election campaigns—The 1974 law was upheld on the financing provisions. Briefly, those provisions were: the major parties would receive $2 million each for their national conventions, and the candidates selected by those conventions would receive $20 million each (provided sufficient funds were generated by individuals checking off the $1 campaign subsidy item in their income tax returns). Candidates in presidential primaries could receive matching federal funds for each dollar raised (up to a $10 million public-private total, plus $2 million for fund raising) if they demonstrated broad national support by raising at least $100,000, with at least $5,000 coming from each of 20 states, and no individual contribution counting for more than $250. Finally, minor and new party candidates would receive funding in proportion to their votes, provided they obtained at least 5% of the total.

The court observed that these provisions were challenged "because [according to the claims of the appellants] they work invidious discrimination against minor and new parties in violation of the Fifth Amendment." The court disagreed. It held that the major parties had historically demonstrated their difference from other parties, and went on to say that, "Sometimes the grossest discrimination can lie in treating things that are different as though they were exactly alike... Since the Presidential elections of 1856 and 1860, when the Whigs were replaced as a major party by the Republicans, no third party has posed a credible threat to the two major parties in Presidential elections." The court further stated that the "appellants have made no showing that the election funding plan disadvantages nonmajor parties by operating to reduce their strength below that attained without any public financing."

Chief Justice Burger dissented from this part of the ruling on the grounds that public financing of presidential campaigns was "an impermissible intrusion by the government into the traditionally private political process."

Justice William H. Rehnquist dissented on the grounds advanced by the challengers. He argued that, while Congress could demand new or minor parties to show some evidence of support before granting them public funds, "Congress in this legislation has done a good deal more than that. It has enshrined the Republican and Democratic Parties in a permanently preferred position, and has established requirements for funding minor party and independent candidates to which the two major parties are not subject."

Expenditures and contributions—The court generally accepted the contention of the challengers of the law that, in modern society, effective political speech required money, and limitations on the use of money were limitations of speech. However, it distinguished between political expenditures and contributions. Limitations on expenditures, it held, directly violated the First Amendment. The court thus struck down several provisions of the campaign law: the ceilings on expenditures by congressional candidates in their campaigns; the $1,000 a year limit on expenditures by an individual in independent efforts for or against a specific candidate (and the $25,000 limit on all such expenditures by an individual in a year), and the ceilings on campaign spending (from either their own, or contributed funds) by presidential candidates who did not accept federal subsidies. The court ruled, however, that candidates who accepted

federal subsidies were subject to the limitations on spending specified in the act. (All of the major candidates for the presidency in 1976 have accepted the subsidies, so they remained bound by the ceilings.)

Justices Marshall and White dissented in favor of sustaining the limit on expenditures by a presidential candidate from his own or family funds. Justice White also dissented in favor of sustaining the other spending limits.

On the point of political contributions, however, the court sustained the ceilings provided for in the election law. It said: "It is unnecessary to look beyond the act's primary purpose—to limit the actuality and appearance of corruption resulting from large individual financial contributions—in order to find a constitutionally sufficient justification for the $1,000 contribution limitation." It held that the "limited effect upon First Amendment freedoms" was outweighed by the purposes served by the act.

Chief Justice Burger dissented from the ruling sustaining contribution limits, saying that the "limitations infringe on First Amendment liberties and suffer from the same infirmities that the court correctly sees in the expenditure ceilings." Justice Blackmun also dissented.

Disclosure requirement—The court upheld the law's requirements that the names and addresses of contributors of more than $10, and the names, addresses and business occupations of contributors of more than $100 be reported. The decision observed that three interests were served by disclosure: the public gained more information about the candidate, the requirement deterred both the actuality and the appearance of corruption, and the reporting and record-keeping would aid the government in enforcing the limit on contributions. Against these interests, the court acknowledged, had to be weighed the danger that public disclosure of contributions might inhibit some people from contributing, and "in some instances, disclosure may even expose contributors to harassment or retaliation." Challengers of the law argued that these dangers, especially in regard to contributors to minority or new parties, were such that the disclosure requirement should be voided. The court disagreed, but it did allow that "only a reasonable probability" of harassment or injury contingent upon disclosure need by proved by minor parties to gain exemption from the requirement.

Chief Justice Burger dissented, saying that the "act's disclosure scheme is impermissibly broad and violative of the First Amendment as it relates to reporting $10 and $100 contributions."

The Federal Election Commission—The court unanimously held that the Federal Election Commission (FEC) as then set up was unconstitutional. The FEC, it reasoned, in enforcing the election law performed executive duties. Therefore, according to the doctrine of the separation of powers, its officers should be appointed by the executive branch. The 1974 law gave Congress the power to appoint the majority of the officers.

(The court did not object to the composition of the FEC in respect to those of its duties which might be considered as delegated from Congress—investigating and making public campaign practices.)

The court gave Congress 30 days to refashion the FEC, or enact some substitute means of enforcing the election law, before its ruling would take effect. It also validated all of the actions of the FEC to date. Chief Justice Burger dissented from the 30-day extension and validation of past actions.

The 137-page decision was not signed, but rather delivered per curiam, "by the court." Justices Brennan, Stewart and Powell concurred with the decision in its entirety. Justices White, Marshall, Blackmun, and Rehnquist and Chief Justice Burger dissented in part. Justice Stevens did not participate in the ruling, having been sworn in after oral arguments were heard.

Appeals Court opinion—Prior to the Supreme Court action, the U.S. Court of Appeals for the District of Columbia had upheld all major provisions of the law Aug. 15, 1975 with only partial dissents by three of the eight judges.

Citing the historic abuse of political funding, its undue influence on public policy and the "circumvention" of past federal election laws, the court said the government's latest efforts "to cleanse its democratic processes should at least be given a chance to prove themselves." There was "a compelling governmental

interest," it said, "both as to need and public perception of need, that justifies any incidental impact" on the freedom of expression guaranteed under the First Amendment.

"The corrosive influence of money blights our democratic processes," the court declared, and the past record and growth of campaign funding "support the legislative judgment that the situation not only must not be allowed to deteriorate further but that the present situation cannot be tolerated by a government that professes to be a democracy."

The court urged that "a careful scrutiny" be kept on implementation of the law's provisions.

The court did declare unconstitutional the provision of the law that set extensive financial disclosure regulations for nonpartisan public interest, political reform and civil liberties groups. The provision was "vague and overbroad," the court found, and "seeks to compel disclosure by groups that do no more than discuss issues of public importance on a wholly nonpartisan basis."

Campaign fund procedures. The Federal Election Commission had approved some ground rules Dec. 4, 1975 to govern campaign debt settlements between a candidate and a corporation.

It said it would handle specific cases on an individual basis, but it issued guidelines under which campaign debts could be cancelled or settled "in certain extenuating circumstances" when the corporation involved "has treated the outstanding debt in a commercially reasonable manner."

The latter condition would be met, the commission said, if the credit was extended on the same terms as to a nonpolitical debtor, if "an exhaustive effort" was undertaken by the candidate to satisfy the outstanding debt and if the corporation's effort to collect the debt was "similar in intensity to that employed in pursuit of a nonpolitical donor."

Among other decisions, the commission ruled that:

■ Sept. 4: The cost of a presidential candidate's campaigning in a special election on behalf of a Senate candidate would be counted in the spending totals for the Senate and not the presidential candidacy. The ruling applied in particular to New Hampshire appearances by President Ford and Ronald Reagan on behalf of the GOP senatorial candidate Louis C Wyman.

■ Oct. 16: Fees paid by candidates to lawyers and accountants for political services would be counted as part of the spending to come under the ceiling imposed by law.

■ Nov. 13: An industry lobby organization, in this case a milk lobby, would not be permitted to establish committees in various states that could then each contribute the legal maximum of $5,000 to a single candidate. The commission said the lobby could establish the state units but their contributions would be counted along with any from the national group as one total, subject to the $5,000 overall ceiling for any one candidate.

■ Nov. 18: A corporation, in this case Sun Oil Co., would be permitted to use corporate funds to set up a political committee that could solicit voluntary contributions from stockholders and employes to be disbursed to candidates selected by the company officials managing the fund, subject to the mandated campaign contribution ceilings.

■ Nov. 20: A presidential candidate's campaign travel expenses in 1975 would not be counted against his 1976 campaign spending ceiling in most cases. The decision applied in particular to President Ford, who had traveled quite extensively this year for appearances before Republican audiences. A different interpretation was applied to Ford's 1976 campaign travel expenses. From Jan. 1, 1976 on, the commission held, all of Ford's domestic travel would be presumed to be on behalf of his candidacy and the cost would be counted as subject to the spending limit for presidential candidates for primary elections.

The rule of thumb apparently was that the 1975 travel costs would be construed as expended on behalf of the party, not the individual.

■ Dec. 2: An annual payment for broadcast commentary, in this case $1,-800 a year paid by CBS to Rep. Barbara Jordan (D, Tex.) for monthly television commentary, would not be construed as an honorarium subject to the mandated ceilings on individual and total honoraria for members of Congress.

N.Y. campaign rules nullified. The U.S. Supreme Court ruled unanimously Jan. 12, 1976 that provisions of New York State's fair campaign practices plan were unconstitutional.

The provisions struck down were those that restricted the speech of candidates. Under the New York State fair campaign code, candidates were barred from making racial attacks on, or deliberately misrepresenting the qualifications of, opposing candidates. The court ruled that these provisions conflicted with the First Amendment guarantee of freedom of speech.

The opinion delivered with the lower court ruling said: "When the state, through the guise of protecting the citizen's right to a fair and honest election, tampers with what it will permit the citizen to see and hear, even that important state interest must give way to the irresistible force of protected expression under the First Amendment."

The opinion did, however, say that the freedom of speech guarantee did not extend to statements made with "actual malice." Presumably, this meant that campaign laws could be written that would not be struck down as unconstitutional.

N.Y. political penalty voided—The U.S. Supreme Court June 13, 1977 ruled illegal a New York State law forcing political party officers to waive immunity and testify before grand juries. The decision affirmed a lower court ruling.

The case, *Lefkowitz v. Cunningham,* concerned a 1976 challenge to the law by Patrick J. Cunningham, then chairman of the New York State Democratic Party. He had refused to sign a waiver of immunity when subpoenaed by a grand jury investigating the alleged sale of judgeships in New York City. Under the law in question, the state had the power to remove him as party chairman for not signing the waiver.

The majority in the 7–1 high court decision found that the law violated Cunningham's Fifth Amendment protection against self-incrimination. Justice John Paul Stevens dissented. Justice William H. Rehnquist did not participate.

Michigan campaign reform law enacted. Michigan Gov. William G. Milliken (R)

Aug. 27, 1975 signed a bill that he called "the most comprehensive political reform law of any state."

The new statute, scheduled to take effect in April 1976, set limits on political spending and contributions, provided for the public financing of gubernatorial races, and required that the state's 20,000 public officials disclose their finances. An independent state agency with subpoena power also was established to enforce the new campaign law.

The spending limit for gubernatorial candidates was set at $1 million; a $15,000 limit was set for state representative races. Individual political contributions were limited to $1,700 in statewide races, and less in district contests; organizations, such as labor unions, were permitted to contribute 10 times the individual limit. Candidates were required to disclose the names of those who donated at least $15, and the occupations and employers of donors who gave at least $100. Gifts and contributions from lobbyists also were restricted.

Major party candidates for governor, beginning in 1978, could obtain up to $667,000 in matching public funds for their primary campaigns, and $750,000 for the general election. The subsidies would be raised by a $2-a-year voluntary check-off on personal state income tax returns. (New Jersey was the only other state that had incorporated a public-financing provision in its campaign fund law, according to the New York Times Aug. 30.)

In San Francisco, total campaign spending by each mayoral candidate was limited to $127,600 under a law passed in 1974 by the city's Board of Supervisors, the New York Times reported Sept. 8. The law also set ceilings on political contributions from individuals and groups.

Opponents of the law contended that the spending and contribution limits favored incumbents and established political figures, because only those candidates who were well-known could afford to restrict their campaign activities.

N.J. disclosure order upheld. In New Jersey, the Appellate Division of Superior Court had upheld Gov. Brendan Byrne's order that all high state officials make public financial disclosures, it was reported Oct. 6, 1976. The order, issued Jan. 7. 1975, affected about 150 directors and assistants in state departments and divisions.

The order had been challenged by two officeholders, Assistant Secretary of Agriculture William E. Kenny and Catherine McGovern, director of field services for the Department of Education.

Mercer County Superior Court Judge Samuel D. Lenox Jr. later rejected the officials' contention that the order had invaded their privacy. The Appellate Division upheld the lower court decision.

As to the merits of the order itself, the appellate court found that the governor had the authority to insure efficient and honest performances by state employes under his jurisdiction and that he had the power to issue orders to achieve that purpose.

Public lobby issues campaign code. The national citizens' lobby, Common Cause, promulgated a code of standards for presidential candidates Nov. 5, 1975. The code, sent to declared and major potential candidates, called for disclosure of personal finances, participation in public debate, authentication of private poll contentions, renunciation of media attacks against an opponent and a ban against use of taxpayer funds for staff or transportation.

The presidential contenders also were being asked by the lobby to draft an estimate of a federal budget that would justify their spending and tax programs.

The code was designed to counteract "campaigns characterized by issue evasion, image manipulation, manufactured 'media events' and outright exploitation of our communications systems," Common Cause chairman John W. Gardner said at a news conference in Washington. "We propose that citizens and the media make it as difficult as possible for political managers to deal in plastic images, to manipulate events and to avoid authentic give-and-take with the voters."

The lobby planned to monitor campaign activity of the candidates for code infractions and inconsistency of policy positions.

President Ford and 10 Democrats agreed to abide by the new standards, a Common Cause spokesman said. The Democrats who pledged observance were Sens. Bayh, Bentsen, and Jackson; Rep. Udall; Govs. Wallace and Milton Shapp (D, Pa.); former Sen. Harris; former Govs. Carter and Sanford; and Shriver.

Two candidates reject code—Common Cause said Jan. 9, 1976 that two presidential contenders refused to observe campaign standards drawn up by the group. Refusing to abide by the nine-point code of standards were former Democratic Sen. Eugene McCarthy of Minne-sota, an independent, and former Gov. Ronald Reagan (R, Calif.).

Fair campaign group complaints. The Fair Campaign Practices Committee had received a total of 42 complaints from candidates in the 1976 elections, it was reported Jan. 4, 1977. The total was the lowest since the group had begun monitoring campaigns in 1954. The committee had received 57 complaints in 1974 and 82 in 1972.

The committee, a private, nonpartisan clearinghouse for candidates' allegations of unfair campaigning, had also noted a drop in 1976 of personal attacks and charges of corrupt practices, it was reported.

Continuing Attack on Corruption

Action Against Accused Officials

Indictments of public officials increase. The Justice Department's first study on public integrity, reported Feb. 10, 1977, showed that the number of officials indicted by federal grand juries had risen during 1970–76. There were 63 indictments in 1970, 160 in 1971, 208 in 1972, 244 in 1973, 291 in 1974, 255 in 1975 and 337 in 1976.

Of the 1,598 public officials indicted during the seven-year period, a total of 1,081 were convicted of corruption charges. Richard Thornburgh, head of the Justice Department's criminal division, said most of the cases involved extortion and bribery charges related to racketeering, gambling and prostitution "protection schemes."

The highest number of indictments, 135, was in the Northern District of Illinois (Chicago), where prosecution had been under the direction of former U.S. Attorney James R. Thompson, currently governor of Illinois. New Jersey had 66 convictions and the Southern District of New York (New York City and Westchester County) had 62 convictions.

Maryland Gov. Mandel, 5 others convicted. Gov. Marvin Mandel (D, Md.) and five associates were convicted by a federal jury Aug. 23, 1977 of mail fraud and racketeering involved in an influence-peddling scheme. The prosecution charged that the scheme had brought Mandel over $350,000 in personal profit and enriched his codefendants' racetrack investment.

The 10-week retrial ended with a 113-hour jury deliberation that extended over 13 days, considered by legal experts to be the longest on record in a federal criminal case. (A mistrial had been declared in December 1976 after two attempts at jury tampering were alleged.)

Mandel, who was found guilty on 17 counts of mail fraud and one of racketeering, was automatically removed from office Oct. 7, the date he was sentenced to serve four years in prison.

Mandel's five co-defendants were sentenced as follows: W. Dale Hess, Henry W. Rodgers 3rd and Irvin Kovens, four years in prison and fines of $40,000 each; William A. Rodgers, 20 months in prison and a $40,000 fine, and Ernest N. Cory Jr., 18 months in prison.

District Judge Robert L. Taylor said he did not impose a fine on Mandel because he believed he was unable to afford it. Mandel could have been sentenced to up to 105 years in prison and fined a maximum $42,000.

Maryland Attorney General Francis B. Burch had ruled Aug. 25 that when he was removed from office, Mandel would lose all powers and perquisites of the governorship, with the exception of his title. Lieut. Gov. Blair Lee 3rd would remain acting governor until Mandel either resigned or exhausted all possible legal appeals. If vindicated, Mandel could reclaim his office.

(Mandel, 57, had transferred all the formal powers of his office to Blair June 4 on the advice of physicians, who said Mandel may have suffered a mild stroke in April.)

Mandel became the first incumbent governor convicted of a federal crime since 1924, when Indiana's Warren Mc-Cray was convicted of mail fraud. He was also the highest-ranking government official ever convicted under a federal anti-racketeering law—the Organized Crime Control Act of 1970. The law gave the government the power to confiscate all assets gained in an illegal plot.

Mandel was accused of accepting bribes—in the form of business interests, cash and bonds guaranteeing his divorce settlement, clothing and jewelry—from his five codefendants, who were described as his friends; the five codefendants had purchased the Marlboro Racetrack secretly in 1971. In exchange, the prosecution alleged, Mandel had successfully encouraged the state legislature in 1972 to override his prior veto of a bill doubling the number of Marlboro's racing days. The action had greatly enhanced the track's value.

Mandel claimed that his friends had concealed their ownership of the Marlboro track from him until 1975, well after he had promoted the beneficial legislation. His codefendants said they had kept the truth from the governor to spare him "political embarrassment."

Each of the six men was convicted of 17 counts of mail fraud and acquitted of three counts. Corey and Kovens each were convicted of one racketeering count and Hess and the two Rodgers brothers were convicted of two racketeering charges each.

Gov. Moore acquitted. Gov. Arch A. Moore of West Virginia was acquitted by a federal jury in Charleston May 5, 1976 of conspiracy to extort $25,000 from a state banker during Moore's 1972 election campaign. His fellow defendant, William Loy, 43, a former aide, also was acquitted.

Shapp ordered to repay funds. The Federal Election Commission May 12, 1977 ordered Pennsylvania Gov. Milton J. Shapp to return $299,066.21 in federal matching funds paid during his brief campaign for the Democratic presidential nomination in 1976.

The agency said a six-month investigation had revealed that the Shapp campaign organization made false claims to qualify for the federal funds. The law required that a candidate raise $5,000 in contributions of $250 or less in each of the 20 states to become eligible for the matching grants.

The agency said the Shapp organization had contributed some of the $5,000 donated in each of five states—Alabama, Georgia, Nevada, North Carolina and Texas.

The FEC also fined 22 of the 43 persons it said had made or solicited illegal contributions on Shapp's behalf in the five states. The fines ranged from $25 to $750. An investigation of possible criminal wrongdoing in the Shapp fund-raising operation would continue, the FEC said.

Shapp May 13 agreed to repay the nearly $300,000 in matching federal funds, saying he would not contest the FEC's disclosures. Shapp also denied "any knowledge of improper fund raising."

Ex-Gov. Hall guilty of bribery. A federal jury in Oklahoma City, Okla. March 14, 1975 found former Gov. David Hall (D, Okla.) guilty of four counts of bribery and extortion. At the same time, Texas financier W. W. Taylor was found guilty of three bribery charges. The former governor was sentenced April 25 to three years in prison on each of the four counts, to run concurrently. Taylor received 18 months on each of the three counts against him, also to run concurrently.

The government had contended, in an indictment handed up Jan. 16, three days after Hall left office as governor, that the men had conspired to bribe Secretary of State John Rogers Jr., who was then chairman of the board that administered retirement funds for the state, to vote to invest $10 million in such funds in one of Taylor's companies, Guaranteed Investors Corp. (The investment was eventually approved by the board but the indictments were handed up before the money was turned over.)

In addition to the bribery charge, Hall was convicted of extorting $50,000 from Taylor and his associate, R. Kevin Mooney, to take part in the scheme. During the trial Mooney pleaded guilty to a single conspiracy charge and two other charges against him were dropped in return for his testimony as a Government witness. The trial, which began Feb. 24, included the presentation of taped conversations made with the conspirators by Rogers who acted as an undercover agent for the Federal Bureau of Investigation. Hall, who lost a reelection bid in the wake of a corruption scandal in 1974, had accused U.S. Attorney General William R. Burkett of prosecuting him for political reasons.

Senate report criticizes Callaway. A Senate subcommittee report released Oct. 5, 1976 charged that Howard H. (Bo) Callaway, former secretary of the Army and former campaign director for President Gerald Ford, had used his post to exert pressure on the U.S. Forest Service. Callaway had sought approval to use government-owned land for the expansion of a Colorado ski resort.

The report was backed by the five Democratic members of the Senate Interior Committee's subcommittee on environment and land resources. The four Republican members of the panel opposed the report. In a minority report, they maintained that none of the charges against Callaway had been substantiated by the subcommittee's inquiry and that the report unfairly damaged Callaway's reputation. The Republicans conceded that Callaway had shown "poor judgment" in using official stationary for correspondence concerning his personal affairs and in holding a meeting with Agriculture Department officials in his Pentagon office. (The Forest Service was part of the Agriculture Department.)

At subcommittee hearings in the spring, Callaway had denied acting improperly or trying to do any more than expedite the Forest Service decision on the land. Officials of the Agriculture Department and the Forest Service testified that Callaway's position had played no part of the decision to allow the ski resort to expand. (The Forest Service at first had opposed the expansion.)

The subcommittee's majority report concluded that "concern expressed in Washington may have tipped the scales in favor of a recommendation in Secretary Callaway's interest." In reaching the conclusion, the majority report drew particular attention to Callaway's meeting in his Pentagon office on July 3, 1975 (Callaway's last day as Army Secretary) with Agriculture Department officials. J. Phil Campbell, former undersecretary of agriculture; Richard Ashworth, Campbell's deputy, and Rex Resler, deputy chief of the Forest Service, attended the meeting.

Callaway used the meeting, the majority report said, "to press for a decision favorable to Crested Butte [the site, and also the name, of Callaway's ski resort]." The firm that built the resort was the Crested Butte Development Corp.

The report noted that after the meeting Campbell wrote a memorandum to then Agriculture Secretary Earl L. Butz urging Butz to "push" for a Forest Service decision favorable to the ski resort. The memorandum noted that "the Crested Butte development will be 'out of business' without this language in the statement [i.e., without an environmental impact statement by the Forest Service that would permit the ski resort to expand onto the federal land]."

Butz sent the Campbell memorandum to an aide after adding the words "Phil [Campbell] thinks Bo [Callaway] is right on this. ELB [Butz]—Call Rex Resler." At a May 13 subcommittee hearing, Butz testified that all he meant by the note was that the Forest Service should expedite its decision.

The majority report maintained, however, that the note showed that Butz had a "manifest" intention to "exert high-level pressure on the Forest Service." However, there was no evidence, the report said, that Butz's message had ever been conveyed to the Forest Service. "Doubts remain," the report concluded, "as to whether intent to interfere became interference in fact."

The majority report termed the affair "a sorry history of partiality and favoritism." The result, the report said, was to "undermine public confidence in the conduct of the government."

Callaway said Oct. 5 that the subcommittee investigation and report represented "a new political dirty trick." He called the report's criticism of Butz "the cheapest shot of all." Callaway said: "They just found out that Earl Butz was down and decided to kick him because he was down." (Butz resigned as Agriculture Secretary Oct. 4 after a derogatory remark he had made about blacks caused a furor.)

The Republican minority on the subcommittee agreed with Callaway that the investigation had been "an exercise for political advantage and excoriation."

The Civil Aeronautics Board March 31 dismissed a separate charge that Callaway had violated CAB regulations in obtaining special exemptions for charter flights to carry skiers to an airport 30 miles from Crested Butte. The CAB said there was "insufficient evidence" to sustain the charge. The CAB did find it "regrettable" that Callaway had talked with two board members regarding the charter flights. The discussions, the CAB said, "created the appearance of soliciting preferential treatment."

Ford backs Kelley on favors, gifts. President Ford said Sept. 4, 1976 that he would not fire FBI Director Clarence M. Kelley, who had admitted Aug. 31 that certain of his house furnishings had been provided by the FBI without charge and that he had received gifts from his top aides. Ford issued his statement after he had read a report on Kelley prepared by Attorney General Edward H. Levi. In the report Levi said that Kelley should be neither formally disciplined nor asked to resign. Ford, who Sept. 1 had asked for the report, said that he believed Kelley had "the capacity to meet the essentially high standards of the FBI."

Kelley, in response to a story published Aug. 31 in the Washington Star, admitted that day that FBI employes had installed some window fixtures in his apartment shortly after he took office in 1973. He said that it had been done "without [his] knowledge." (Kelley Sept. 2 gave the bureau a check for $335 to cover the cost of the labor and the fixtures.)

Bureau sources quoted in the Sept. 1 Washington Post recalled that when J. Edgar Hoover headed the FBI, it was common practice for the director and other top executives to receive special favors.

In light of this history, the bureau sources said, the fixtures might have been installed by overzealous employees without a request from Kelley.

Kelley also admitted Aug. 31 that at his request bureau employes had built a portable cabinet for his use at home. Kelley said, however, that he considered the cabinet to be FBI property and intended to return it when he left the bureau. The cabinet was used to house FBI stationery and related materials, Kelley said.

Kelley said that he was "prepared to make restitution" for the gifts he had received from his personal staff and from some executive aides if his acceptance of them violated federal regulations.

The day after Kelley's statement, Ford asked Levi for the report on Kelley. The Washington Post carred a story that day saying that a Justice Department investigator had recommended that Kelley be fired. The investigator's superior had toned that down to a recommendation that Kelley be publicly reprimanded, the Post said. The recommendation, which reportedly had been sent to Levi three weeks before the Post story, was made by officials in the Justice Department's Office of Professional Responsibility, the Post said. That office was investigating charges that FBI executives had abused their powers.

The Justice Department, in a Sept. 4 statement on the Kelley probe, said that gifts accepted by Kelley from his subordinates did not violate federal regulations. The statement said that the most expensive of the gifts—including a chair and a clock—cost $105. The statement noted that individuals had pooled their donations so that only "nominal" amounts—as required by federal regulations—had been given by any individual.

The window fixtures, the statement said, had not been requested by Kelley. The statement said that Kelley had offered to pay for the fixtures once he discovered they had been installed by the bureau. That offer had been rejected by bureau officials at the time, the statement said, on the grounds that the security of Kelley's apartment necessitated the installation of the fixtures by FBI personnel.

The Justice Department statement said that the security rationale was applicable to some of the "goods and services" afforded Kelley. It said that other such goods and services "were requested and provided to assist the director to work at home, particularly during the period of his wife's terminal illness."

The statement noted that there had been concern that unless Kelley were forced to resign there would be "an aura of special treatment because of his high position." It said that Kelley's conduct, however, was "different in kind" from that which deserved disciplinary action or prosecution.

"The caliber of government service [would not be] improved in situations such as this, where there is every evidence of an intention to be honest, by a reading of human conduct in its worst possible light," the statement said.

(On Aug. 13, John Dunphy, head of the exhibits section of the FBI, resigned from the bureau and pleaded guilty to a misdemeanor charge of using government lumber for a birdhouse at his home. Dunphy's action followed an agreement with Justice Department prosecutors that reportedly included a promise to give grand jury testimony on similar misuse of government property. The exhibits section prepared models of crime scenes for use in trials.)

Young cleared in prisoner aid charge. A Justice Department spokesman Oct. 19, 1977 said his department had no evidence to support an allegation that U.N. Ambassador Andrew Young had improperly used his influence to have a federal prison inmate transferred to a medical facility.

The inmate was Atlanta businessman Michael G. Thevis, who in 1974 had been convicted of transporting obscene material across state lines and was incarcerated at the federal penitentiary at Terre Haute, Ind. Thevis was transferred to the federal prison hospital at Lexington, Ky. in 1977.

Allegations surfaced in the press that Young, a former Atlanta congressman, had been instrumental in obtaining the transfer. Nicholas Kasemehas, an ex-convict associate of Thevis, told the Federal Bureau of Investigation that Thevis had funneled $400,000 into Jimmy Carter's 1976 presidential campaign. According to Kasemehas, $250,000 of the illegal contribution had gone through former Budget Director Bert Lance and $150,000 through Young.

Young had written letters to prison officials in 1976 and 1977 in Thevis' behalf, including a February 1977 letter on U.N. stationery. Young claimed that he had not made an extraordinary effort to obtain the Thevis transfer and that his aid was a routine, humanitarian action for a constituent of his congressional district. Young's congressional office had continued to function until April 5, 1977, when a successor to Young was elected.

Both Young and Lance denied receiving any money from Thevis. The Justice Department said it would continue to investigate this aspect of the allegation.

Former Eximbank head accused. The former head of the U.S. Export-Import Bank, Henry Kearns, was accused Sept. 30, 1975 of having received, while in office, part of the proceeds from the sale of stock believed to have been placed in a blind trust.

The disclosure was made by Sen. William Proxmire (D, Wis.), who made public a letter from Richard L. Thornburgh, assistant attorney general, declaring that although there was "insufficient evidence" to "support a criminal charge" it appeared Kearns had been "less than candid" about his financial dealings in testimony before a Senate Appropriations subcommittee in 1972 and 1973.

According to the letter, Kearns had placed shares of a Thai firm called Siam Kraft Paper Co. in a blind trust, over which he supposedly had no control. The shares were sold at $5 apiece to Mitsui Co. (USA), and $293,000 proceeds from the sale were transferred by the trustee, Bank of America, to "a commercial account under the exclusive control of Mr. Kearns" before he left office as president of the Export-Import Bank.

Sen. Proxmire described himself as "flabbergasted" by Thornburgh's "outrageous decision" not to bring criminal charges against Kearns, adding that it "makes a mockery of the confirmation procedures if a man can enter into a blind trust agreement as a condition of confirmation for public office and then violate both his promise and his agreement with impunity." Proxmire said Kearns "clearly lied" to the Senate. "Further," he said, "he obviously feathered his own nest at a time when he was president of the bank and openly solicited the purchase of his stock from a company with which he was dealing officially as president of the bank and for whom he was not only in a position to help but did help."

50 convictions in Los Angeles FHA & VA home frauds. A two-year inquiry by a federal task force in Los Angeles had led to over 50 convictions of persons for defrauding the Federal Housing Administration (FHA) and the Veteran's Administration (VA), the Wall Street Journal reported Aug. 15, 1975. The Journal said the VA fraud was found in its home-loan-guarantee program. The FHA corruption was uncovered mostly in its property rehabilitation and resale programs, the Journal reported July 17.

Among those sentenced were Michael J. Whelan, a former FHA area management broker, and William Radich, a contractor, who together set up six fictitious contracting companies to defraud the FHA. In addition, the companies received kickbacks from various contractors. Whelan was sentenced to five years probation and fined $2,500 and Radich received a six-month prison term, it was reported July 17.

Alabama PSC official guilty of bribery. Kenneth J. Hammond, president of the Alabama Public Service Commission, was convicted in Montgomery, Ala. on a charge of soliciting a bribe to get vending machines placed in telephone company service buildings (reported Dec. 13, 1975). Hammond was sentenced to three years in prison and removed from office as required by state law.

Hammond's conviction was largely based on the testimonies of Rex Moore, an Alabama businessman, and Charles Price, a vice president of the South Central Bell Co.

Hammond, according to Moore, had helped arrange for Moore's company to get its vending machines into the telephone company's properties through the efforts of Price. Price said that he agreed to intercede because he thought that if he did not do so Hammond would vote against a pending increase for the telephone company. (An increase, lower than that requested, was subsequently approved by the commission.)

Testimony further revealed that Moore went to Alabama Attorney General William J. Baxley following a demand by Hammond for $10,000 which Moore said he could not afford.

The attorney general's office arranged to record Moore's conversation with Hammond at which the payoff was discussed.

Moore and Price were not indicted and the attorney general indicated that they were granted immunity in return for their testimony as state witnesses.

Payoff to N.J. Turnpike aide charged. A Gulf Oil Corp. executive vice president testified in a report to the U.S. Securities and Exchange Commission (SEC) that the company had paid $10,000 as a "thank you present" to New Jersey Turnpike Authority Executive Director William J. Flanagan in 1965, the New York Times reported Jan. 1, 1976.

The Gulf official, William L. Henry, told a special review committee investigating alleged bribes paid by the company that the payment was made a year after Flanagan had been of "tremendous help" to Colonial Pipeline, in which Gulf controlled a major interest.

The pipeline, which carried oil and chemical products from Texas up the eastern seaboard to New Jersey and New England, had faced serious problems in planning a right-of-way through Woodbridge.

According to the Times' report of Henry's testimony, Flanagan had given Colonial advance information on the Turnpike Authority's plans to build a new interchange on the east side of the highway where Colonial was planning a pipeline terminus. Henry said he had used this information to pursue an alternate route on the western side of the Turnpike.

Flanagan had also allegedly informed the company, the Times said, that Woodbridge officials would have to be paid off in return for granting the company construction easements. (In 1973, former Woodbridge Mayor Walter Zirpolo and former Council President Robert Jacks admitted extorting $110,000 in bribes from Colonial and were sentenced to two to six years in prison.)

Flanagan, a former Hudson County sheriff and one time deputy to the late

Mayor John V. Kenny of Jersey City, conceded that he had given some advice to Colonial, but he "categorically" denied ever receiving any money in return. He said Jan. 2 that turnpike engineers had advised Colonial on where to locate the pipeline as a matter of course.

The Times reported Feb. 19 that statutes of limitations prevented federal and state prosecutors from pursuing bribery and tax-evasion allegations against Flanagan.

Md. official sentenced. Alford R. Carey, former chief of Maryland's school construction program, was sentenced Jan. 9, 1976 in Baltimore to three years in prison. He had pleaded guilty to charges of forgery and false pretense in connection with the embezzlement of $22,105 in state funds.

Carey was accused of having obtained the money by falsifying an invoice for work supposedly done in the state's $6 million portable school program.

A number of other charges, including state tax evasion, were dropped in return for Carey's guilty plea. He had entered a plea of not guilty in July 1974.

Bailey cleared in Connecticut. A judge's report made public Jan. 12, 1976 cleared the late John M. Bailey of charges of having accepted a $250,000 influence-peddling fee in Connecticut's jai alai scandal.

The report was released in Hartford by Superior Court Judge Harold M. Mulvey, who sat as a special one-man grand jury investigating the charges. Mulvey made no recommendation for criminal prosecution but he criticized many figures in the scandal, which involved allegations of corruption, fraud, tax evasion and organized-crime influence.

The scandal broke in the fall of 1975 when David Friend, who headed a company that had built a jai alai fronton in Bridgeport, allegedly approached state police investigators in Florida and told them that he had "bought" Bailey, the former state and national Democratic Party chairman.

After hearing secret grand jury testimony on the charges, Mulvey found that "there is no evidence approaching even a minimal standard of credibility that

John Bailey ever received any money or any valuable thing whatsoever from David Friend or from anyone else on his behalf."

Also cleared of any wrongdoing were nine members of the State Gaming Commission, four state legislators who met with Bailey to discuss the fronton, and J. Brian Gaffney, the former Republican state chairman.

Those criticized by Mulvey included John L. Sullivan, the 77-year-old former state tax commissioner, who testified at public hearings that he had accepted $7,000 in return for introducing Friend to Bailey. Mulvey urged all state officials to avoid dealing with Sullivan.

Paul Manafort, a former state public works commissioner, also came under attack in the Mulvey report. Manafort, whose family demolition company was contracted to clear the fronton's building site, had arranged a meeting between fronton officials and officials of the State Department of Environmental Protection that resulted in a waiver of a state air-pollution permit requirement, which Mulvey said had been fraudulently obtained.

Asbury Park ex-mayor fined. Joseph F. Mattice, former mayor of Asbury Park and long-time figure in the area's politics, was fined $3,000 by Superior Court Judge John Bachman in New Brunswick, N.J. Jan. 19, 1976. Mattice had pleaded guilty in November 1975 to three counts of violating the state's election laws by falsifying nominating positions in 1973 in an attempt to retain political power. Other charges in the 79-count indictment were dropped.

Specifically, Mattice was fined $1,000 on each of three counts of filing false nominating petitions for three candidates in the 1973 primary race for Monmouth County Democratic committee.

Besides having served as the municipal attorney for several shore communities and as a District Court judge, Mattice served on the Asbury Park City Council from 1957 to 1969 and as the city's mayor from 1969 to 1973, when he was defeated for reelection.

Lodi ex-officials sentenced. Ronald Gasalberti, former Lodi, N.J. borough manager, and Salvatore DeRosa, former borough water superintendent, were sentenced Jan. 26, 1976 by Berger County District Court Judge Paul R. Huot to two to three years in prison. The pair was convicted in October 1975 of conspiring to defraud the borough of $43,000 through a phony voucher scheme using water meters that were never installed.

Ex-senator admits perjury. Former state Sen. James M. Turner of Woodbury, N.J. Jan. 28, 1976 pleaded guilty to three counts perjury stemming from testimony before a state grand jury in which he denied having accepted a bribe to help a convicted gambler win early parole from the state prison in Trenton.

In return for Turner's plea, the state agreed to drop a bribery charge at the time of sentencing. In addition, the state recommended that Turner receive one- to two-year prison sentences for each of the perjury counts and that they be served concurrently with the three- to five-year term he was already serving.

In June 1973 Turner was convicted of conspiring to discredit a political rival, Assemblyman Kenneth A. Gewertz (D, Deptford), by planting illegal amphetamines in Gewertz's home and car.

Before his 1973 conviction, Turner was chairman of the legislature's Joint Appropriations Committee.

SCI probes Middlesex kickbacks. Winding up three days of public hearings in Trenton, N.J. on alleged kickbacks related to Middlesex County's multimillion-dollar park program, State Commission of Investigation Chairman Joseph H. Rodriguez Jan. 29, 1976 urged state action "to put an end to the proposition that you have to pay monetary tribute to get government work" in New Jersey.

During the hearings, two real estate appraisers—Jerome Gall and John Galaida—testified Jan. 27 under immunity that they had paid kickbacks totaling some $8,000 to Nathan DuBester, administrator of the Middlesex County Land Aquisition Department, and also had made contributions to the local Democratic Party at DuBester's request in order to be awarded real-estate appraisal contracts. DuBester admitted in testimony that he had sold tickets to party

functions to the two men but denied that he had ever received money for himself.

Other testimony during the hearings indicated that the $1.5 million the county paid for a total of 43.5 acres for the proposed Ambrose and Doty's Brook Park in Piscataway Township might have been double what the land was actually worth. DuBester testified that he had authorized payment of $35,000 an acre.

In the statement released at the end of the hearings, Rodriguez was critical of "serious deficiencies" in the state's Green Acres program, which paid for half of county parkland purchases, saying the program had not adequately reviewed the appraisals submitted by Middlesex County. He urged Gov. Byrne to issue an executive order requiring more thorough review of all appraisals received from local governments.

Rodriguez also said new legislation might be needed to tighten state review of land purchases by local government agencies. Middlesex County, he said, had already moved to improve controls on land acquisitions. Had it acted sooner, "some of the failures and abuses aired at these hearings might have been cut off at the pass," he said.

Portash convicted in N.J. Joseph S. Portash, 43, a former Ocean County, N.J. freeholder, was convicted by a Superior Court jury in Toms River Feb. 11, 1976 of unlawfully taking $31,730 from a developer seeking favorable treatment on building- applications before county and Manchester Township utility and planning boards.

The seven-man, five-woman jury, which deliberated for 16 hours over two days, found Portash not guilty of a second charge of misconduct in office.

Portash had been indicted by a state grand jury in April 1975 on charges he accepted $31,730 during 1971–72 from Leisure Technology Inc. and its president, the late Robert J. Schmertz, through a Lakewood real estate agency associated with Schmertz. According to the charges, Portash's connection with the agency was a "no-show" job funded by Schmertz. Portash was alleged to have used his influence to gain approval for water and sewer franchises for the senior citizen communities that Leisure Technology was building in Manchester Township.

Portash, who did not take the witness stand, maintained through his attorney that he earned the money as a consultant.

Portash, at the time of his conviction, was mayor of Manchester Township, a member of the township's planning board, a member of the municipal utilities authority and director of the state Pinelands Environmental Council.

Schmertz, who owned the Boston Celtics of the National Basketball Association, was indicted by the grand jury Feb. 5, 1975 but died the following July 23 before being brought to trial.

Donald Safran, 45, owner of the defunct Lakewood real estate agency through which Schmertz was alleged to have funneled payments to Portash, was also indicted Feb. 5, 1975. He died, however, of an apparent heart attack Feb. 8 while on an airline flight.

Portash was fined $1,000 and given a suspended six-month jail term March 12.

Portash, despite his conviction, apparently had retained support in Manchester Township, where he had held numerous positions in local government for the past decade. A cocktail party in behalf of Portash March 7 had raised $6,000 to defray his legal expenses. Some 5,000 local residents were said by township Republican officials to have signed petitions in support of Portash.

Portash's wife, Adelaide, March 18 was appointed to fill her husband's seat on the township council. She was also named police commissioner, finance committee chairwoman and to her husband's seat on the municipal utilities authority. Portash himself was appointed an unpaid, special adviser to the council and promised his council seat "as soon as he is legally able" to regain it. His post as Manchester mayor was left unfilled. (Under state law, Portash was required to resign his municipal government posts on the day of sentencing.)

Gregorio bribery case dismissed. Charges that Assemblyman John T. Gregorio (D, Linden) had solicited a $25,000 bribe were dismissed by N.J. state Superior Court Judge Cuddie E. Davidson Jr. Feb. 25, 1976. Davidson held that

testimony by the state's chief witness, contractor Thomas Siggia, was "vague and wanting" and would not support allegations that Gregorio had asked for a bribe to ensure Siggia would receive a $4 million contract to build a high school in Linden. A perjury charge against Gregorio, who was also the mayor of Linden, had been severed from the trial two weeks earlier. The perjury charge was dropped March 4.

New Jersey corruption convictions. A father-daughter team that ran a construction company in Brooklyn and New York City's chief rent stabilization inspector were found guilty by a federal jury in Newark, N.J. March 17, 1976 of conspiring to pay $3 million in bribes to Jersey City's housing director in return for $33 million in municipal contracts.

John Ai, a fourth defendant, was found not guilty of charges he acted as an intermediary for the New Yorkers. A fifth defendant, Brooklyn contractor John J. Hart Jr., won a directed acquittal March 16 from presiding trial Judge Herbert J. Stern, who ruled Hart had become unwittingly involved in the conspiracy.

Convicted were Salvatore Visconti, 45, vice president of the Adjustment Construction Corp. of Brooklyn; his daughter, Valerie Visconti, 20, president of the family-owned concern; and Raphael Bressler, 57, chief inspector for the New York Conciliation and Appeals Board. Each was found guilty of attempting to bribe Neil S. Piro, Jersey City's housing director.

Piro, according to evidence presented at the trial, had been offered $3 million in bribes in May 1975. Cooperating with Federal Bureau of Investigation agents, however, Piro strapped a tape recorder to his body, subsequently met with the Viscontis and Bressler, and pretended to go along with the bribery scheme. Piro was the chief witness at the trial.

Ai, an engineer with the Jersey City housing department before his indictment, remain suspended from his job after being acquitted. He was ordered by the city to face disciplinary action for "conduct unbecoming a public employe." At the trial Ai's attorney had claimed his client had been duped by the other defendants.

Thomas Milano, former commissioner of housing for the Morris County Town of Dover, and Raymond LaBadie, a Hackettstown businessman, were convicted by a Morris County court jury March 25 of conspiring to bribe the former mayor of Dover, L. William Newkirk, in 1974 to obtain a zoning variance.

According to the indictment against the pair, they had offered Newkirk a $5,000 bribe to use his influence to secure a zoning variance that would allow the building of two-family homes in a one-family home area. LaBadie was found guilty of the conspiracy charge but was acquitted of a bribery count. Milano was convicted on both counts.

Milano, who was suspended Feb. 9 as assistant deputy director of the state Division of Alcoholic Beverage Control, had been found guilty Feb. 6 of unrelated charges he and Morristown health inspector Stanley Buglione had attempted to bribe Newkirk to get him to use his influence to have the Town of Dover sell garbage trucks to a friend of Buglione at an artificially low price. Buglione was also convicted.

Buglione subsequently pleaded guilty Feb. 18 to unrelated charges that he offered to inform Morristown Community Medical Center officials in advance of all health inspections. In return, Buglione admitted in Morris County District Court, he asked the hospital officials to award garbage removal, vending and other contracts to his friends.

In addition, Milano had gone on trial on charges he and Buglione had conspired to break into Dover Town Hall, steam open sealed property revaluation bids and possibly rig them. A mistrial was declared March 3 by presiding Morris County Judge Arnold M. Stein when the jury was unable to agree on a verdict. Buglione had pleaded guilty to the charges Feb. 20.

Milano was sentenced April 2 to serve consecutive one- to three-year prison terms and fined $1,000 for both his convictions. Buglione was sentenced March 12 to one to three years in prison for his two convictions. LaBadie was sentenced April 30 to six months in jail and fined $1,000.

N.J. ex-mayor & mayors found not guilty. Malcolm W. Hill, former mayor of the Bergen County Borough of Little Ferry, N.J., was acquitted by a county court jury April 3, 1976 of extortion, misconduct and perjury in connection with an alleged $10,000 bribe paid by developers to gain municipal approval of a controversial garden apartment complex.

Former Little Ferry Councilman Robert Simon, convicted of the same charges in a trial ending Feb. 10, was sentenced to seven to ten years in prison March 6. (Simon and other former Little Ferry officials had been convicted in September 1975 on unrelated charges stemming from a state grand jury investigation into payoffs in connection with other building projects.)

■ A perjury indictment against Camden Mayor Angelo Errichetti stemming from an investigation into charges that he was part of a conspiracy to violate state bidding laws in the handling of city painting contracts was dismissed April 13 by Superior Court Judge George Y. Schoch at the request of the state attorney general's office. Errichetti had been acquitted of the conspiracy charge in a trial in January 1975.

■ East Orange Mayor William S. Hart Sr. was acquitted July 22 of misconduct in office and bribery. An Essex County jury returned the verdict after deliberating for two hours on charges that Hart had paid an Essex County freeholder to influence the appointment of a municipal court judge, Stanley Silverman.

During an 11-day trial, Hart had testified he had given Freeholder Thomas H. Cooke Jr. $1,000 as a peace offering for the expenses he had cost the freeholder when he had opposed him in a 1975 county primary election.

Hart July 29 requested the return of the $1,000 that prosecutors had charged was the bribe. In the papers filed with the court, Hart contended the money had come from personal funds and therefore should be returned to him. The money had been held as evidence by Essex County Prosecutor Joseph Lordi.

N.Y. cases dismissed. New York State Supreme Court Justice Aloysius J. Melia April 13, 1976 dismissed all charges in a perjury and bribery indictment against Albert H. Blumenthal, New York State Assembly majority leader. An original perjury indictment against Blumenthal in December, 1975 had been superseded with another on March 12 that added the bribery accusation.

Melia was critical of the case brought against Blumenthal by special state prosecutor Charles J. Hynes. The judge said that Hynes utilized "gross specula- tion" and "inference upon inference" that had "unduly coerced" the grand jury.

The case involved Blumenthal's rela- tionship with indicted nursing-home pro- moter Bernard Bergman.

An indictment charging New York State Assembly Speaker Stanley Steingut and his son, Robert, with "corrupt use of posi- tion" in offering a job in return for a cam- paign contribution was thrown out Nov. 15 by the State Supreme Court's Appellate Division in Brooklyn. The appeals court voided the indictment on the basis that it had been returned by a Brooklyn (Kings County) grand jury that lacked jurisdic- tion. The Steinguts maintained that if the alleged misconduct had occurred at all, it had occurred in New York City's Borough of Manhattan.

Two of four indictments against Bronx Democratic leader Patrick J. Cunningham were thrown out Dec. 22 by New York State Supreme Court Justice Leonard H. Sandler on grounds that evidence given to a special grand jury had been insufficient to sustain the charges.

Sandler dismissed the indictments for bribery and official misconduct against Cunningham and also charges against Judge Anthony J. Mercorella, involving an allegation by former special New York State prosecutor Maurice H. Nadjari that Mercorella had wrongfully obtained his office by Cunningham's help.

A major setback for Nadjari's efforts had occurred June 3 when the New York State Court of Appeals ruled, 4–3, that Nadjari's jurisdiction was limited "strictly to the criminal-justice process or system." The opinion held that the 1972 executive order by then-Gov. Nelson Rockefeller, which established Nadjari's office, forbade his prosecution of cases involving civil jus- tice.

Citing this ruling, the Appellate Divi- sion of State Supreme Court in Brooklyn held unanimously Aug. 12 that Nadjari had no jurisdiction to prosecute Fred G. Moritt, a retired Brooklyn Civil Court

judge. It transferred his indictment to Brooklyn District Attorney Eugene Gold.

In the meantime, Gov. Hugh L. Carey and State Attorney General Louis J. Lef- kowitz had dismissed Nadjari June 25, 1976 from his job as investigator of New York City's criminal justice system.

The Appellate Division in Manhattan Nov. 4 dismissed charges against Manhat- tan Surrogate Samuel Di Falco, saying their presentation to the grand jury by a lawyer from the special prosecutor's office was illegal under state law.

Sandler Dec. 1 threw out a perjury in- dictment against Joseph A. Brust, former Supreme Court justice, because one of Nadjari's aides had improperly questioned Brust before the grand jury. State Supreme Court Justice Leon B. Polsky Dec. 17 dismissed a perjury indictment against Carmine De Sapio, the former Tammany Hall leader, because of insufficient evidence.

Compton councilmen sentenced. Two Compton, Calif. city councilmen, Hillard Hamm and Russell Woolfolk, were sen- tenced June 21, 1976 to three years in prison and fined $10,000 each for defrauding the federal government and extorting $40,000 from the owner of a piece of property by threatening to disapprove its sale to the city's redevelopment agency.

Ex-SBA official sentenced. Thomas F. Regan, ousted chief of the Richmond office of the Small Business Administra- tion, was sentenced June 25, 1976 to 19 years in prison for fraud and bribery in connection with a scheme to defraud the government agency and Virginia banks of more than $800,000.

Ten years of the sentence on one count of fraud and one of conspiracy were sus- pended. He was placed on five years' pro- bation on each of the remaining 11 counts, most of them charging Regan with racketeering and accepting gratuities. A U.S. District Court jury had convicted Regan June 5.

Federal prosecutors claimed that in 1973 dummy corporations had been set up solely to receive SBA-guaranteed loans which Regan approved. Four men had al- ready pleaded guilty to participating in the fraud scheme and had received sentences ranging from 17 months to seven years.

Troy pleads guilty. New York City Councilman Matthew H. Troy Jr. pleaded guilty July 1, 1976 in Brooklyn federal court to a charge of filing a fraudulent income tax return for 1972. He was sentenced Sept. 29 to two years in prison and fined $5,000, in addition to which he would have to pay tax and fines on the $37,000 he failed to report. The judge suspended all but two months of the prison term. Troy resigned Sept. 30 as chairman of the City Council Finance Committee, although council rules did not require such action. Troy went to jail Oct. 22.

Nine indicted in Alaskan conspiracy. Richard L. McVeigh, former U.S. attorney for Alaska, was among nine persons indicted July 8, 1976 by a federal grand jury in San Francisco on charges of promoting gambling and prostitution activities in Valdez, Alaska, a major pipeline construction center.

Also charged with the use of interstate facilities for racketeering and conspiring to transport women across state lines for prostitution were Charles Tourine, 69, a widely-known organized-crime figure and Alexander Miller, 54, a former legislative assistant to Alaska ex-Gov. William Egan. McVeigh, 43, an Anchorage lawyer, served as Alaska's U.S. attorney from 1964 to 1968.

The seven-count indictment charged that the conspiracy began in 1974 and said that the accused had expected to net up to $1 million in six months.

Pennsylvania officials accused. The state special prosecutor for Philadelphia filed criminal charges against two legislators Sept. 27, 1976 for allegedly demanding $15,000 from a Delaware County man for having his son admitted to the Temple University School of Dentistry. State Rep. Stephen R. Wojdak and state Sen. Francis J. Lynch, both Philadelphia Democrats, were charged with conspiracy, bribery and wagering on official actions.

In a similar case, a federal grand jury Oct. 5 handed up an indictment against Martin Abrams, 51, a Philadelphia Housing Authority executive and former Democratic city committeeman. Abrams was charged with lying to the grand jury when he denied having received $37,500 for helping two students gain admission to the University of Pennsylvania Veterinary School.

According to the indictment, the charges against Abrams were part of a larger federal investigation into allegations that certain public officials had "solicited and accepted bribes and/or extorted money from parents of applicants to various professional schools."

Herbert Fineman, speaker of the Pennsylvania House of Representatives until he resigned from office May 23, 1977, was sentenced June 10 to serve two years in prison and pay a fine of $5,000. The Philadelphia Democrat had been convicted May 20 of trying to obstruct a federal investigation into alleged blackmail and influence peddling by state legislators in connection with admissions to medical schools.

In the state House since 1955, Fineman had been one of the most powerful politicians in the Pennsylvania government.

Former State Sen. Henry J. Cianfrani began serving a five-year sentence at the Allenwood, Pa. federal prison Feb. 20, 1978 for racketeering and mail fraud. Cianfrani had pleaded guilty in December 1977 to 106 counts of a 110-count federal indictment, which had charged that he took $52,500 in bribes from parents of children seeking admission to state professional schools.

Bellis fined in two bribery cases. Former Philadelphia City Council Majority Leader Isadore H. Bellis was fined $8,500 and put on two years' probation Oct. 7, 1976 for taking $56,000 in bribes for his influence to secure concession contracts for three companies at the Greater Philadelphia International Airport.

A Philadelphia Common Pleas Court jury had convicted Bellis in April 1975 of taking payoffs from ARA Food Services and two of its subsidiaries. The jury had found that Bellis had solicited a total of $214,000 in bribes—accepting $56,000 in cash and the remainder in stock, which was worth some $400,000 at the time of sentencing. He had not been charged with accepting the stock as a bribe.

Visiting Judge John A. Cherry of Clearfield County fined the former Democratic councilman $500 for each of eight counts of bribery, eight counts of misconduct in office and one count of election law violation. He sentenced Bellis to one year of probation for each count, all but one to be served concurrently.

Cherry did not order the 56-year-old Bellis to make any restitution for the bribes. He said the "conviction was the punishment in this crime. I think . . . Bellis lost everything—his career, his political future, his dignity, his health."

In a separate case in Philadelphia Municipal Court, visiting Judge Carson V. Brown placed Bellis on two years' probation Oct. 6 for accepting $9,000 in illegal campaign contributions from a Norristown architect who had been awarded a $180,-000 no-bid contract for work at the airport. Brown ordered Bellis to make restitution of $9,000 to the city, not to John R. Betts, the architect.

The judge said that "in my county this would be considered a very serious crime and the penalty would be more severe. But I must consider the political atmosphere in this city in determining sentence."

The prosecution in both payoff cases had urged that Bellis be imprisoned.

Hoboken gambling payoffs charged. Hoboken, N.J. police and city officials were being paid more than $10,000 a week to overlook widespread gambling activities, The Dispatch of Union City reported Oct. 19, 1976 in a copyrighted article.

The newspaper, which said its report was the result of a two-month investigation, asserted that money was paid by gamblers to police officers, who in turn channeled it to members of the administration of Mayor Steve Cappiello. The report did not name specific officials.

Knowledge of the payoffs was so widespread in the police department, the newspaper said, that the local Patrolmen's Benevolent Association had attempted to gain leverage in labor negotiations with the city by shutting down the gambling operations. The action was presumably designed to result in the cutoff of payoffs to city officials.

The Jersey Journal had published a report Oct. 18 saying that PBA leaders—not city officials or police superior officers—had told patrolmen to warn gamblers, bookies and others of an impending crackdown. The Journal's story, denied by the PBA, said the PBA's action was linked to "problems the PBA had been having in getting city officials to agree to a contract."

The Dispatch said Hoboken police had made only 16 gambling arrests on their own in 1975. In a report Oct. 20, The Dispatch said outside law enforcement agencies did not notify the Hoboken police of planned gambling raids for fear suspects would be tipped off in advance and because the Hoboken vice squad had such a poor record of arrests on its own.

Mayor Cappiello and Police Chief George Crimmins denied knowledge of any payoffs and called the accusations politically motivated.

Former Mississippi official convicted. E. L. Boteler Jr., former Mississippi highway director, was convicted Jan. 8, 1977 in state court of stealing $100,000 in highway funds. Boteler was the first Mississippi official since the 1930s to be prosecuted for converting state funds to his own use.

Boteler, 56, had testified that he had passed the money to Hershel Jumper, a former state highway commissioner.

Georgia senator acquitted. A federal jury in Atlanta May 20, 1977 acquitted Georgia state Sen. Culver Kidd, 62, of charges of conspiracy and bribery. Also acquitted was Kidd's co-defendant Donald Gilbreth.

The men had been accused in connection with an alleged attempt to fix a drug-possession case against Hugh Lowe (Jimmy) Jordan of Centre, Ala. in 1975. Jordan had filed a lawsuit in August 1976 claiming Kidd had taken $10,000 to fix the case and seeking to recover the money.

Chicago Mayor Bilandic fires accuser. Chicago Mayor Michael A. Bilandic Nov. 21, 1977 fired a city official who had accused him of having "greased the way" for an unjustified taxicab fare increase.

A fare increase was required under city law to be justified on the basis of a firm's financial data.

Jane M. Byrne, commissioner of consumer sales, said she had informed Bilandic of an audit revealing errors in financial data of the taxi companies. But, she said, Bilandic had told a taxi executive to get the figures to "add up right" for an increase, which was subsequently approved by the city council.

Bilandic denied any wrongdoing. In announcing Byrne's dismissal, Bilandic said he had passed a lie-detector test administered by the firm that had given a similar test to Byrne. Byrne's test, which she also passed, had been commissioned by the Chicago Daily News.

Trial of Honolulu mayor folds. State bribery charges against Honolulu Mayor Frank Fasi were dismissed Dec. 27, 1977 as the key prosecution witness continued to refuse to testify against him.

The witness, Hal Hansen, had told a grand jury at one point that he had made payments to Fasi's campaign fund in return for being selected to build Kukui Plaza, a Honolulu redevelopment project.

After Hansen was indicted by a federal grand jury on charges stemming from his Kukui Plaza dealings, he refused to testify in the state case against Fasi on the ground it could jeopardize his own defense.

The refusal put him in jail. After two weeks, during which he maintained his silence, Circuit Court Judge Toshimi Sodetani decided that Hansen could no longer be held and special prosecutor Grant Cooper was forced to move for dismissal of the charges against Fasi and his codefendant, Fasi's former campaign treasurer, Harry C. C. Chung.

Fasi had protested the whole thing was a "political vendetta" against him by Gov. George Ariyoshi to keep him from running for the governorship.

Former Justice Yarbrough convicted. Donald B. Yarbrough, a former Texas Supreme Court justice, was sentenced to five years in prison Jan. 27, 1978 after conviction on a charge of aggravated perjury.

Yarbrough had been accused of lying to a Travis County, Texas grand jury in connection with a meeting he had with a former business associate. At one meeting with the former associate, John William Rothkopf, Yarbrough allegedly had had Rothkopf forge a title transfer to obtain a clear Texas title for Rothkof's car. At that meeting and others, Rothkopf was secretly wired with a tape recorder.

Other Developments

CIA funds for foreign leaders reported. The Central Intelligence Agency had made secret payments totaling millions of dollars to King Hussein of Jordan each year since 1957, the Washington Post reported Feb. 18, 1977. News stories the following day named a number of other heads of state or high government officials who had allegedly received secret CIA payments. The Post story and other news accounts were based on information supplied by unnamed sources.

According to the initial Post story, President Carter had learned of the payments only a few days earlier. Carter had then ordered that the payments cease, the Post said.

At a Feb. 18 White House news briefing, Press Secretary Jody Powell read a statement saying it was the "Administration's policy not to comment on—either to confirm or deny—any stories concerning alleged covert activities."

The statement went on to note that "all sensitive foreign intelligence activities" had been the object of an "intensive and comprehensive review" begun almost immediately after the Carter Administration took office. The purpose of the review, the statement said, was to ensure that all such activities were "proper," that oversight procedures were fully complied with, and that "what can be done openly is not done secretly." After studying the findings of the review, the President would make "basic decisions" about the future of covert activities, the statement said.

The statement gave particular praise to Hussein as an "outstanding national leader" who had helped reduce tensions in the Middle East.

The alleged payments came up as a topic at a Feb. 23 news conference Carter gave. Carter said he would not comment directly on "any specific CIA activity." He said he had reviewed the "more controversial revelations that have been publicized in the last few days" and found some of those revelations to be "quite erroneous," others to have "some degree of accuracy." He said, however, he had not found anything "illegal or improper."

In response to another question, Carter conceded that it was a "value judgment" on his part to say that none of the CIA actions in question had been "improper." Carter said the Intelligence Oversight Board created by former President Ford in 1976 had made the same judgment. He added that the Senate Intelligence Committee and the appropriate committees in the House of Representatives had been informed of the CIA activities.

Carter added that he thought San. Daniel Inouye (D, Hawaii), chairman of the Senate Intelligence Committee, shared his belief that there was not any "impropriety" or "illegality" in "any ongoing CIA operation."

Carter's use of the adjective "ongoing" was noted by some observers as possibly indicating that CIA payments of questionable legitimacy had in fact occurred but that Carter had terminated them prior to the news conference.

Carter also observed that public disclosure of "these kinds of operations which are legitimate and proper" could be "extremely damaging to our relationship with other nations [and] to the potential security of our country even in peacetime." Carter said he would try to reduce such disclosures by limiting the number of persons with access to information about such operations. He said any measures he took to reduce leaks would be "within the bounds" of observing propriety, legality and the American dislike of secrecy.

Payments detailed—According to the original Post story, the Intelligence Oversight Board had learned of the alleged payments to Hussein and had labeled them improper in a formal report given to Ford. Nevertheless, Ford did not act to end the payments, the Post said.

According to the Post, in 1976 Hussein received $750,000, which was down from previous levels. The Post said the CIA had justified the payments to Hussein on the ground that Hussein permitted U.S. intelligence operatives to work freely in Jordan, a country of strategic importance. Hussein also himself provided information to the CIA and channeled some of the CIA money to other Jordanian officials who cooperated with the CIA, the Post said.

Sources cited in the Feb. 19 New York Times said that the payments had been aimed at insuring Hussein's continued survival and sympathy. One source quoted by Times said that the payments had in large part been used for legitimate purposes and indicated that it was the secrecy rather than the use of the payments that had caused them to be called into question.

However, the payments were viewed by some CIA officials simply as bribes that enabled the king to afford an affluent lifestyle, according to the Post. The Post also reported that the CIA had provided Hussein with female companions.

Among the other foreign heads of state or high government officials named in the press Feb. 19 as allegedly having received secret CIA payments were: Chiang Kai-shek of Nationalist China (Taiwan) (deceased); Ramon Magsaysay of the Philippines (deceased); Syngman Rhee of South Korea (deceased); Mobuto Sese Seko of Zaire; Eduardo Frei Montalva of Chile; Ngo Dinh Diem (deceased) and Nguyen Van Thieu of South Vietnam; Luis Echeverria Alvarez of Mexico; Carlos Andres Perez of Venezuela; Archbishop Makarios of Cyprus; Jomo Kenyatta of Kenya; Holden Roberto of Angola; Forbes Burnham of Guyana, and Willy Brandt of West Germany.

Most of those named in the press denied, either directly or through spokesmen, having any covert financial links with the CIA.

Perez, president of Venezuela, said the charge that he had received CIA payments while minister of the interior. was "vile and false." Venezuela recalled its ambassador to the U.S. and on Feb. 22 protested the charge at a Washington meeting of the Organization of American States. However, Venezuelan Foreign Minister Ramon Escovar Salom said Feb. 22 that the "very delicate" situation had been closed in a satisfactory fashion by a letter from Carter to Perez. Carter had dismissed the charge as "groundless and malicious," Escovar Salom said. The White House Feb. 23 acknowledged that Carter had sent Perez a letter but refused to release its contents because it was "a personal letter." A White House official quoted in the New York Times Feb. 24 said, "If it [Escovar Salmon's description of the letter's contents] wasn't correct we would tell you that."

The Wall Street Journal reported Feb. 22 that CIA money had also gone to the Israeli government. According to the Journal, the payments—totaling in the millions between 1964 and 1968 and perhaps later—had been channeled by Israel to various African nations in an attempt to win support for Israeli positions on Middle East issues, particularly in debate at the United Nations.

Jordan assails report—The Jordanian government Feb. 18 denied as "a fabrication and distortion" the report that King Hussein had received payments from the CIA for 20 years.

The government statement said Hussein had "led Jordan into a close cooperation with the United States on the basis of mutual respect and friendship." It insisted that "the Jordanian leadership has not engaged in improper practices or pursued personal interests."

A Radio Jordan summary of the government declaration later Feb. 18 made no mention of Hussein. The broadcast called the Post story "lies" and charged that "the writer of the article [Bob Woodward] is known for his Zionist attitude."

Saudi cited as CIA liaison—The Washington Post said Feb. 22 that, besides Hussein, the CIA had also cultivated ties with another powerful figure in the Arab world: Kamal Adham, head of national security in Saudi Arabia. The Post did not say the CIA had made payments to Adham. However, it identified him as Saudi Arabia's liaison with the CIA. The Post also said Adham had profited considerably from commissions on Middle East sales of American products, including aircraft.

The Post said Adham had close ties to the Saudi ruling family and to Egyptian President Anwar Sadat. The Post said

that according to one "authoritative source" Adham had at one point provided Sadat, then Egypt's vice president, with a steady private income.

CIA ex-head gets fine, suspended prison term. U.S. District Court Judge Barrington Parker fined Richard Helms $2,000 Nov. 4, 1977 and gave him a suspended two-year prison sentence. Helms, a former director of the Central Intelligence Agency, had pleaded no contest Oct. 31 to two charges of failing to testify "fully, completely and accurately" to a Senate committee that was inquiring about CIA activities in Chile.

Parker severely criticized Helms for his testimony to the Senate panel. Helms, Parker said, had "dishonored" his oath, and as a consequence now stood before the court "in dishonor and shame." Parker further observed that "if public officials embark deliberately on a course to disobey and ignore the laws of our land because of some misguided and ill-conceived notion and belief that there are earlier commitments and considerations which they must first observe, the future of this country is in jeopardy."

In a plea for lenient sentencing, Helms' lawyer, Edward Bennett Williams, argued that Helms had been "impaled on the horns of a moral and legal dilemma" in being questioned by the Senate committee. The obligation to testify accurately to the Senate panel, Williams said, conflicted with Helms's oath as CIA director to keep certain matters confidential. Williams also noted that "there was no self-interest at work" when Helms testified before the Senate panel.

Williams told the judge that Helms would "bear the scar of a conviction for the rest of his life."

Once sentence was passed, however, Williams told reporters outside the courtroom that Helms would "wear this conviction like a badge of honor." Helms agreed with his lawyer, saying he did not "feel disgraced at all. I think if I had done anything else, I would have been disgraced."

The Justice Department, as part of the plea-bargaining agreement that led to Helms's no contest plea, had recommended to the judge that Helms not be required to go to prison.

More than 400 former CIA employes, meeting at a country club in Bethesda, Md. after Helms was sentenced, took up a collection to pay Helms's fine. One of the former employes at the meeting commented that it was "safe to say there was more than enough contributed to pay the $2,000 fine."

Senate committee says FBI offered political services. The staff of the Senate Select Committee on Intelligence issued a report Dec. 3, 1975 accusing the Federal Bureau of Investigation of providing political services for Presidents from Roosevelt to Nixon.

According to the report, the FBI in 1940 ran "name checks" (checks of its files) and supplied reports on persons opposing the foreign policy of President Roosevelt. In 1949, an investigation by the FBI of the National Lawyers Guild was passed on to President Truman. And in 1956, when President Eisenhower asked for a report on racial tension from the FBI, the report contained information "not only of incidents of violence, but also on the activities of seven governors and congressmen in groups opposing integration, as well as the role of Communists in civil rights lobbying efforts and the N.A.A.C.P.'s [National Association for the Advancement of Colored People] plans to push legislation."

Under the Kennedy administration, the Senate committee report said, Attorney General Robert Kennedy authorized wiretaps on newsmen, as well as on government officials, two lobbyists, and a Congressional staff member.

President Johnson received information from the FBI on seven newsmen, on members of the staff of his 1964 presidential opponent, Barry Goldwater, and on persons opposing his foreign policy, according to the report. The report stated that the FBI also sent to the White House information drawn from wiretaps on civil rights leader Dr. Martin Luther King Jr., at the time of the Democratic National Convention in 1964.

President Nixon, according to the report, had the FBI carry out wiretaps of newsmen and White House officials.

The report left open in several cases the question of whether the activities described of the FBI had been motivated politically, or by a desire to preserve national security, or prevent violence.

Politics cost bank $232,300. Politically-related transactions involving bond deals and trust funds cost Missouri's largest bank, Mercantile Trust Co., $232,300 from 1964 through 1970, according to the report of a special review commission Feb. 27, 1976.

The audit committee was established by the board of Mercantile Bancorp Inc., a holding company created in 1971 with Mercantile Trust as its lead bank, to investigate charges of improper political activity.

A federal grand jury in Kansas City was investigating possible wrongdoing by the administration of former Missouri Gov. Warren E. Hearnes (D). Attention was focused on the bank's dealings with the late J. V. Conran, a Democratic boss of southeastern Missouri and political ally of Hearnes.

Donald E. Lasater, chairman and chief executive officer of both the holding company and the bank, was indicted in 1975 on four counts of perjury before the grand jury.

The audit committee concluded that Lasater "acted in the best interest of the company at all times," but determined that the late Kenton R. Cravens, former chairman of the bank, had initiated the bond deals with Conran and set up a private political trust fund that cost the bank money.

Meat-purchasing scandal charged. A Senate subcommittee heard testimony May 10, 1976 that two New England firms had charged the Defense Department top prices for inferior cuts of beef, using payoffs, gifts and prostitutes to persuade Army meat inspectors to go along with the fraud. One witness testified that in some cases knuckle meat (priced at $1.85 a lb.) had been substituted for sirloin ($3.85 a lb.) that was specified in government contracts.

The Senate Government Operations Committee's subcommittee on federal spending practices, efficiencies and open government had conducted a nine-month investigation of military meat-purchasing. The companies that came under fire at the hearings were the G & G Packing Co. of Roxbury, Mass. and the Blue Ribbon Frozen Food Corp. of Hamden, Conn. The companies—both co-owned by Harry Goldberg and David Goldberg (not related)—went out of business in July 1975.

In the year that ended June 30, 1975, the two companies together had sold the Pentagon 15.3 million pounds of beef for $21.9 million. (The Pentagon had been spending about $110 million annually on domestic beef.)

Edward Kehl, the witness who told of the substitution of knuckle meat for sirloin, was a former employee of G & G Packing Co. He said the company had made up to $960,000 a week in illegal profits. Manuel Pacheco, a civilian inspector, testified May 10 that he had received between $100 and $200 a week from Harry Goldberg to "refrain from hassling the employes." Pacheco admitted, in response to a question, that he had known about the inferior meat being substituted for expensive cuts. Two army meat inspectors—one no longer connected with the service—also testified May 10. Charles Reidinger, a former sergeant, said he had received payments and the free services of prostitutes. Sp. 4 Nadja Hoyer-Boots admitted that she had received free clothes, plane tickets and weekend trips from G & G officials while she was assigned to their plant.

Sen. Lawton Chiles (D, Fla.), the subcommittee chairman cited two factors May 7 that he said contributed to the "breakdown" in military beef procurement. One, he said, was the rigid and burdensome contract specifications that the Pentagon imposed on beef items. Since most meat packers would not go to the trouble of trying to meet the specifications, the standards, in effect, stifled competition, Chiles said.

(Chiles noted a Pentagon requirement that steaks be nearly identical in size. He said that this forced manufacturers to process the steaks through special machines. "The housewife," Chiles said, had "a much better chance of getting her money's worth at any store.")

The other factor Chiles cited was what he called the Army's laxness about selecting and training personnel to inspect meat. The subcommittee, Chiles said, "found that young kids recruited into the system were inadequately trained, unsupervised, and encouraged to steal meat." Chiles added that "the kids also quickly learned to accept gratuities from the meat vendors they were supposed to be monitoring."

Lawyers for the Goldbergs charged May 12 that the subcommittee's public reports on its investigations had smeared the reputations of their clients and violated their rights to a fair trial.

FDA probe criticized. A panel of experts May 23, 1976 recommended further investigation of allegations of undue drug industry influence on the Food and Drug Administration.

The panel, appointed by Health, Education and Welfare Secretary David Mathews, criticized a previous investigation of the allegations by FDA Commissioner Alexander M. Schmidt, who had said in his report that he had found "no industry domination of the Bureau of Drugs or industry protection by the bureau or agency."

The panel noted improvements in FDA procedures since Schmidt joined the agency, which was after the incidents involved in the allegations occurred. The panel did not question the fairness of Schmidt's investigation, but it claimed "serious deficiencies" elsewhere. It faulted the in-house nature of Schmidt's probe and said "a significant number of important allegations" were left unresolved.

Besides a probe of industry influence, the panel recommended an independent reinvestigation of allegations concerning personnel shifts, use of advisory panels and possible in-agency bias favoring drug approvals.

Dr. Thomas C. Chalmers, the panel chairman who also was president of the Mount Sinai Medical Center in New York, disagreed with the report. Schmidt also criticized the report, as did Sen. Edward M. Kennedy (D, Mass.), chairman of the Senate Labor and Public Welfare Committee's health subcommittee. The subcommittee held hearings in 1974 during which the original allegations were made. Kennedy said that the latest report was, "in essence, an investigation of an investigation, which concludes by recommending an additional investigation."

LBJ Senate primary fraud? A former Texas voting official July 30, 1977 admitted that he had knowingly certified 202 fraudulent ballots to enable Lyndon B. Johnson to win the Aug. 28, 1948 Texas Democratic primary runoff for the U.S. Senate. Victory in the Democratic primary then was tantamount to election.

Johnson won the primary by 87 votes out of a total of nearly one million ballots cast, defeating former Gov. Coke R. Stevenson. The official, Luis Salas, who had been the election judge for Jim Wells County's election Box 13, said, "Johnson did not win the election—it was stolen for him. . . ."

Stevenson had defeated Johnson in the June primary but failed to win a majority, forcing the August runoff. Three days later, Aug. 31, a nearly complete count showed that Stevenson was leading Johnson by a narrow margin. According to Salas, South Texas political leader George B. Parr that day directed that the 202 names appearing on a poll tax list in Jim Wells County be added to Box 13 in Johnson's favor and ordered Salas to certify their validity. Salas complied and Johnson was declared the winner. The decision to stuff the ballot box was made at a meeting Aug. 31 between himself, Parr, Johnson and other political leaders, Salas said. (Parr committed suicide in 1975.)

After a protest by Stevenson, a federal court judge in Fort Worth Sept. 14, 1948 signed a temporary restraining order barring certification of Johnson's victory pending a probe of the voting in Jim Wells County. Johnson petitioned the Supreme Court and Justice Hugo Black Sept. 29, 1948 voided the restraining order. Black's action, in effect, validated the primary results and ended the investigation.

Three of Johnson's aides in the 1948 election Aug. 1 denied that Johnson had any part in the alleged voting fraud. They also insisted that Johnson was not present at the Aug. 31 meeting with Parr and the others.

A Johnson memo released Aug. 3 by the Johnson Library in Austin also denied that he had attended the alleged meeting at which plans were made to alter the primary election results. According to the statement made public for the first time, Johnson was quoted as having said: "I am without knowledge concerning the ballots in either Duval, Jim Wells or Zapata Counties. I have not been to any of those counties and have not conferred with the officials in those counties."

Harvard Professor Doris Kearns Aug. 6 said Johnson may have lost a 1941 bid for the Senate because of a voting fraud scheme similar to the one he was accused of taking part in in 1948.

Kearns, a confidante and biographer of the late President, said her research had uncovered widespread discrepancies in the 1941 election. Johnson was initially declared the winner by 5,000 votes against incumbent Tex. Gov. W. Lee O'Daniel, but lost in a subsequent recount. (O'Daniel had a 1311 vote margin when the ballots were counted again.) Kearns said she had "no proof one way or the other" concerning the 1948 election, but said the similarities with the 1941 race "say something about the political ethics of the times."

Judicial misdeeds charged. Rep. Paul Findley (R, Ill.) asserted in a statement in the Congressional Record Oct. 5, 1977 that "not all federal judges" were "hardworking, honest and extremely capable." He said:

"For example, a Federal district judge in Philadelphia, Herbert A. Fogel, has invoked his constitutional right against self-incrimination before a Federal grand jury investigating the questionable 1971 award of a $78 million General Services Administration lease to his uncle, Philadelphia developer Mathew Weinstein. As reported in the Washington Star:

The lease was given to Weinstein even though his bid was millions of dollars higher than two other bids and did not meet legal requirements, according to a study made later by the Government Accounting Office.

"For some time, Justice Department officials have been trying to persuade Judge Fogel to resign, but currently there is nothing that anyone can do, but politely ask him. Under the Constitution, as Fogel is quick to point out, a Federal judge 'is a lifetime appointee.' Today there is no way that he can be forced to leave office short of impeachment.

"A few years ago, a judge of the U.S. Court of Appeals continued to hold office and receive compensation for an extensive period of time while appealing a conviction for perjury and conspiracy. Once the possibility of appeal was exhausted, the judge wisely chose to resign. But the decision to resign was his own. Even in these circumstances no external authority forced him to leave the bench."

Judge recalled in rape case—A Madison, Wisconsin judge who had espoused the theory that women provoked sexual assaults was defeated Sept. 7 in the state's first judicial recall election. The drive to oust Dane County Judge Archie Simonson stemmed from remarks he had made depicting rape as a "normal" response to women's provocative clothing and Madison's climate of sexual permissiveness.

Simonson made his controversial statements to Assistant District Attorney Meryl Manhardt May 25 at a disposition hearing for a 15-year-old youth accused of raping a 16-year-old girl. The youth pleaded no contest to delinquency and Simonson sentenced him to a year's probation in his parents' custody. Manhardt had urged a more stringent sentence to show the community "that such conduct cannot and will not be tolerated."

Simonson's treatment of the case provoked a public furor, particularly among feminists who urged him to apologize or resign. Simonson refused to resign and requested that a complete transcript of the courtroom conversation be released. He believed the news media had distorted the issue and that the recall effort would be aborted if his comments were considered in context.

At one point in the courtroom dialogue, Simonson told Manhardt, "I'm trying to say to women to stop teasing." He then added, "and are we supposed to take an impressionable person 15 or 16 years of age who can respond to something like that and punish that person severely because they react to it normally?"

Simonson, 52, faced five opponents in the election. He was defeated by Moria Mackert Krueger, 33, who became Madison's first elected female judge. Her campaign received a boost when it was reported Aug. 27 that the rape defendant Simonson had released had been arrested on burglary charges.

Index